PRAISE FOR *OUT HERE*

"You are a readable writer and a likeable writer which is to say a good writer. This book is not recommended for people who need to quit reading and go to work. *Out Here* clearly is the right place for you."

—Wendell Berry, Kentucky novelist, poet, essayist, environmental author, cultural critic, and farmer

"If I wrote like Bob Hill I could get a job with decent hours. He looks like a macho, trench-coated reporter of another decade, but his prose gives him away. Through Bob's column, a reader meets people making heroic efforts to muddle through. They're the people we might never hear if Bob hadn't stopped to listen."

—The late, great Bob Edwards, Louisville native and NPR host of *Morning Edition*

"*Out Here* is a fascinating journey through the icon Bob Hill's love of family, delicate story telling and working the soil. *Out Here* is a roadmap for everyone. Don't drop your dreams. Pursue the best vision of yourself. Savor every second of life."

—Terry Meiners, Louisville WHAS Radio host

"Hang with Bob Hill long enough, and he'll find you a time, place and character that will cause you to come away feeling good about humanity."

—Dave Kindred, author of eight diverse books, former Louisville *Courier-Journal* and *Washington Post* sports columnist

"At a time when many Americans no longer appreciate journalism, Bob Hill shows us what an honorable and essential profession it is. He makes easy work of political poseurs and focuses on telling the stories of little-known lives that say something meaningful about the human condition. His work is plainspoken and solid, like Shaker carpentry, with little adornment except the perfect adjective, metaphor, and turn of phrase. His wood and pegs are the English language, used to lasting effect. Read him."

—Al Cross, political reporter and columnist for the *Courier-Journal* for 26 years, where he shared a 1989 Pulitzer Prize, Director Emeritus of the Institute for Rural Journalism at the University of Kentucky, former national president of the Society of Professional Journalists and member of the Kentucky Journalism Hall of Fame

Out Here
Essays and Encounters from the Heart, Soul, and Left Field

By Bob Hill

OLD STONE PRESS
LOUISVILLE, KENTUCKY, USA

Out Here: Essays and Encounters from the Heart, Soul, and Left Field

Copyright © 2025 by Bob Hill

All rights reserved.

This book may not be reproduced in whole or in part without written permission from the publisher, Old Stone Press, or from the author, Bob Hill, except by a reviewer who may quote brief passages in a review; nor may any part of this book be reproduced, stored in a retrieval system, or transmitted in any form or by any means, electronic, mechanical photocopying, recording or other, without written permission from the publisher or author.

For information about special discounts for bulk purchases or autographed copies of this book, please contact J. H. Clark, Old Stone Press at john@oldstonepress.com or phone 502.693.1506. Also, contact the author Bob Hill at farmerbob@hiddenhillnursery.com or phone 502.744.6242.

This is not a work of fiction. It is a "memoir" and a labor of love by Bob Hill a.ka. Farmer Bob of Hidden Hill Nursery Utica, Indiana for his family, friends, and newspaper journalists at large and anyone that believes in the stories of our human race.

Out Here: Essays and Encounters from the Heart, Soul, and Left Field

Library of Congress Control Number: 2024918252

ISBN: 978-1-938462-69-6 (Paperback)
ISBN: 978-1-938462-70-2 (eBook)

Cover photographs by John Nation

Published by Old Stone Press
an imprint of J. H. Clark & Associates, Inc.
Louisville, Kentucky 40207 USA

www.oldstonepress.com

Published in the United States

This book, our good lives, and our wonderful family would not have been possible without Janet Hill, my wife of 63 years, who got us through the better and worse parts of marriage until it was all only better.

Contents

Acknowledgments	9
Preface/Prologue	11
PART ONE	**19**
PART TWO	**35**
From Singac To Sycamore	41
Basketball, Slide Rules And Larry McMurtry	56
What Do You Mean There Are No New Jobs	68
It All Began With $500 And A '52 Buick	77
Show Up, Shut Up And Wait For The Pension	82
Game On	86
How Do You Spell Awkward Transition	90
It All Began With A Guy Named "Scummy"	94
What Do You Mean I Have To Learn How To Type	98
A Lot Of Very Interesting Dead People	108
I Still Want To Write A Damn Column	115
Nothing Beats Three Friends And A Grain Truck	123
Good Journalists Are Best People In The World	126
Ready For Deeper Water But Unsure Which River	132

All I Knew For Sure Is They Have Some Horse Race   153
This Is Going To Work—I Hope   158
I Know I Am Better Than This   163
Nothing Beats On-The-Job Training   168
So When Do I Get To Write A Column Again   174
Column Writing As A Sport   176
Enjoy The Process—You Could Have A Real Job   182
From Hickman To Gravel Switch To Butcher Hollow   185
Not Exactly Full Circle But Close Enough   243
And Some Days There Is No Equal Justice   251
So You Want To Be A Columnist. No Problem   255
Columns Can Find You   275
More Columns From The Louisville Days   296
Stay Tuned. Bob Interviews A Gas Pump   315
Mcdonalds, My Father's Chair, A Wedding   328
Full Circle In A Boxing Ring   345
Epilogue   348

ACKNOWLEDGMENTS

This book, a product of 40 years of serendipity, memories, old newspaper columns, and spell check, is a testament to the power of collaboration. It would not have been possible without the contributions of a fine group of co-conspirators.

That would include Jim Tomlinson, a high school classmate and football teammate who is a fine book author. Our football team was undefeated two years in a row.

The hometown history in this book was only possible with the help of Rob Glover, director of the Joiner History Room at the Dekalb County History Center in Sycamore Illinois, who provided years of printed memories, and Michelle Donahoe, the center's executive director, who inspired the center's vision.

Add *Courier-Journal* writers and friends Dianne Aprile, John Hughes, and C. Ray Hall, who nudged the book in just the right places.

Former *Courier-Journal* copy editor Ed Heath spent many days diligently pursuing proper spelling, grammar, punctuation, and headlines, instantly banishing any and all semi-colons.

Photographer and good buddy John Nation not

only provided the book's cover photos but also offered constant encouragement, in-focus suggestions, and the occasional breakfast. His unwavering support was a driving force behind the book's completion.

Computer Guru Byron Graham was ever-helpful with minor book details such as organization, layout, design, printouts, page numbers, and author-publisher-copy-desk coordination.

Then, in the beginning, Old Stone Press publisher John Clark, a man I had never met, came to our house, sat on a sofa, and said, "Hey, Bob, why don't you write another book?"

Well, OK then.

PREFACE/PROLOGUE

The old saying "Life is what happens while you are making other plans" pretty much assumes there are other plans. In my youth among my peers that would have included becoming a cop, a fireman, a soldier, a pilot or a teacher. More modern youth might prefer to emulate tech and entrepreneurial giants Bill Gates or Elon Musk, or the talent and business savvy of Taylor Swift. Including social media, working at home and occasional hikes into the Grand Canyon with family and friends. And also, ditch the 40-hour work week. Add pricy weddings with family and friends in exotic places. Progressive politics. Hip-hop. Environmental work. Diversity. Pizza.

Truth be told, the only thing I have ever truly and deeply wanted to do was play centerfield for the New York Yankees, but Mickey Mantle had the job. Leaving me and John Fogerty pretty much lamenting life without a centerfield.

So, I ended up with a long and happy career as a writer, newspaper columnist and author, including writing 4,000 columns and 14 books. With a lot of time planting flowers, shrubs and trees and losing money in the nursery business.

This lesser tome of column-essays and reminisces will cover all that, including why I always preferred to live, work and be satisfied "out here," away from the news-dominated worlds on both coasts, with its occasional, almost self-conscious peeks at the nation's middle. Many journalists and others, of course, are very happy, productive and satisfied working in major metropolitan areas. All good and understood. To each his—or her—own. It's hard to become a world class ballerina living or staying in South Dakota,

That is really the larger point of this book. I was eventually lucky enough to be able to write many tales from both coasts, Washington D. C. to Orange, California, touch those sacred journalism bases and return home safely. Happiness is inside out. Hang on to it. If anyone in almost any profession eventually believes he or she is good enough to work anywhere, but finds security, peace, satisfaction and happiness in a place at least somewhat away from the Madding Crowd, why not live there? It will be a hellavu lot shorter drive to work.

Mine was eight miles.

The book will feature many of my favorite newspaper columns written for fun, good reason or because I had a damn deadline and space to fill. One longer tale will be an almost obligatory visit to Elvis Presley's birthplace in Tupelo. Another is a memorable visit drinking moonshine with Loretta Lynn's brother in Butcher Hollow, KY., and more important, feeling her sense of home.

But this book ain't all hound dogs and drunk husbands with lovin' on their minds. It covers presidential visits, brutal murder, justice delayed, interesting dead bodies, interviewing a talking gas pump, and political satire—is there any other kind?

There's failing at job hunting, an oyster dinner for a 104-year-old lady, lessons on how to write columns, the necessary blessings of serendipity, finding a home and staying there 50 years, and creating just the right mix of pumpkin pie aroma and lavender to produce an erection. Drinking for the latter was never mentioned.

Slight warning: This book will also meander some—nicely. It was never intended to be read all in one sitting, busting through in a few hours to get to the next book. Where's the fun in that? Slow down. Read some journalism history, a few old columns—there are plenty here covering a lot of time and territory. Think them over, enjoy the moments with the subject matter. Start a conversation.

My journey was less than a straight line. Along the way the Inner Writer in me kept struggling to get out, needing to be heard, sometimes banging loudly inside my head, but more often it was stalking me in the quiet of night asking pithy questions about my early vocational efforts.

Among them: As a college graduate could I be happy selling baseball bats at a suburban mall Montgomery Ward or ordering parts for police cars at a massive Chrysler assembly plant? Was that the best I could do for myself and my family? More important, was that what I was supposed to be doing with my life?

The theory "Bloom where you're planted" would suggest that personal misery should be endured for a decent salary, medical benefits, a pension and a pat on the head for rearranging widgets for 30 years. However, my career path involved backing away from widget rearranging as fast as possible, while keeping the family housed, clothed and fed until the right job came along. Both our children followed that same wandering path to success.

Janet Hill, my wife of 63 years, has always made that possible with endless love, patience and household skills while mothering our children, along with in-home transcribing, story-idea-offering, copy editing and critiques. She found happiness in a job as a teachers' assistant, mediocre pay but a chance to use her management skills and work with dedicated people while having the same hours and vacation as our children. She has been with me every step of the way, including the wrong ones. It can be hard to go forward when you have no idea where you're going.

As I finally found my designated career, that Inner Writer stayed with me, cheered me on, even occasionally helped with my spelling. It always seemed like a separate person, mostly showing up as needed, but willing to take a day or two off, perhaps to attend some seminar on Writers Block.

If someone praised something I wrote, I would always credit Inner Writer. It was responsible when the right words showed up, and often when a needed idea or burst of inspiration appeared at three o'clock in the morning. I was just the bearer of good words, the human vessel that drove the car to work to finish the job, to write the story. To be sure, not all Inner Writers are created equal, but I had no complaints.

My early newspaper career was somewhat hampered by the fact I had never taken a journalism class, had never taken a focused writing class, and I was writing by pencil in longhand. Still, I ended up producing more than 4,000 columns and feature stories and 16 books using my two fingers.

I also ended up winning many awards, my most cherished among them the Ernie Pyle Legacy Award given me for "Lifetime Achievement" by the National Society of Newspaper Columnists. Pyle was a legendary national Scripps-Howard columnist who wrote about life in America, and the men in the trenches in WWII. He was killed by a sniper's bullet in the Pacific Islands.

Bob Hill given the Ernie Pyle Legacy Award for his work.

Politics, per se, never interested me much. Mocking the process and its occupants, however, was mandatory. I grew up Eisenhower Republican and moved over to "Flaming Moderate," not seeing much productive legislation or co-operative instincts from extremists on the far left or right, although they could get the ball rolling on some needed changes.

My newspaper career began at my hometown

bi-weekly newspapers in Sycamore IL, then on to Rockford IL and the final 33 years at the *Louisville Times* and *Courier-Journal*, the latter then a family-owned, top 10 paper in the country that made staying out here all that easier. I did eventually write columns or stories from Europe, Czechoslovakia, Africa, South America and Canada, but mostly hung out in the Midwest and Kentucky, maybe even to write a book about all that titled "Out Here".

It's a book roughly divided into my three newspaper stops, with slices of life and thoughts about each stop, then favorite columns from each era. Looking back was fun, educational, necessary and somewhat humbling. With beer.

To keep you interested in the early chapters, I shall include bits and pieces of columns that just fit in with the narrative, in italic. The longer columns are coming later from each stop. Some so old they seemed new.

I have watched and lived with the sad demise of the newspaper business in many parts of the country, especially in small towns where it is needed most. In larger cities the talking heads and teams of "analysts" have turned sportscasts and news into loud entertainment, scatter-shot opinions and outright lies, many directly tied to particular political audiences.

I've witnessed the inevitable decrease in print editions and advertising as television, the internet, digital media and cell phones took larger slices of the pie. Scheming, self-serving politicians hammering away at "fake news" have seriously damaged credibility in a business filled with good, honest, caring people. What's the alternative, you might ask?

Please do.

Anyway, this is what happened in one very good life.

PART ONE
ON THE ROAD TO WRITING

In June 1975 I walked through the front door of the *Louisville Times and Courier-Journal* newspaper on my second day at work at the Times; Muhammad Ali was in the spacious lobby, autographing books. Yes, Muhammad Ali. The Louisville Lip. The Greatest.

I had grown up in a small mid-American corn-field town. All Eisenhower Republicans by default. My early journalism career had not placed me around many famous people. But there was Muhammad Ali. By himself, or as much as that could ever be. He had finished signing books and was headed out the door. A few more minutes and I would have missed him. Serendipity has always been a needed and necessary asset in my news career—and my life.

I turned around and followed him out the door, wondering where he was going. A few others in the lobby also followed him. Muhammad Ali had left the building. On foot. Headed east on Broadway. There was no waiting car. No entourage. Just Ali.

He was soon recognized. A few men in a bar peered out the window, even came out the door to watch, beers in hand. Others on the sidewalk turned to follow him. No idea where they were going. Just following Muhammad Ali. Walking. Ali was famous and infamous, respected and mocked, loved and hated. He had become a national hero by winning a gold medal in the 1960 Olympics and was happy to talk about it.

"Float like a butterfly, sting like a bee, the hands can't hit what the eyes can't see."

He created a national firestorm in 1964 when he changed his name from Cassius Clay to Muhammad Ali for his new Muslim religious beliefs. He refused to be drafted into the Vietnam War on those beliefs. I saw and felt both sides of that. Many others, some high school and college classmates included, had avoided the draft through deception or personal medical connections. I would have gone, but, including college deferments and a pregnant wife, my number never came up.

As we walked down the street, Ali, buoyant and on cue, began talking with his followers, his performance art on display. A live production. He tossed imaginary punches as they trailed behind him. Traffic on Broadway slowed, then stopped, drivers honked their horns, passengers frantically waved their hands. *"Hey, that's Muhammad Ali."* Second day in Louisville and my new job expectations had already been exceeded.

Ali's pursuing posse grew as we all walked west, a mix of about 20 people. I stuck with the parade for several blocks, enchanted by it all, taking mental notes, wondering where it all would lead. I later learned he was headed to the Louisville Free Public Library a few blocks up Broadway to sign more books. Right. Muhammad Ali in a "quiet please" library sanctuary. With mixed feelings I turned around and headed back to the paper. I couldn't be late on my second day of work, which would last in Louisville another 33 busy years, including Muhammad Ali's funeral.

Spending time with the world famous does polish the silverware on a reporter's resume, and I've had some of that beyond Ali. I've covered presidential politics and bar-fights, not always seeing much difference. The annual Kentucky Derby brought British royalty to town, and vivid memories of Louisville native Hunter S. Thompson, whose epic article "The Kentucky Derby is Decadent and Depraved" offered truth for years after he left town. John Wayne showed up, bent down to one knee beside a very short Courier-Journal photographer, the much beloved Bill Luster, and asked, "How's this little fella?" Baseball Hall of Famers came to the Louisville Slugger Museum from Ted Wiliams to Derek Jeter.

Many New York plays and famous performers showed up in Louisville's active art community, albeit a year or two after Broadway productions. I've watched the Supreme Court argue how old one must be to be charged with murder and heard America's best writers try to explain their genius at Kentucky Author Forums. The bottom line: Basically, you can do it well or you can't.

But over a 40-year columnist career covering two states and three newspapers I preferred to write about the people standing alongside a parade route, or who stayed home to raise dwarf goats in their basement, content in their place, if not willingly oblivious to the outside world.

It's all about timing. Everyone is a story at some point in his or her life. There are no new stories, only new reporters. On some days I would just get on a city bus to see who and what showed up. Or just write about the scenery. The bus driver. The tiny lady in the back row clutching a bright pink purse. Our son asking me to go fishing with him:

> *The boy had never asked me to go fishing with him before. He normally slips out the side door at sunrise, fishing pole in hand, headed for the creek to meet a buddy.*
>
> *The boy never goes fishing without announcing his intent the night before. Then he leaves a one-word reminder scrawled across the kitchen message board. It is as tender in its thoughtfulness as it is alarming in its composition.*
>
> *"Fishin'," he writes.*
>
> *This time the boy asked me Saturday afternoon if I would like to go fishing with him Sunday morning. The question warmed me. I try to tell my son once a day I love him. It is not very often that 11-year-olds return the favor.*
>
> *He woke me at 6:30 a.m., Sunday, edging into our bedroom and reaching out suddenly from its darkness to grab my shoulder,*
>
> *"Dad, are you still going fishing?"*
>
> *"You bet."*

Along my journalism journey I met a 78-year-old woodworker in the Eastern Kentucky mountains. He had spent almost 60 years hand-crafting dulcimers and caskets, spending about 100 hours on each casket. His nicely worn tale was that he kept trying to make one final casket for himself but ended up selling it to close friends. We sat at his bench and talked for hours, his tools of trade in hand. He laughed as he reported that he was willing to try his casket one more time, "I ain't ready to die no how."

I met a 94-year-old Black man in Western Kentucky who, as a son of slaves, had lived our complex and bitter American history. His sagging wood-frame house was only two miles from the farm where he had been born. As we talked, we walked deep into the woods searching for his parents' graves, so poorly marked and far back in the trees and weeds we couldn't find them.

I spent time with a Louisville woman who stood in her back-yard garden and sang happy songs about her home-grown tomatoes. Her smiles lit up the garden. As a hugely sophisticated local columnist I also got to wrestle a live bear in a downtown motel parking lot—had a column due the next day—and rode an elephant in a circus parade.

Bob wrestles a benign bear in a downtown Louisville motel parking lot.

I spent another few hours with a Rockford IL man, who, at 78 and needing something to do, rented a small downtown parking lot. Capitalism on a string. We sat together in his old wooden shack as he explained that on nights when he felt like it, he would just park 17 cars at 50 cents each, then go home. That's $8.50 for a summer evening.

I watched a golf-ball-hunting spaniel at work in the thick grass at the edge of a city golf course, his proud owner dumping the find in a five-gallon bucket. I sat talking to an animated Pee Wee Reese, a Louisville and Brooklyn Dodger legend, who I had watched on television in hundreds of games, World Series included, whose voice I first heard in the announcer's booth with another legend, Dizzy Dean.

Bob Hill living large on a circus elephant.

Baseball was my game. My good buddy, Joel Winkowski, and I had mown down the grass in a pasture to fashion our Field of Dreams, played there for hours in the summer, looking for our chance at the majors. We were both Yankee fans.

Now there he was, Pee Wee Reese, talking baseball and Jackie Robinson. Pee Wee, "The Captain," 18 years in the major leagues, later gave me an autographed picture of the famous incident where he put his arm around Jackie's shoulder in public support of a teammate in a very racist world.

He autographed it, *"To Bob, a dear friend..."*

I wrote a column about Dick Vitale, the name-dropping, cliché-ridden, basketball announcer and his propensity for the phrases "Diaper Dandy," and "prime-time, P-T-P player" and got a phone call from Dickie V. himself asking what's the problem? His support group included my sportswriter friends that knew and liked the guy, and, of course, the funds he raised for cancer research. What's a columnist to say? I just told him while my face-to-face sports buddies liked him, I found his on-air persona annoying. We left it at that.

I wrote about meeting Micky Mantle, my absolute childhood idol. I would write one of my very first columns about meeting him in a major league ballpark. Keep reading, it's in the book. I later sat on a couch next to Stan Musial as he played "Take Me Out to the Ballgame" on his harmonica as we all sang along. And I was sitting behind Dodger's legendary announcer Vin Scully, who had 66 years in the booth, when I reached up and snagged a foul ball as it came whistling into the booth over his head.

Being there always mattered in the column business. I spent a day in a primarily Black community in the Eastern Kentucky hills with NBA star and coach Bernie Bickerstaff, a mountain native whose father and grandfather worked in the coal mines after moving north to find work.

I wrote the horrific story of a Holocaust survivor finally ready to talk about her experience before she died, the first reporter she had ever spoken with. I wrote of a WWII combat veteran with his harrowing tale of luck and survival hiding in a grove of trees from the Nazis, and then how he became my dentist. I became investigative reporter Bob when the City of Louisville ordered the demolition of a doghouse. A dog story barking to be told.

Very early in the game I wrote all my stories with a pencil—the only equipment with which I was familiar. It did take me a while even to learn to use a typewriter. But once that became part of the process, our young daughter, when asked what I did for a living, provided an answer covering all areas of my journalistic experience, if not almost all writing experiences.

"Daddy types," she said.

Nobody has ever topped that.

Daddy types.

Our elder child will register for her high school classes today. She is now the same age her mother was when we first met and traded incredibly self-conscious notes on three-ringed line paper in freshman study hall.

Our elder child took to school as easily as a six-term congressman takes to equivocation. We had crammed her preschool years with candy-cane stories of the wonder of education to emotionally prepare her.

It wasn't that long ago that she had ridden the kindergarten mini-bus to her first day of classes. It was a crisp, blue September morning framed in glowing sunlight. She waited for that first ride perched in an aluminum lawn chair at the far end of our sidewalk, her yellow hair neatly combed, her feet dangling 10 inches above the cement.

The bus made a tight circle in the farmyard and stopped directly in front of the chair. The elder child popped up the stairs and disappeared inside, not even looking back at us as the bus doors folded shut behind her.

We had never intended that she be that emotionally prepared.

―――

My journalism career came with some travel, too. Writing took me to the World Ice Skating Championships in Czechoslovakia. It also led to a nighttime walk into Butcher Hollow KY to visit Loretta Lynn's actual homeplace, and on a daylight trip to a Southern Indiana nudist colony. The lesson learned there: There is zero sex appeal in a swimming pool full of naked people.

I Interviewed a still-coherent old man holding in his guts with two bloody hands following a shotgun blast at close quarters. His assailant was never charged because he had terminal cancer. I spent a long day in the not-so-sacred halls of the U.S. Supreme Court as it discussed the nuanced details of a horrible, abusive murder during a convenient store robbery and could a 17-year-old be sentenced to death?

I covered two NCAA basketball championships, one victory each for Kentucky and Louisville, in a basketball-crazed state. Newspaper journalism took me way up into Minnesota to write of the "Cornbread Mafia," a tight-knit group of Kentuckians with a massive Midwestern marijuana empire featuring hundreds of acres of pot hidden away in the middle of corn fields.

Not one of the many arrested agreed to testify against the others, serving prison time instead. The code unbroken.

Louisville photographer John Nation and I made a 5,700-mile trip to Ghana to write about Louisville doctors caring for pregnant native women under a tent in an open field. Some of the women, barefoot and already mothers, were carrying small children in crude packs on their backs.

Then there was a live Louisville NPR radio show offering commentary on all things local and national, another NPR show on gardening and a few hundred Louisville newspaper garden columns labeled "Down and Dirty."

All of that from being based "Out Here."

My journey eventually included writing books whose opportunities all came to me as a long-time local newspaper columnist, such recognition placing me ahead of many very good and frustrated writers who never had a book published.

Right place. Right time. Inner Voice.

Two of my books on gardening came just using the scripts of Fred Wiche, a very popular Louisville TV personality with a horticulture bent. We sold almost 25,000 locally, figuring every gardener in Louisville was gifted six.

My book on the history of the Louisville Slugger came with the territory, my love of baseball, and included an interview with Yankee Captain Derek Jeter.

A book on bi-polar illness came following a column about a man trying to deal with the issue, his life a constant emotional adjustment. He wanted to say more in a book, needed to say more, to explain the uncontrollable urges that came with it. The book, *"Survivors: Five Stories of Depression & Manic Depression,"* would include the life stories of five very interesting people, their highs and lows, financial losses and gains, their personal lives torn apart and never rebuilt.

"Double Jeopardy," was a book about a Louisville man who got away with murder, proof of his crime only found after his acquittal. I interviewed 10 of the 12 jurors who exonerated him. One juror said he was certain the defendant was guilty, but he wanted to get home by Christmas.

The book earned a visit on "Geraldo," the national TV show that was more spam entertainment than journalism, but at least I managed to include a sun-splashed walk in Central Park.

"Always Moving Forward," is a 2024 book about the life story of Louisville native David Jones, who grew up poor in blue-collar Louisville. He and partner Wendall Cherry each borrowed $1,000 in 1961 to found what became the Humana Corporation, which had $90 billion in earnings in 2023.

His was a tale of genius, humility, philanthropy and changes in medical care. He gave back his life's lessons and hundreds of millions of dollars to Louisville and beyond. The award-winning book gave needed recognition and inspiration to a very successful man who didn't want his name on any building or park he helped create, always insisting, "You don't pray in public."

Humana co-founder David Allen Jones is wearing his casual black shoes and slacks, a slightly wrinkled Parklands of Floyds Fork shirt and his ever-present confident smile. He is standing in an empty lot, once the site of his small, crowded boyhood home at 1737 Garland Ave. in Louisville KY.

We had come to visit and talk about a place—even time—that he had never really left: this neighborhood, this house, who he was, who he became. His roots were here in blue-collar West Louisville, where his dreams began in the 1930s. The many neighborhood problems that needed changing then are still here now.

The stories of home included his part-time jobs: pumping gas at all-night gas stations, handing out hundreds of flyers door to door and repairing and replacing windows with his father.

He told of old-world grocery stores whose owners gave the needy neighbors credit, the local saloons serving take-home beer in buckets, the poker games in back rooms.

His life memories are vivid, heart-felt and picture perfect. He can just as easily tell of his father's backyard vegetable garden on Garland Avenue as his later experience walking the debris-laden streets of New York on 9/11 as the city crashed down around him.

Along with all this came the creeping death of the newspaper business, the profit-first newspaper chains, the loss of family ownership, the explosion of social media news outlets and "alternative truth" sycophants. Nostalgia comes easy, the resurrection more difficult.

Journalism was never about money to the people who worked and lived it. It rarely is in the land of newspapers. Our pay was about the same as good schoolteachers, but without the 30 needy kids eight to ten hours a day. I just loved the business and the good people in it. They come from diverse backgrounds, most bringing the cheerful cynicism about the job and the world required us to deal with its many faults and still be dedicated to fixing it. At least as we saw it. There is some truth to the old cliché that an objective reporter is one whose prejudices you agree with. But it's now all much more complicated than that with our profession so diminished by self-serving, political bullshit and charges of "fake news." I fear it will only get worse.

PART TWO
FIGURING IT ALL OUT

My career began, as few journalism careers have, as a management trainee sitting on an overstuffed sofa in a Montgomery Ward store in Houston. With somewhat different chairs waiting ahead in Illinois, Indiana and Kentucky. Along with typewriters, hot lead and Linotype machines. Then came digital, cell phones and storing stuff in a cloud.

My life's path was not neat, tidy, direct or even expected. At 26, I had just figured out that I wanted to write for a living, needed to write for a living, and newspapers were how I could get there. I explained to people that I didn't go forward into my career path. I "backed" into it, basically refusing to do for very long what I didn't want to do until I found out what I did. Then stuck with it.

But it was never quite that simple. At 26, married, with kids, requiring clothes, food, schoolbooks and rent, I needed jobs, any jobs. So, the backing up began. In forward steps, my Montgomery Ward experience was quickly followed by sitting in a big office with about 30 other automatons at a Chrysler assembly plant in Belvidere, IL, ordering literally millions of car parts by telephone from Detroit. Not much poetic license allowed there. Just mostly grizzled, hard-nosed men on the other end of the phone meeting constant deadlines and not always happy about it. I made one trip to Detroit to meet them. Suspicions were confirmed.

My find-your-happiness process wasn't all bad. It helped me develop and retain a better understanding of the real working world in which I had grown up, but never much thought about. Like selling baseball bats and catchers' mitts in a Montgomery Ward store in suburban Houston. Or watching people fasten 60 mufflers an hour onto the metal frames of Plymouths relentlessly flowing down a huge Chrysler assembly line built in Northern Illinois corn fields. It was make-a-living and pay-the-bills kind of work.

Later, as a journalist out in the nation's midlands, I would watch with some fascination as national elections brought the seasonal river of famed journalists out to the Midwest from both coasts to determine what we locals were thinking.

I watched Dan Rather taking stock of regular folk in Louisville by asking questions of them while wearing a brand-new pair of blue jeans. He and his peers would hang out in Midwestern diners and coffee shops, microphones in hand, asking softball cultural and political questions. They still do, only in larger volumes in select states. Yet nobody ever suggested I reverse the trend and head into Katz's Delicatessen in New York City to discuss what those urban locals were thinking over a pastrami sandwich.

By the time I saw that journalism truth, I figured I was good enough to work anywhere. Many of my peers had taken jobs with The *New York Times*, the *Washington Post* and the *Los Angeles Times*, all places I had thought about as necessary bookmarks for success, but never really lost any sleep over it. My biggest chance at that would come when I was offered the job as sports editor for the *Kansas City Star*. I was an ex-jock. It would have put me onto the circuit of all that mattered in sports—Super Bowl, World Series, NBA finals, NCAA football and basketball finals, et al.

When I arrived in Kansas City for an interview, I was told the former occupant of the Kansas City job was on the road almost 200 days the previous year. I was already hesitant. By then our family, my wife and two young kids, were happily settled in an 1860s farmhouse on six acres of Southern Indiana only eight miles from the Louisville office. Twenty easy minutes to work. All that would have been lost in an endless rush of cross-nation deadlines, airports, coliseums, stadiums, rented cars, traffic and hotels. But with the chance to cover such as Walter Payton, Kareem Abdul-Jabbar and George Brett.

As I was mulling over the job, Ed Bennett, a *Louisville Times* editor and friend, came to my house to talk about the potential move. He brought along a six-pack of beer. We climbed into the loft of the small wooden barn some friends and I had built on our place, sat in a couple of folding chairs and looked out an open loft door at our green pasture below and talked.

Game over. I decided right there I would prefer to watch my own kids grow up and play sports rather than watching someone else's kids play games two time zones from home. It's a price many sports writers and columnists pay, and few of their devoted readers think about. What's more important, being at an NBA finals or your daughter's high school graduation? Sure, a couple of laps around the Big Time Circuit would have been nice, but that wasn't the game I wanted. I've never really regretted the decision, but I did save those empty beer bottles.

FROM SINGAC TO SYCAMORE

But long before making that Kansas City decision, there was that job as a Montgomery Ward trainee, my first out of college. I launched that career—go figure—in its sports department. If all went as the Retail Gods had planned, it was a program that was to last six months before perhaps moving on to a promotion to assistant housewares manager.

The job defined my desperation. I had just graduated from Rice University in 1964, consistently ranked as one of the nation's best universities, with a Bachelor of Commerce degree. I didn't choose commerce, it chose me, my only hope of graduation in four years. I still had absolutely no idea what I wanted to be when I grew up. Actually, less than no idea. Rice had been free with a basketball scholarship, including a grand adventure in Texas, the place as much a state of mind as a state in the union. All I really wanted was to just get the hell out of Rice with any degree in four years . . . while married. More on that later.

In retrospect, writing should always have been a career option. I had always enjoyed reading, the disappearing into myself that came with it. I was a natural writer, but I didn't know it. I was always much more comfortable with writing my thoughts than vocalizing them. And better at it. I'm still that way. My writing did get my high school teachers' attention and good grades. It felt good. But compared to what? I had to find that out.

I had gone to Rice from Sycamore IL, then a classic Midwestern corn-field community of 5,000 about 60 miles west of Chicago. Except for Chicago Cubs, White Sox and Bears broadcasts, Chicago could have been 6,000 miles away. It was a rarely visited place, if not planet, its suburbs already edging out.

I was eight years old in 1951 when my parents moved us to Sycamore from Singac NJ, maybe 20 miles from New York. Our father, a mid-level engineer with only two years of college, had been transferred there by a company producing electrical wire. The move meant leaving our East Coast family behind, save occasional and ever-diminishing visits back home.

The strongest memories of my New Jersey years are the stuff of Mafia movies. On one summer visit to see family in the crowded New York milieu, some bigger kids grabbed me and held me in front of a fierce gush of water pouring from a fire hydrant. They laughed and let me go, washed downstream in terror.

As a kid in Singac I was paid 50 cents a day by a neighbor to feed his fighting-cock roosters living in coops about 50 yards from our house. I had no real idea of their deadly end game. Each had sharp spurs attached to its legs. White feathers flying, they would tear each other to bloody death in a wooden ring in a nearby filthy barn as dozens of men crowded around, placed bets and cheered. One of my best friends lived upstairs above the ring. I would stay overnight in his house with the smell of straw, dirt and dead fowl floating up from below. When my parents found out, they ended my cock-feeding employment, my first job.

We lived for a time in a very small, rented yellow house with wide stone steps and the Passaic River flowing past just across the way. It was an all-blue-collar world with some hollyhock and lilac bushes, a small garden and a burning barrel out back for trash. Some days my mom would tie me to the trash barrel with a rope to keep me in the yard. I needed it.

World War II had just ended. Milk and ice for our ice box came in a horse-drawn wagon, the delivery man using metal tongs to haul big blocks of ice up those stone stairs, leaning into the task, is a picture that lingers.

On summer afternoons the ice cream man would come into our neighborhood, peddling his cart, ringing his bell. This stopped rather abruptly when a neighbor who worked nights and slept days got irritated with the noise, came out of his house and decked the ice cream man with one punch. Game over. What greater trauma for a six-year-old kid than witnessing our Eskimo Pie guy get flattened. Memories of Jersey. Worse, we never saw the ice cream man again.

In retrospect, with then four kids in our family and constantly moving from house to house and then living with our grandparents, money was always an issue. My father went to work on a bus. My mom worked as a waitress. The neighbor raised fighting cocks. We never took vacations. A TV sitcom on a 13-inch, black-and-white television. It was all we knew and nothing to compare it to.

We would walk a couple blocks to the neighborhood grocery store for eggs and bread, the purchases kept on a tab. In winter we would glide our Flexible Flyer sleds down a steep hill past parked cars and out onto a highway. Our weekly allowances were a nickel a year for every birthday. Six-year-olds got 30 cents. But 60 cents never seemed near enough once turning 12. By then there were five kids with our hands out.

Part of our regular entertainment was swimming in the Passaic River at a place called Stoney's, an easy walk down a narrow dirt path. In those pre-EPA days the Passaic had caught on fire years earlier from heavy industrial pollution. Agent Orange was being produced in nearby Newark, with residue being dumped in the river, all unknown to us neighborhood swimmers. One day a stranger, a painter, gave me 10 cents to sit on the edge of a rowboat in the middle of the river to pose for his work. If I had fallen in I never could have made it to shore. Never told Mom about that one.

When we moved to a bigger house in Singac, our grade school was only two blocks away. I ran away from home at four years old and tried to enroll myself in kindergarten a year early. Mom came and got me. She worked irregular hours as a waitress. Irish and very protective, there was the day she was told a man had threatened to beat me up. I can still see her, marching down the street, with a big brown beer bottle in her hand, ready to clobber some guy to defend her son. Ring up Martin Scorsese.

Just to get her dander up, we five kids would later

ask Mom which of us she liked best. Her answer: "I never liked any of you sons-a-bitches." We were all reasonably sure she was kidding. Her beer bottle had established that.

Years later I met a guy who penned a letter to his mom on his 28th birthday figuring out, a little belatedly, how that came to happen:

> *To my Mom,*
>
> *I have been thinking about this for a lot of reasons, I guess. Been thinking a lot about family and the big changes going on now. Been thinking about my birthday and the celebration of it. It seems the celebration is always on the bornee and not the borner.*
>
> *Then each year it was more of the same, but also more different. I began to notice that I was celebrating my birthday, that I was the center and the cause of all the hoopla, and you have begun to fade into the background. You wanted me to have it all.*
>
> *When I became a living member of the outside world that day. I came from you. One minute we were one and the same, the next, two very different, and alike, people.*
>
> *And so, on this my 28th birthday, I join you in celebration for that day in 1954. And to thank you for that day, and all those that*

have followed.
I love you Mom.
Bobby.

———

For me, there were brighter East Coast memories, like a trip to Yankee Stadium to see Mickey Mantle. I was eight years old. As we crawled through the Bronx in heavy traffic with three-story brick buildings pushing out to the street, I kept wondering how anyone could play a baseball game here. We parked in front of the huge, curved stadium with giant light towers. Our stadium seats were up high and deep, and as we walked out way above center field, my first glimpse of all that emerald-green grass spread out below, with Mickey Mantle in charge, was a religious experience.

A short time later we were off to Illinois, located somewhere out there beyond Chicago on a map our parents had shown us. Dad and four of us kids—ages ten, eight, five and three - and our large Collie, Lassie, were all stuffed into a new, rented car for the journey. Our family had never been anywhere near a new car. Our mom, very pregnant with her fifth child, flew out to Chicago later to be met and taken into our new world.

All new, this. Our 840-mile trip west on mostly two-lane highways took three days. With big, black clouds of steel-mill smoke pouring out above as we drove through Pittsburgh, the big soft beds in hotels and restaurant food day and night. We were amazed. Lassie stayed in the car.

Once in Ohio and Indiana there were corn fields.

Lots of corn fields. And farmhouses and animals straight out of our children's books. We took turns sitting in the front seat with Dad, and then the back seat with Lassie, looking out the windows, wondering, the images piling up.

Once transplanted to Northern Illinois, we lived first in a two-story house on the east end of Sycamore as all our landscapes noticeably widened. The sun was more of a presence, arching overhead and dropping over the flat horizon on a regular basis.

Sycamore, a world of tidy Republicans with its churches, busy downtown shops, good schools, a community park and small-town flavor, was a good place to grow up. I bonded with it all, the fields, the broad sky, the nearby Kishwaukee River.

Kishwaukee was a Potawatomi word for "river of the Sycamore," those huge, white-barked trees that grew along its banks from which the Native Americans carved dugout canoes. The river came with the freedom to fish it, wander it, skip rocks in it, walk the railroad tracks along it. Without being held captive to a gushing fire hydrant. Or worrying our parents.

The rich Midwestern Illinois prairies were created by millions of years of glaciers, swamps and decay leaving 20 feet of rich soil. Then came the farmers creating miles of flat corn and bean fields. Then came the crunching fall harvests as bug-like, monster combines turned the fields to ragged stubble. Then to see the fields plowed and planted again in spring, the seedlings rising in the black dirt. Up the corn and beans went. Down they came. Year after year. Mine was a good life lived in ancient poetic agriculture circles not realized at the time, the fields just something to be endured on the way to fishing the Kishwaukee River. Those images stuck and came in handy later.

Hot summer jobs came with that turf. As a 16-year-old teenager I joined my peers in big fields of hybrid corn, hand-pulling tassels from the tops of each six- to eight-foot stalk to prevent cross pollination. We began about 6 a.m., the male and female teen-agers understandably pulling tassels in separate fields to keep things moving, working eight-hour days.

We had to reach up and bend each stalk without breaking it, the dew fresh on razor-sharp leaves, walking and yanking in 100-yard rows. Our pay was 65 cents an hour, 75 cents if you didn't quit before all the yanking was done. Most of us stuck it out. My total detasseling paycheck was something like $58, enough to buy a portable radio requiring four D-size batteries. A memory there, too, carrying the radio on mile-long walks to the community park, listening to Elvis, Brenda Lee and Buddy Holly.

In high school I worked at the nearby stockyards stacking bales of hay in precise patterns in huge, open sheds. That earned a then-princely $1.50 an hour in the 1950s working 12 hours a day, seven days a week. At break time we grabbed clubs and tipped over stock yard feed stalls, hunting rats. I later lived and worked on a high school classmate's family-owned dairy farm. It paid $300 a summer, with room and board and endless adventures for man and cow, not all of them particularly useful or environmentally friendly.

Another summer I worked in a Wurlitzer piano factory unloading enormous oak and mahogany planks from the gloom of huge boxcars onto forklifts. My partner in this clumsy balancing act was a very handsome, frustrated musician who talked constantly of wanting to go to California, maybe in a boxcar. With him it seemed possible.

Sycamore was all so clearly Midwestern as later defined to me by writers and poets such as Willa Cather, Edgar Lee Masters and later, Garrison Keillor. All their stories were told from inside out.

I read a lot as a kid—the usual Tom Sawyer and Huck Finn, then Isaac Asimov, then on to John Steinbeck, J. D. Sallinger and Jack Kerouac. I cannot remember a single book I read in college. One favorite sixth-grade teacher would put stars on the wall next to our names for each book read. My stars were lined up down the wall and around the corner.

Some nights our whole family would be sitting in chairs around the living room reading. Then it was off for more books. Many days I would walk the mile—uphill of course—to the Sycamore Public Library, erected in 1905 with an Andrew Carnegie grant. Our librarian was Cleta Harr, who held sway over the place and her books like a Prussian guard. In summers she would insist on checking my hands for dirt before letting me in. One day I checked out a book, walked across the street to read it on the courthouse lawn, and tried to take it back the same day. She wouldn't let me. She didn't believe I had finished it.

My early Sycamore was the world of status quo. In 1952 our Central Grade School had a mock election for the Dwight Eisenhower--Adlai Stevenson presidential race, with Stevenson being a former Illinois governor. The result was like 121 to 1 for Eisenhower. We all wondered who the traitor was.

Come the Eisenhower inauguration, our fourth-grade class walked about five blocks to Bobby Waller's house to watch it on a small, black-and-white TV. Eisenhower was right there in front of us. The president. My first live glimpse. So was Washington. It was an enduring memory of my youth.

Living inside the Midwest could disguise its ugly truths, another journalistic lesson. You must leave a place, then look back to see it. Sycamore had a small Black population—very rare for small Midwest towns. Most had moved there to work in the several factories in Sycamore, their housing strictly limited to "North Avenue" on the so-described north edge of town.

But we kids—white and Black—all attended the same schools, joined in the same school groups, played on the same athletic teams, and, yes, some became best friends for life.

When you think about it, racism is learned in ignorance, then taught, stereotyped and used for personal gain. That was much less of a problem for us kids just standing together in the same lunch lines. But we all lived with our enduring, unconscious racism and stereotypes. They don't go away at any age until you become aware of them. Even then they linger. It takes work to change.

Our Black community had a separate restaurant and bar, "Dixie's," owned by a man named Dixie Sims. In its day it was all-you-could-eat chicken or duck and strawberry shortcake on Wednesdays for 25 cents. In the early 1900s Sims was a local prize fighter. He gave lessons in the "Dixie Gym." His son, Allen, and wife, Fannie, ran the restaurant and bar for years after he died. Fannie was on the Sycamore planning commission, library board and human relations commission for many years.

In later years back in Sycamore I would hang out with friends and customers in Dixie's bar. One was a Black Vietnam combat veteran who spent too much time at the bar. After a couple beers we would go outside and sit on the steps to talk. One night he told of a Vietnam experience, a fierce jungle battle during which a bullet entered his mouth and blew out his cheek. A small scar remained. He was a man allowed to fight and die for his country but could only live on one designated street in his town.

As I grew up, sports entered my life, pushing aside real academic achievement and even any possible thought of being a writer. My dad, never much of an athlete, was a big baseball fan. I grew tall and skinny—six feet tall at age 12—but very clumsy, with low confidence.

Baseball was a way out of that. Our Little League manager, Wilber Kocher, would hit long fly balls at practice in our community park, which was then circled by farm fields, now pricey subdivisions. The balls would hang up high in the soft summer air, carefully poised at the top of an arc, waiting for me to run them down just as Wilbur had shown us.

Hunting fly balls took some practice. They defined my summer, my early athletic success: *I can do this.* One night Wilbur leaned over my shoulder and whispered, "Bobby, you're going to be in the major leagues someday."

That thought hung up there for years like a high fly ball. Almost 60 years later, for his 98th birthday I gave Wilbur a Louisville Slugger bat with his name on it. He said he remembered those fly balls, too.

Basketball popped into my life at the original Sycamore Community Center, a solid red-brick building built in 1875. It was first a Universalist church, then an activities center, then the Midwest Museum of Natural History. Then, incredibly enough, a country and western saloon. In my day it was a basketball court in a box, with tall wooden walls about a foot off the sidelines and big, square wooden backboards.

The community center was about a mile from our house. At 10 years old I'd walk up Saturday mornings, dribbling a cheap rubber basketball all the way. I played in stocking feet, throwing up shots and chasing down the results. The fabled "Chucks" tennis shoes—named for 1919 Columbus IN high school basketball star Chuck Taylor—came later at $7.95. On some Saturday mornings my shots would drop into the basket. It was a nice surprise, a whole different feeling that needed to be repeated.

My first organized basketball games came in the fourth grade at Central School. Our principal, Burdette Peterson, was coach and keeper of the real basketballs. He was as Midwestern tight and fit as a drill sergeant, all about sturdy discipline, raising an arm and standing still to get his attention. Another lesson learned—temporarily. We won our first game 3-0. Grant Henry got all three points. We still laugh about it.

We had no goal at home. Most days I would cut through a neighbor's yard to practice shooting for hours at a netless metal rim attached to a round steel backboard bolted onto a pole stuffed into an asphalt high school parking lot. On cold days I would shoot until my fingers turned red and numb.

Some coordination showed up just in time for high school. Suddenly one summer I could dunk a basketball in our tiny, Quonset-hut gym. It was supposed to be locked but we would go in through a locker room window. The coaches knew it. I still remember that first dunk, the absolute surprise and joy of it, the ball slammed *downward* through the goal and net. *What the hell was that?*

As a 6-foot-2 freshman I played some varsity games. At 6-foot-4, I started on the varsity team for the next three years, pushing up to 190 pounds. I remember dunking in our warmup lines, with grade school kids leaning over the balcony cheering me on. Oh, to be 17 again and be cheered.

I would eventually letter in four varsity sports at Sycamore High School, football, basketball, baseball and track. I was an all-conference tight end on two undefeated football teams, with BIG 10 scholarship offers from Iowa and Northwestern. I was second-team all-conference in basketball. I had peaked out in baseball in Little League and ran, threw the discus and competed in hurdles in track.

By then any thought of academics—or writing—had totally slipped away. I was happy with a "B" grade average and a better jump shot. Given the family finances I was counting on an athletic scholarship to get me into college, the school's size and location was almost immaterial.

So, it was, the door to somewhere, still waiting to find me. In the big high school writing picture, I had a knack for cranking out essays. I was popular, even elected class president, with no leadership skills. Nobody ever told me that writing could be a way to make a living.

The closest I came to high school encouragement was my English teacher, Virginia Garland. She praised my essays, told me I had talent and encouraged me to write more. She watched me very nervously give a book report on John Hersey's *Hiroshima*, to a sophomore English class. My hands were shaking so badly I had to push them down to the lectern to keep them still. Afterward, she sent me a note saying, "Good report, Bob, good use of hands."

I always wanted to thank her for first stirring the latent writing fire in me. I heard she had married and moved off to Texas. Many years later I wrote a Louisville Courier-Journal column about her. Afterward I learned she had been living in Madison IN, just 40 miles away, but had recently died. I met with a relative in Madison who had read the column. We went to her grave where I gave muted thanks.

Even in high school, I had a knack for writing goofy poetry, a talent, in retrospect, I could have used for country songs or beer commercials. But years later it would turn up in a newspaper on occasion: What else could you do with a water-skiing squirrel in a huge convention center?

Bob Hill

Of Twiggy I sing, a florida gray
a squirrel of homeric adventures
for Twiggy floats not on feet of clay
but on Styrofoam extenders.

Now Twiggy's new, and a little bit more
of new waves she's the curl
she's what the public is crying for
a water-skiing squirrel

Twiggy trained for two short months
and daily she stood taller
as she became the less a klutz
her skis were whittled smaller

Something there is, says Robert Frost
that doesn't love a wall
and something there is, says Robert Hill
that loves a skiing squirrel

———

But even way back in my adolescent, goofy-poems phase, I'm sure there were some discussions with my parents, and our high school guidance counselor, trying to figure out a serious future education.

Football was out. It was my best sport, and we all loved our Illinois Hall of Fame coach, Pete Johnson, but I hated football practices. Baseball, my favorite sport, was out. I had peaked at 12. Track? Hurdles? No way.

BASKETBALL, SLIDE RULES AND LARRY MCMURTRY

I had one interview with a football/academic recruiter from Dartmouth but was soon told by a favorite teacher "*You* don't want to go there." I've thought that over for about 60 years, too. Why not? The recruiter seemed to think I could make it in the Ivy League, a whole different world that a few of my Sycamore schoolmates had already conquered. But my teacher was right. I think.

That left basketball—and Rice University, an academic, engineering school in Houston in football-crazed Texas with 1,600 undergraduate students and a 70,000-seat football stadium it would fill for games against LSU, Texas, Texas A&M and such.

It had a 5,200-seat gymnasium and a basketball coach named Johnnie Frankie, who knew Illinois high school basketball was then much better than Texas high school basketball. So, he came to our house in Sycamore and sat down in our living room to talk about it with my folks and me.

Rice had never been on my radar. It was 1,066.4 miles from Sycamore. I knew nothing of the old

Southwest Conference, had only a TV western sense of Texas. And there we were: my dad, an engineer with a mid-level job and two years of college. And my mom, the high-school-graduate waitress who was a good, funny natural writer herself. She had worked for years trying to sell a satirical piece to the *New Yorker* written in longhand. She and Dad, without degrees, had always preached college to all us kids. And Mom's stories never made the New Yorker.

And then Rice, the engineering school where it never snowed, and some students walked around in pre-calculator days with slide rules on their hips. And me, who had one day of high school calculus and no interest in math or engineering, or even Texas at that point. But Texas turned out to be interesting and Rice was free with basketball.

To seal the deal the Rice Athletic Department flew me down to Houston for a visit, my first ever airplane ride. Where, not wanting to appear to be a dumb Midwesterner while eating shrimp at our recruit dinner, I didn't ask any questions about the method of consumption. I had never seen a shrimp. I ate the tail and threw away the meat. My Texas teammates loudly reminded me of that for the next forty years.

So, Rice it was, with the decision being made just to get a free education from a damn good school and worry about the job thing later. I was an engineering major for about two weeks until confronting head-on the horrors of slide rules—one of which I had never owned or operated—and calculus. As soon as possible I flipped over to the newly introduced Bachelor of Commerce program and gently rode that out for a degree. It was later framed, hung high on the wall of our large TV-watching room and largely forgotten.

As far as basketball was concerned, I had three prime skills. I could shoot, I could shoot, and I also could shoot. Pass some. Rebound a little. Defense never much interested me. At 6 foot 4 I was then the wrong size for any position having never learned how to dribble.

I did have a good time playing at Rice from 1960 to 1964 with a bare modicum of success in the then all-white and very mediocre Southwest Conference basketball world. Freshmen were not eligible then. I started a few games my junior year but mostly sat my senior year when a new coach was hired. He was a disaster. After the Frankie-recruited players graduated Rice won only three games in two years, going 1-22 and 2-23 in a weak basketball conference.

Bob Hill 40 pounds and 60 years ago.

My strongest basketball memory is of playing SMU in Dallas a few weeks after President John F. Kenedy was assassinated. Before the game I walked down from our hotel by Dealey Plaza and looked up at a sixth-floor window of the Texas School Book Depository where Lee Harvey Oswald had been kneeling when he shot the president. I just stood and stared at that window. Later in life as a tourist at a National Society of Newspaper Columnists convention in Dallas I got to stand on the sixth floor and look out toward Dealy Plaza.

It all then seemed a little too touristy, to come see where a president was murdered, but that image lingers, too.

My first college roommate was Kendall Rhine. He was from Dupo IL, another small town just outside St. Louis. He was by far the best player on our team and later played with the ABA Kentucky Colonels for a year. We quickly bonded. We were both dead broke most of the time. We walked three miles from Rice to the downtown movies to save money. We hunted for golf balls at night, wading in a nearby upscale country club lake until I got chased out by a guard with a .22 rifle pointed at my back. Long-legged Kendall was long-gone by then.

We hitchhiked home together from Houston to Illinois one spring. We were 6-foot-9 and 6-foot-4, standing along country roads, tall and needy, thumbs out, day and night. I had farther to go up to Northern Illinois, so it took me 33 separate rides over 36 hours to cover my 1,064.6 miles. I kept a notebook, documenting all the people and places along the way, thinking I might chronicle the trip one day. I lost it. Jack Kerouac kept his. But now I can just make things up.

Between my sophomore and junior years at Rice I married Janet Dieterlen, my Sycamore High School sweetheart, just to get us together again. We didn't have to get married. No children then. I was 19 and she was 18. We had no idea what was involved. None.

We were one and two years out of high school, the senior prom. We lived on a $65 monthly stipend from Rice, her $240-a-month secretarial salary and young love as we understood it at the time. We now have 63 years of marriage and counting. We live on love now.

College was a blur. I was there because I was supposed to be there to play basketball and get some degree. Studying and learning seemed a part of that, but only to take the next test, with basketball practice to follow. I've always thought I'd like to go back to college some day and do it right. Maybe learn something and hold on to it for further discussion.

My best classes—and grades—were in history and English, although it never really occurred to me at Rice to think *why*. They were just my easiest classes. I saved many of those essays and term papers with their good grades and comments, just thinking it was a good idea to keep them. Wasn't sure why. All of it written in long hand. They all got accidentally tossed out in a house remodeling.

It was a time at Rice when novelist Larry McMurtry, author of "Dead Man's Walk," "Lonesome Dove" and "The Last Picture Show," among others that became movies, was teaching there. I remember being in an English class with a very confident teacher sitting cross legged on a desk talking. I've since seen pictures of McMurtry sitting on a desk, talking. I keep thinking it had to be him and wishing I had paid more attention. What would have happened if I had stuck around after class to talk to the guy, paid attention, gone to more of his lectures, sought his advice. Where could that have led?

"Lonesome Dove"—a novel by Larry McMurtry

When Augustus came out on the porch that morning blue pigs had eaten a rattlesnake—not a very big one. It had probably just been crawling around looking for shade when it ran into the pigs. They were having a fine tug-of-war with it, and its rattling days were over. The sow had it by the neck, the shoat had the tail.

"You pigs git," Augustas said, kicking the shoat, "Head on down to the creek if you want to eat that snake," It was the porch he begrudged them, not the snake.

My summer job in Houston before my senior year with the Walter Mischer Construction Company was an education in itself. The firm was constructing massive subdivisions at the edge of Houston, a town without real edges as it madly pushed outward with no zoning. Houston's population was less than a million in the 1960s. Houston's metropolitan area is now almost eight million.

That job, arranged by the Rice University Athletic department, was to work with a crew laying water lines beneath flat Texas fields in 100 degree-plus summer temperatures. More specifically, I was handed a paint brush and a can of black protective goop and told to paint the ends of each section of clay pipe before they were glued together by a crew working in trenches often 10 to 15 feet below ground. I was also taking a summer course at night at San Jacinto College seeking a credit in some math course needed to graduate in four years.

I was the only white guy in the pipe-laying crew. The foreman, a soft-spoken man, and the backhoe driver, a racist asshole, were white. I was paid $1.50 an hour for being white. The Black guys, who worked down in those deep dangerous trenches, got $1.25 an hour with no medical or insurance benefits. Any overtime pay came after 40 hours of work a week. You could work 36 hours in three days, get rained out the next two days, and no overtime in the paycheck.

This was the early 1960s. I suspect my co-workers knew the salary differential. That's the way it was. We got along, at least as far as I understood it. We talked a little during breaks about our life and families, but never the pay. I was always the white college kid. Just there for the summer. I could move my work into the shade, take breaks as needed. Their lives would remain sweating down in the trenches. A few times that summer I went down there with them, looking up at those steep clay walls to see and feel what it was like working 10 feet underground, trying to earn a little respect.

Their leader above and in the trenches was Raymond Nunn, a stocky, muscular Black man who just radiated leadership with very few words. Everyone in our crew respected Raymond. He was just Raymond.

Years later I would write a column about him, the world in which he and his co-workers lived, the leadership that came so naturally to him and other people I would meet along the way.

The folks who really get the work done aren't always the ones in charge

Sometimes when I watch alleged leaders—or even fellow office workers—circle one another for weeks at a time trying to exercise control or solve some argument or dispute, I think about the work ethic of Raymond Nunn.

Raymond was not born to be a diplomat. He was a construction worker, a man of limited formal education who never would have felt at home in an office, much less at a banquet table. But he had a way of getting his message across.

Raymond was the most naturally muscled man I have ever known. When he lifted things, the cords along the back of his neck would knot up and thick slabs of muscle would gather across his back and shoulders and down across his thighs and calves.

Just watching Raymond walk across a field, his shirt unbuttoned, his arms as thick and taut as ship's rope, you could see the power in the man and sense his presence.

Raymond knew this, of course. There were buttons on his shirt. He could have buttoned them. But that wouldn't have been Raymond.

Raymond had come by this muscle the old-fashioned way; he earned it. He'd been digging trenches and lifting pipes since he was a kid. He had never been in the mainstream of public educational or social concern. To Raymond Nunn, Head Start was something you got on Friday nights to beat the traffic on the way home.

We met during a summertime construction job in Texas. We were laying a waterline across a flat field so some developer could fill it with streets and houses. There were about 15 laborers in our crew, and 14 of them—the black laborers—were being paid $1.25 an hour. I got $1.50 an hour because I was white.

I'm sure that kind of pay structure really bothered Raymond, but we never got close enough to talk about it; that's just the way things were then in Texas.

It was lousy and dangerous work at 10 times the pay. Often the temperature would be in the high 80s when we went to work at 7 a.m. and would be well over 100 when we quit at 5 or 6 p.m.

It was my job to stay above ground and slop some goop on the end of the pipes to better seal them. The rest of the crew—the Black guys—worked down in trenches 10 to 12 deep laying the water pipe, while another white guy on a small bulldozer would fill in the trenches right behind them.

There were almost no safety precautions. One rainy morning a trench caved in, and two terrified men scrambled nearly 10 feet up the sheer face of a dirt wall as tons of thick, wet earth slid in behind them.

The crew took a 10-minute break to clear the trench, added a couple of supports and went back to work.

Raymond was the crew boss. We had crane operators, bulldozer jockeys and even an official foreman—all white, of course—but Raymond was the man, the sergeant, the ramrod.

He just did it naturally. The other people made more money, drove nicer cars and huddled together when things went wrong, but not much moved unless Raymond said it moved.

It wasn't that he talked much or even raised his voice; Raymond came of more heroic proportion than that. Raymond really was the strong silent type. He could give orders without even opening his mouth. A guy could look at Raymond and understand he'd better go pick up a shovel and get in the trench.

I don't know how he did it. But I know I have watched dozens of other people over the years try to give orders, people who were supposed to be in charge but who had no natural leadership ability, and none of them could do it as well as Raymond; it takes a heckuva man to get somebody in the bottom of a wet, 15-foot-deep trench at 7 o'clock on a rainy morning.

Like I said, Raymond knew it, and he took no small pride in that. In a way, that was his extra pay, his other 25 cents an hour. The better-paid people were playing a game; they could all pretend to be in charge, but everybody in the field or down in the trench knew the real score.

Sometimes I think the world is run by the people like Raymond, people who are either denied the chance to be placed in charge or are just more comfortable operating a few notches below the firing line.

It is almost always they—the upper-level city or

county employees who stay while elected bosses come and go, the secretaries who run the office for 20 years while bosses are promoted upward—who get the real work accomplished.

And they know it.

July 22, 1989

There were obviously no life guarantees working at the bottom of the trenches, no wall supports. Any safety was in the hands of the asshole backhoe driver and his far-reaching bucket, pushing out and coming down. The human lives didn't seem to matter all that much.

Another day we were all sent to another job on the far side of Houston. Not wanting to drive there and back, several of us got there sitting in the open air behind the cab of the flatbed truck used to haul the backhoe. As we pushed through busy Houston traffic the asshole backhoe driver, also driving the flatbed truck, deliberately weaved it back and forth, looking out his rear window laughing as we hung on with both hands for dear life.

When we reached the new construction site the asshole driver climbed up on the flatbed truck. I decked him with one punch. He left me alone after that. I only missed one day of work all that summer. I was worn out from helping lay pipe beginning at 7 a.m. and stopping by San Jacinto Junior College on the way home for a sociology class, mostly to earn credits to graduate in four years. It was 14-hour days in the open fields and hurried classes living off packed lunches.

The one day I was absent the foreman called me that morning to ask what the problem was. I told him I was sick, would be in the next day. I was. On my last day of work, he said I was the only college kid he ever had who stuck it out all summer.

WHAT DO YOU MEAN THERE ARE NO NEW JOBS

In the spring of my senior year at Rice I began going to the placement center to cash in my four-year degree from a marvelous academic institution. I was also a very unsure interviewee with a Bachelor of Commerce degree. The people representing the engineering companies were alternately kind or condescending. With reason. Either way I didn't fit their needs. I had an overall "C" average and no real interest in engineering or business. I just needed a job. Both sides of our employment discussions knew it.

I routinely put on a suit, skinny tie and played the game . . . poorly. Then on one very bleak and memorable day I went over to the job center and the Rice guy in charge of job interviews basically told me, "Sorry Bob, there are no more interviews scheduled this spring. We are done for now."

And I am thinking: *Wait a minute. What the hell is this? I am married and have a degree from a very good educational institution, the very best in all of Texas, and I can't get a job.*

Finally, a former basketball teammate, a math

major who did get a job, suggested I try retail giant Montgomery Ward, a company, somewhat ironically, actually involved in commerce.

I forget how that interview happened, but I was hired as a management trainee in a sports department in a suburban mall for $440 a month. Two weeks in I wanted out. Janet insisted I wait six months—traditional good form at the time.

About two months into the job the Montgomery Ward regional manager came to visit. We met in the store's furniture department, all employees spread out across soft chairs and sofas. He was a big, burly, blustery, self-confident guy who quickly informed us he was making $40,000 a year in 1964 wages managing 40 stores while I was literally sitting on $440 a month.

The talk did turn out to be a gamechanger. The guy was ego-entertaining. He suddenly went all football-coach, halftime pep talk, revving us up with the wonders of Montgomery Ward, the kind of speech I had heard maybe 250 times before. But he was pretty good at it. He ranted on, words flying across the sofas, then reached a thunderous crescendo and screamed, *"Everyone who wants to sell a sofa stand up and holler."*

He looked damn proud of his sofa speech, but it was perhaps the most crucial turning point of my young life. Seriously. I looked around to discover I was the only one in the room still sitting. All the rest had jumped up eager to sell a sofa, or at least kiss the regional manager's ass. A room full of sofa-selling-crazed adults.

No thanks, regional bossman. It was reflection time. I found myself looking back on the encouraging words of former high school English teacher Virginia Garland. I'm thinking maybe I could be very happy as a writer. Maybe even get into newspapers, which I had always read cover to cover, especially the columnists.

I told Janet I was gone from the sofa-selling world. I was off to become a writer. Local Montgomery Ward management was not surprised. At six months I gave notice and spent the last two weeks of my retail career playing Santa Claus, making soft promises to little kids sitting in my lap and then riding around the store on a bike in a Santa Claus suit honking its horn. Perhaps the finest exit in the history of retail sales.

With no experience in the writing business—I couldn't even type—my first stop was a University of Houston freshman journalism class. All I remember of that was an older, slim-trim former newspaper guy who preached that a good journalist always goes out armed with five, maybe six questions: Who, what, when, where and why. And sometimes how?

As the guy spoke—this in the mid-1960s—he held up folded sheets of typewriter paper, which he very carefully tucked into left jacket pocket, showing off his magic. Good journalists, he said, should always carry folded paper and two sharp pencils.

What could be easier than that? Paper and sharp pencils. And I already knew about pencils. And five solid questions. Who needs to finish this class? What else was there to know about journalism? So, I bailed out early.

Janet and I had already been having serious discussions about heading back north toward home to start over. She wanted out of Houston. I wanted a job. Our decision to move back home had roughly coincided with another possibility about our future. Even before being rejected by business school recruiters at Rice, I had tried to sign up for the U.S. Navy Officer's Candidate School.

It made some sense at the time. As a kid I had always been fascinated with military history, primarily World War II in the South Pacific. I read extensively of the bloody Marine landings on Guadalcanal, the Solomon Islands and Iwo Jima. I had memorized all three verses of the Marine Corp Hymn. An uncle, a tail gunner on a B-17 bomber, died when his plane was shot down off the coast of France. His picture in uniform is pinned above my desk to this day, a faint, told-you-so smile on his face, dark eyes staring off into space.

I was a full-bore, patriotic Midwest American with no idea what to do with my life, and the Navy seemed a possibility. One downside was that I was a lousy swimmer. I had almost drowned in the Atlantic Ocean at a family outing at Jones Beach NY and never would get over it, with a lifetime fear of large bodies of water.

This was 1964, when the Vietnam War was beginning to escalate, but with no thought or understanding where that might lead, a horrible waste of 58,000 lives created by the "Red Scare" and then prolonged by disingenuous, lying politicians.

My attempt to become a Navy officer didn't get past the first physical. I was born with poor vision in my right eye—amblyopia or "lazy eye muscle." I was instantly disqualified. Years later, as the Vietnam War escalated and more bodies were needed, I was given another physical at the U.S. Army draft center in Chicago.

Retreat to Canada never crossed my mind. Attendance was mandatory. Duty called, but not quite as loudly as my earlier attempt to join the Navy. By then it was obvious our government needed more bodies for a cause without end.

Dozens of us possible draftees were herded on buses in DeKalb IL and shipped into Chicago where we stood in long lines for hours in our underwear being poked and prodded like cattle. It was a bizarre, surreal experience being suddenly yanked out of the civilian world and paraded toward a possibly frightening and unknown future.

The doctor assessing my eyes this time decided my Navy experience with amblyopia was no longer a problem. Your eyes are fine, son. Uncle Sam and Vietnam need your body. The next man up was measuring my height. He slammed the metal bar down on my head so hard I measured 6-foot-2, two inches below normal. I then weighed about 245 pounds. At 6-foot-2 I would have been a little too heavy to be labeled 1A draft material. My Vietnam military future had come down to being slammed on the head with a metal bar.

The man doing the slamming looked at me again, and asked how tall I was. I owned up to being 6-foot-4, and I was back to being Vietnam draft eligible. I was never called. College deferments, Janet becoming pregnant and a high draft number—chosen at random—kept me out of a war fought by those who couldn't find ways to beat the system.

Vietnam forever took away my automatic Midwestern belief in government, a helpful if not necessary trait for a journalist. I have twice since been to the Vietnam Memorial to touch the name of a good friend's dead brother. Many others joined me along the wall, heads bowed, some of us crying.

I would later write in Rockford a column about another sad Vietnam experience:

Untold story buried in yellow envelopes

Newspapers bury the dead in small yellow envelopes and place them in alphabetical order in their libraries so they can be more easily exhumed.

In time, the newspaper clippings become creased and torn and the pictures fade. In time, the deaths pile up until a broader category is needed. All the suffering must be consolidated into other envelopes in the interest of more efficient newspapers.

So we have three thick envelopes and one much thinner, labeled: VIETNAM WAR—RFD AREA FATALITIES.

We have 241 people buried in those little yellow envelopes, but the stories are very incomplete.

Our clips do not say that 1st Lt. Stanley F. "Fred" Patterson is buried under a pine tree in Little Harlem Cemetery at Alpine and Harlem Roads.

Our clips do not say that Tuesday afternoon the flag

over his bronze grave marker was snapping defiantly in the wind.

Our clips do not say that almost eight years after the death of their only son, Stanley and Ruby Patterson, 2003 Exeter Ave. are still heartbroken.

They do not say that after the United States finally abandoned the bloody quagmire of Vietnam to the Communists, Stanley and Ruby feel their only son died for nothing.

THEY HAVE his last letter. It came the same day the war department notified them their son had been shot. The letter opened with a complaint about the weather. It closed with the report his platoon sergeant and three of his four platoon leaders were dead.

"I am the only one left," their son wrote. Lt. Patterson had named his tank "Leigh Ann" after a baby daughter he never saw. His wife remarried and has moved to California.

Stanley Patterson was bitter about the war. He said wars are started by governments, but must be fought by people.

"War is all politics," he said. "The government starts wars to bring an end to recession. We could have another war now. The government knows if you have a million men fighting you need five million more working at home. A few men come back from war. The rest go to hospitals. I'm with Goldwater. We should have put an atomic bomb on Hanoi and ended the whole thing."

Our newspaper files do not say the Pattersons have placed many of their only son's toys on a shelf in the basement. There is a green and white farm wagon Patterson made for his son along with well-worn tractors *and a combine.*

An August 1953, Sports Afield sits on a table. It tells of Stanley Patterson and his son "Freddie" and the luck they had on the boy's first duck hunt.

There are other pictures of father and son together. Two golf clubs the son had used are mounted on purple felt surrounded by the medals he had won at Harlem High School and later in the Army.

"We were a family," Patterson said. "We did things. Kids don't do that today. Freddie and I promised each other a hunting trip as soon as he got home."

THE NEWSPAPER clips didn't say that Ruby Patterson thinks of her son daily, and often goes to his gravesite.

The don't say that Lt. Patterson's stepsisters still visit the grave for hours on end, talking to their brother.

The clips don't say that Stanley Patterson at once fears a Communist takeover here, but views Vietnam as political folly.

"Freddie" was going to be a lawyer and a senator," he said. "But he died for nothing., President Johnson got into the war but didn't know how the hell to get out. We fought it all for nothing"

The clips don't say what the parents of the other 240 Vietnam dead are thinking as they watch South Vietnam abandon province after province to the guerrillas.

They don't say that Ruby Patterson still breaks into tears talking about her son.

They can't explain the agonizing dilemma of our withdrawal from Indochina.

Out Here

They don't say that on July 7, 1967, as Lt. Stanley F. Patterson lay dying in Chu Chi, Vietnam, he told his captain to tell his father he would never make that hunting trip.

IT ALL BEGAN WITH $500 AND A '52 BUICK

So, the decision was made to move back north to Sycamore. It offered a totally uncertain future, but with an upgrade in transportation and material goods. Our trip south to Houston after our Aug. 25, 1962, wedding came behind the wheel of a 1952 straight-eight Buick. We had purchased it for $150 from Janet's uncle "Tige" Hoffman, who co-owned a Texaco station in Sycamore. The previous owner of the car had died owing her uncle $150 for repairs.

Our assets totaled $500 and the "52 Buick We named it "Old Green" for both its fading, turtle-green exterior paint and disposition. We first headed toward my parents' new home in Holly Springs, MS. Old Green overheated about 170 miles out of town. We finished the next 430 southbound miles driving at night, the air a little cooler, on two-lane country roads at 40 miles an hour, radiator repair to follow.

Our three, penny-pinching years in Houston proved somewhat economically successful. Sort of. We moved on from Old Green to a 1959 Ford Fairlane with a slight uptick in worldly possessions. We had first headed south pulling a 4-by-6 trailer. Our trip back north about three years later required a 5-by-7 trailer. Roughly 11 more square feet of life-sustaining stuff. The American Dream.

Once back home in Illinois, reality reared its humorless head. This writing thing was a nice idea, but we again had bills to pay for such as rent, food and gas. The Chrysler Corporation had just opened a monster assembly plant near Belvidere, IL, about 25 miles north of Sycamore and was needing literally thousands of employees. I had joined that line for a very brief interview and was led to believe I had a full-time job there in public relations, or close. It seemed to offer a brighter future than selling sofas. Oh, yeah, bring along that prized Bachelor of Commerce degree.

When I showed up for my new career in public relations I was informed, with no warning, my new job actually would be in production control. Sorry Bob, that promised job was taken. My actual job would be sitting behind a desk eight hours a day, at minimum, ordering some of the roughly 30,000 parts required for those several thousand people in that huge metal building next door to churn out one new car a minute. That public relations job may be available at some point in the future point, they said. No possible date mentioned.

So, it was back to Priority One, the paying-bills thing. Just roll with it and see what happens. Bloom, ah, where you are planted. This 1965 production control job was way before computers, social media or robots. We were about 30 people in a big room using telephones to call people in Detroit who were connected by telephones to the actual manufacturers of those

30,000 parts. We logged all our orders and inventory by hand in fat ledgers, each of the thousands of parts a separate page, line by line, with various clones handling different parts. It was about the kind of accounting offered years earlier by Ebenezer Scrooge.

Given the relatively limited space available to store parts even in such huge buildings, the inventory churn was incredible, with only a couple days' supply of some larger parts on hand. Keeping Chrysler happy required a constant flow of trains, trucks and delivery vehicles into Northern Illinois cornfields, including a few chartered flights.

I started out ordering parts in general, then was told to become more focused on ordering tires. A promotion of sorts? Entire boxcars of tires of various sizes. Five tires required per car in an assembly plant at one time turning out more than 1,000 cars a day. Do the math. Picture that. Lots of tires. Boxcars of tires. All logged in.

Then, sensing I was coachable, management swung me over to ordering security parts for police cars, door locks, sirens and stuff. Playing Santa Claus in a suburban Montgomery Ward store had never seemed so satisfying. The good news at that time was our daughter, Jennifer, was born on September 26, 1966, healthy and happy, with almost all that bill paid with an excellent Chrysler insurance program.

There was also the day the plant ran out of a particular part on my part list. We had been frantically trying for two days to get more. They didn't come. Some of the assembly lines were shut down. I remember looking out a window as workers headed to the parking lot. Early. But with union pay. Chrysler opened again by the next shift.

Some days I would take off and walk down to the curling assembly lines to watch the men and women work. The repetition, the coordination required was almost an art—attach a door, turn around and attach another door, then another, another, the line ever-moving, sparks flying, mindless and relentless. Next. Next. Next. The work kept coming. Hours. Days. Months. Years.

Death and disaster showed up the following spring. We had about 30 people in our production control office with thousands more next door. Our vulnerability became apparent on April 21, 1967, when an F-4 tornado landed on a hill southwest of our plant. We had our first Chrysler plant tornado drill only the day before. The workers across the room from us watched as the tornado twisted down from the gray sky, blowing up a barn and heading toward our massive complex filled with millions of metal parts and vulnerable workers.

As practiced, we were quickly herded into cinder-block stair wells. We waited, fearful, clinging together in silent terror as the tornado passed just a hundred yards away with a dull roar, seemingly sucking some air out of our stairwell. We left that possible tomb to see railroad cars sprawled along the tracks, workers' cars tossed 100 yards into nearby fields, but no damage to the main building.

This was long before any community-wide tornado warnings. After just missing the Chrysler plant, the tornado roared over the top of nearby high school just as school buses were being loaded. One bus was tossed beyond the parking lot, its top ripped off, with students inside. The grim total would include 24 killed, 13 of them students, with 410 injured as the tornado damaged or blew away more than 500 homes.

The roads out of the parking lot were filled with crumpled cars, impassable. I ran two miles home through the damage, houses in ruins, cars flipped, residents standing outside in silent shock, with no idea what I would find. I had been able to call home with a frantic phone call just as the tornado roared down the hill outside Chrysler. Janet had grabbed Jennifer and rushed across the street to a nearby hospital for shelter, soon to be filled with tornado victims.

My family was fine. I walked back to the high school to see if I could help, saw a row of bodies carefully laid out on the gymnasium floor. Bleeding, shell-shocked students were being loaded onto buses to be taken to the hospital. Doors were pulled off the frames to be used as stretchers. Groups of volunteers walked the halls, searching rooms for more victims. It was all grim business with little conversation. Outside, a stunned horse stood head-down in a nearby street as people and ambulances hustled past, oblivious to a lone horse in the middle of chaos. I would see much more of that shock and terror in coming years.

SHOW UP, SHUT UP AND WAIT FOR THE PENSION

The Chrysler work was all union, good pay, with lots of overtime, excellent benefits and pension. I worked with good people. One was a Korean War veteran who talked a little about combat, frost and death. We had an Arkansas-native, good-ole-boy supervisor with natural people skills who occasionally led us into a local bowling alley for a party when the work seemed overwhelming, the drinks free, or on Chrysler. That period was our first and last years in a bowling league, almost mandatory in that 1960s, blue-collar world. I think my average was about 145, Janet about 100. Good times.

Most of my co-workers seemed happy with their work, or at least its benefits. The money was good, the extra-pay overtime was part of life. It was easy to get stuck in that ethos, the security, the satisfaction, the pride in the product with a good pension that locked people into a job that was truly impossible for me to like. We were all working on the assembly line, just in different buildings, with no guarantees. In more recent times the whole plant was shut down, thousands of lost jobs devastating the community, then was later scheduled to reopen by Stellantis.

I was then 25, two years in and I needed to get out. I still wanted to get into writing, but I had realistically bent that goal into a slightly different direction. There is in the sports world a job titled "sports information director." It combines a type of public relations work—which never showed up at Chrysler—and a job dealing with the people, reporters and media setting up interviews, handing out statistics and story ideas along with access to damn good seats to big games.

While at Chrysler I had checked into those possibilities at a couple of local universities with no luck. Sports information is often an entry level job, but ordering 500,000 tires and parts for police cars was not the resume they were looking for.

At that point, my frustration owned me. I was drinking too much, wasn't at all useful to be around, although I never thought it approached a continual drinking problem, more a weekend and gone-golfing problem.

That old country song *"I gotta get drunk, and I sure do dread it"* was too often on stage, along with stupid, inmature and a lousy parent and spouse. I was not a happy, fulfilled guy. I slowly got better. Janet again held us all together. My idea of a solution was to quit Chrysler cold turkey, go home and then tell Janet I was out of the police-car-parts business.

Which I did. I did give two weeks' notice. Which left us with no income, a few thousand dollars in the bank, rent and car payments, our six-month-old daughter and no writing opportunities . . . or experience . . . or possibilities. But backing away from something I didn't want to do had never felt better, and I would always take care of my family.

For a little extra money, I cashed in all my savings bonds required to be a Chrysler employee. Time to start doing what the hell you want to do—once you totally figure it out. And faced with that same situation again, at that same time and place in my life, I would do it again.

I immediately took to writing letters to small, local daily newspapers asking for a job, mostly hiding the fact I had no training, no experience and couldn't type. Serendipity was in the saddle. One letter led me to my hometown biweekly newspapers, the aptly named *Sycamore Sun Tribune* and the *True Republican*. The latter, it proudly stated on the masthead, was "a home journal devoted to Republican principles and local interests." The papers had been around under various forms, names and ownership since 1861, about the time an Illinois Republican named Abe Lincoln became president.

I had nothing to show the Sycamore management, no writing samples of any kind. My solution was to create a fictional account of how a drop of water fastened to an old spigot kept growing bigger and bigger until it became a threat to mankind, a story perhaps better reserved for a B-movie script. I don't remember giving it a name, perhaps "The Water Drop from Hell."

That was it. My writing resume. The Sycamore newspapers' manager just kind of grinned about the Big Water Drop Essay. He then explained that the current newspaper editor had just given notice and, with me being from Sycamore and possessing an actual

The Sycamore crew: Dave Ross, Carol Brannon, and Bob Hill.

college degree, I could be their new newspaper editor for $105 a week and no benefits. Neither one of us mentioned the degree was a Bachelor of Commerce.

It was serendipity in a water drop. The $105-a-week was about 40 percent of my salary package at Chrysler, which also included benefits, medical insurance and pension. I instantly took the newspaper job. My copy of the Water Drop Essay got lost in time.

GAME ON

The Sycamore newspapers were owned by John Castle, a local businessmen and lawyer who, with other investors, had visions of merging four local Northern Illinois weekly papers into a morning daily to compete with a long-established afternoon paper, the *DeKalb Daily Chronicle*.

I knew nothing of that when hired. Except for that skinny guy at the University of Houston with some sharp pencils, folded paper and his who, what, when, where and why thing, I had no journalism training. I sought help. I remember an evening spent with a Northern Illinois University journalism professor at nearby DeKalb to get a crash course in the profession.

We talked and shared a bit of bourbon, then more bourbon, perhaps the best and lasting journalistic takeaway from that session. He was a very kind man who well understood my need for on-the-job training. When our meeting ended the professor leaned in my direction and wished me well.

The Sycamore paper offices were in an old two-story building just off its main street. History lived there.

The building was once the home of Linotype machines that created molten-metal words to be attached to old metal presses used to pound out broad-sheet newspaper pages. Many thousands of them. For almost a century. One Linotype machine still resided in the dusty wood-beamed basement.

The first floor was all odd shelves, dusty corners and wooden stairs leading up to the open second floor, with the ghosts of former reporters, editors, columnists and photographers lurking in the shadows. History does not always get its due. Our old building was later torn down and replaced with a drive-through bank.

Our circulation was a few thousand copies, twice a week. The day-to-day work was all done by caring, professional women, most Sycamore natives. They took my initial, pencil-written stories, typed and copied them into an offset production system. The results, with advertising added, were carefully pasted onto newsprint-sized paper, processed onto metal sheets and sent off to the printer. The final product was delivered by the U.S. Postal Service or placed in local grocery stores, restaurants and newsstands.

Newspaper delivery prior to the digital world was always fascinating. In Sycamore, delivery was up to the U.S. Postal Service or Bennie the grocery store clerk. As I later moved forward into the daily newspaper business, delivery seemed utterly backwards:

To create a deliverable product required all adult newspaper planning, endless meetings scheduling stories by day, week, month and season. Teams of good, professional, college-educated editors, reporters and photographers would work for hours, days, even weeks on stories and ship them to equally professional back-shop employees to be printed.

Then that final, very carefully produced and edited product would be dropped off at very early morning hours to be delivered by 12-year-old kids on foot or riding bicycles. The same delivery after school for afternoon papers.

What other multi-million-dollar business would operate that way?

As I worked my way up the newspaper food chain, the one absolute truth I learned was that the bigger the paper, the less the community of readers really cared about it. Our bi-weekly Sycamore papers provided a personal touch—the local news mixed with public gossip, obituaries, birth announcements, wedding and anniversary pictures.

One designated correspondent highlighted who was hosting parties, who attended them and who served the coffee. There were bridge-club results, out-of-town guests and who was in the hospital. The names all came with a certain familiarity. If the papers were kept around long enough, they provided history lessons of at least who and how, always great for 50-year reunions.

All this has been lost—and dangerously so—as social media and corporate journalism pirates forced thousands of reporters and newspapers out of business, from weeklies to dailies, with fewer left to pursue who, what, when where and why. Opinion is for sale to the lowest bidder. So many smaller, remote towns no longer have that personal contact, or worse, anyone keeping track of local government. Facebook is not the solution.

In my case, my early newspaper career was only made possible by the kindness of patient women at the Sycamore papers who had to read my sloppy cursive and check my spelling and punctuation. Only the soft deadlines on our bi-weekly papers made that gothic process possible.

Photographs were taken with a bulky box camera with eight or 12 exposures on 120 film. I would point the box at a subject, peer down at the image and click, I was a news photographer.

The magic came in developing the film in our crude darkroom, then putting the negatives to work. The very images I had just photographed would somehow float up through the liquid developer onto a piece of paper, totally fascinating me at every newspaper stop along the way. The images were gently massaged or burned into life. Digital cameras took away a lot of that art, replacing it with speed and utility. Some poetry was lost in the process.

In Sycamore, being the only reporter and editor in the building at the time, I generally understood that my new responsibilities included covering meetings, hunting up the occasional feature story and writing of the local athletic events. I just had no real idea how to do it.

HOW DO YOU SPELL AWKWARD TRANSITION

It was an awkward transition. I read other stories, understood the process in principle, but putting the alphabet to work describing live events for people who were not there seemed a different matter. Only seven years before I had been a Sycamore Spartan on the football field, an all-conference performer for two undefeated teams. Now I was the guy on the sidelines with a notebook and sharp pencils.

That reporter mode would get a little more uncomfortable when interviewing the parents of former classmates or asking questions of city officials. Or worse, asking questions of my former coaches. I could sense that some long-time Sycamore residents—and me with a college degree—were wondering what the hell I was doing working back here on weekly papers. The boy has been to college. Why doesn't he get a real job?

Nor was I prepared to go all diligent investigative reporter in a place where we all went to the same schools, churches, bars and football games. To wit I walked into the local VFW one night, which was often full of beer-drinking veterans who had seen more brutal war than most, truly members of the Greatest Generation.

I was also there for a beer, and wandered into a room lined with slot machines. They were totally illegal but very good for VFW business, if not morale. Forget journalism. There was no story there for me. Not this hometown kid who grew up fond of the flag-waving marching bands in the Veterans Day parades. I still had to live there.

Still, there were local stories that required a little more gumption. Our very long-time mayor, Harold "Red" Johnson, a legendary auctioneer with his machine-gun delivery and big white hat, worked directly across the street from our office in the Gullberg & Haines Furniture Store. He was a distant family relation to my wife. I was a regular at his auctions. My specialty was wooden pullies, with Red occasionally cutting off his delivery a little quicker if I was ahead on a bid.

"*Allll in, allll done,*" Red would chant, shutting off the competition.

Red and the city council members had a bad habit of meeting an hour before the regular meeting to decide what they would do in the public show. I began going early to listen in, a pretty much unwanted guest protected by my First Amendment right. They began to shut that meeting down a little early, or just moved it.

Occasionally, more serious journalism was required. Red, who would be mayor for 36 years, had the local parking problem figured out. He had a portable parking sign he would lean up against the furniture store wall when he needed a place. More due diligence was required here. I took a picture of the sign up against the wall. It made front page news. Pulitzer Prize stuff—"Parking Gate." Red wasn't happy, but easily won re-election anyway. Another journalism lesson learned: A very popular Red was a lot bigger than any illegal no-parking sign. Much the same remains true in politics today.

My much-needed journalism support came about a month later with the arrival of Dave Ross, and a short time later, his friend Turner Lake. They took over as genuine editors and reporters. Both had degrees in English-journalism from Cornell College in Mount Vernon, IA.

Dave, a gregarious, outgoing Chicago native, exuded take-charge energy and bluster with no argument from me. His first change was to move what had been our very primitive office on the second floor down to near the front door, which, he said, gave us better access to the public, if not a better look at the Gullberg & Haines Furniture Store—and its mayoral occupant.

Next, he took a personal interest in the paper, and my work, including a life-changing suggestion that I begin writing a column for the paper. That really resonated with me. A moment every bit as important in my life as being asked to stand up and sell sofas. I could express myself through my fingers.

My first-ever newspaper column of the eventual 4,000, or so, was written on Jan. 26, 1968, in *The True Republican* and labeled "EXTRA POINTS by Bob Hill." The title was apparently the Inner Sportswriter in me trying to get out. Ross, who became a good friend, then suggested a much less prosaic name for future columns: "The Hill With It." Somewhat smirky in the news business. Almost profane in some small-town circles. We went with it. A new life was born.

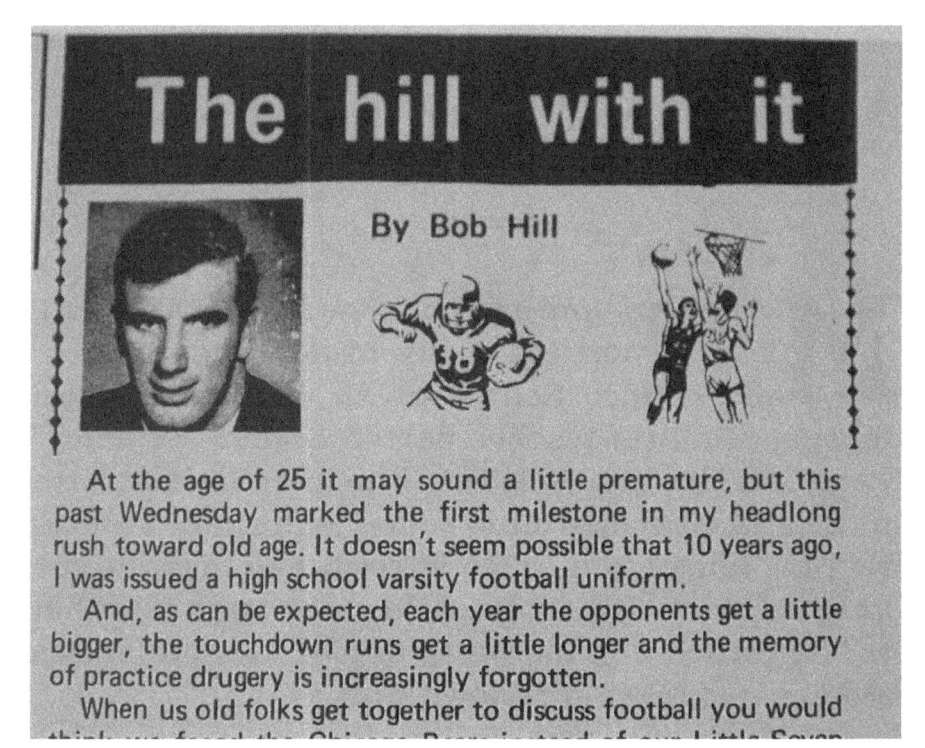

> **The hill with it**
>
> By Bob Hill
>
> At the age of 25 it may sound a little premature, but this past Wednesday marked the first milestone in my headlong rush toward old age. It doesn't seem possible that 10 years ago, I was issued a high school varsity football uniform.
>
> And, as can be expected, each year the opponents get a little bigger, the touchdown runs get a little longer and the memory of practice drugery is increasingly forgotten.
>
> When us old folks get together to discuss football you would

There are no bad puns in sports.

Sycamore gave me that start, offering awkward, self-conscious words written with absolutely no sense where it was all going. I had read a few thousand other columns by then, how hard could it be to write one?

IT ALL BEGAN WITH A GUY NAMED "SCUMMY"

My first column of the following 4,000, or so, was a short testimony to a legendary Sycamore High School coach and mechanical drawing and arts teacher named Leland "Scummy" Strombom. He was a classic, who loved to hold forth in class, was often seen in retirement slowly walking from his house to a coffee shop in mid-town to join other regulars. The story on his nickname was that he had earned it in his youth tipping over outhouses and one had taken him down with it.

> *LELAND STROMBOM, dean emeritus of the high school industrial arts department, is without a doubt one of the most genuinely respected men in the northern hemisphere.*
>
> *Under the concealing alias of "Scum" or "The Professor" he has left the world some monologues that should be enshrined in the great books of the western world.*
>
> *PICTURE if you will, "The Professor" in a battered hat and always slightly crooked*

bow tie expounding in "Strombomese."

WHAT do you think of the referees tonight, Scum?

"I have not had sufficient time to analyze the individual characteristics of the arbitrators in question. My decision will be forthcoming at a later date."

"SURE is a nice day isn't, Scum?"

"The climate conditions that prevail are uniformly pleasant and agreeable. It a pleasure to perambulate in such favorable circumstances."

THEN there is the lowly student whose class attitude does not match the standards set by the "Professor" and is temporarily dismissed.

"You may henceforth take a brief sojourn from your academic pursuits."

Turner Lake, my new friend and journalism mentor, introduced me to another possibility I had never considered: press passes.

Lake had worked on suburban Chicago newspapers, giving him access to press box passes to Chicago Cubs and White Sox games. So why not for the *Sycamore Sun Tribune* and *True Republican*? Just make a phone call. And there we sat drinking free beer watching Ernie Banks in Wrigley Field.

Lake followed that up with passes to professional golf tournaments in Chicago, and then a PGA Championship in Minnesota. All new experiences, and absolutely free. Never thought I'd be here stuff. It didn't take long to get used to that, especially while earning $105 a week. The sunny side of journalism.

With Ross and Lake and other new and very young journalists from Northern Illinois University, we began to publish pretty good newspapers for that time and place. We got into pollution issues, 1960s racial strife, a local teachers' strike and the plight of migrant workers, all way beyond the rote and routine coverage of previous years.

One intern on our staff who would go on to a fine Midwestern career as a reporter, editor and columnist in Ottawa IL was Lonny Cain. A little nervous at first, with no real reporting experience, he recalled our newspaper atmosphere as a "group hug." We held our planning meetings in a coffee shop. There was no bloodletting when his stories were turned in and he learned by watching and doing. He has fond memories of an editor's note given him as he left to cover an archery competition: "Don't get hit in the ass with a broadhead." Actually, pretty good suggestion for many journalism endeavors.

"I've been in several newsrooms since then" Cain said of his internship, "and they all reaffirmed what I learned that summer. Newsrooms are filled with crazy personalities high on the thrill of writing and chasing stories and fueled by the passion to make a difference."

With Ross and Lake around I happily moved over to becoming sports editor and writing "To Hill With It" columns. My idol was and remains *Chicago Tribune* columnist Mike Royko. His Chicago-tough, satirical and bitterly funny Pulitzer-winning columns often featured the fictional, working-class Slats Grobnik. I wasn't Mike Royko. But I would seek out real Slats Grobniks and Sally Grobniks for the next 40 years. That I could do.

WHAT DO YOU MEAN I HAVE TO LEARN HOW TO TYPE

A bout two years after I began in Sycamore, owner John Castle decided to take our weeklies to a daily paper, *The DeKalb Journal*, to compete with the *Daily Chronicle*. Mission was not accomplished. Castle would later sell the *Journal's* circulation to the *Chronicle*.

About the same time, I met a man named Roger Hedges. He was the state editor for the *Rockford Morning News* and *Register Republic* in Rockford IL, about 40 miles northwest of Sycamore. It was a family-owned newspaper sold to the Gannett Corporation a few years before I got there, a sales pattern to be repeated, regretfully, in my journalism travels.

Roger's job—also one I would eventually become very familiar with—was to wander Northern Illinois and Southern Wisconsin hiring correspondents to phone in local news from about 40 small towns, plus managing a regular staff.

Most of those hired were men and women with other jobs who were willing to cover city council meetings, local crime and occasionally write a feature story for fun, some satisfaction and minimal pay, but avoiding any possible mention of slot machines at the local VFW. They often did it for years, and very well, my mother included. She became a correspondent for the Rockford papers, finally her chance at the Fourth Estate.

Hedges had read and liked my stories and columns. He suggested if I wanted to work for a daily newspaper, it might be best if I learned how to type. No sharp-pencil cursive allowed on a copy desk on deadline.

Suggestion taken. I began taking typing lessons, but quickly became frustrated trying to learn to type with 10 fingers while using two fingers at work—an index finger from each hand. So, I stuck with those two fingers, on deadline and off, for the next 40 years. I always claimed I was good for at least 15 words a minute with six mistakes. And I could have been five times better with 10 fingers.

After a couple years, I was ready to move on from Sycamore. My Inner Voice had ambition, too. The papers had folded into the *Dekalb Journal,* which would fail. Hedges got me an interview that included the legendary Rockford newspapers' writing test. I was placed in a small room and given five separate facts covering something about a house, its occupants, a fire and a barking dog.

It did not require typing skills and a master's degree from Northwestern University Medill School of Journalism to figure this one out. Put the barking dog in the lede and you're hired. That's actually a metaphor for life and politics these days.

The only other thing standing between me and a job at Rockford was the equally legendary company physical. It was performed by a guy—I suspect not even a doctor—who only asked, at least this job applicant, to identify the colors of various pencils—red, blue or yellow—as he waved them. I nailed it. No color-blind need apply.

On looking over those early columns written in Sycamore they read like an early dance recital without shoes. But the intent was there, the sincerity was there and the future, as the saying goes, was ahead. I liked being lost in thought. I still had no idea where it might lead. So The Hill With It, get writing. One of the first up, so to speak, was yet another Mickey Mantle sighting, written in the nervous, tentative, self-effacing manner of a rookie trying to move on up to the Bigs.

Another old column about my coaching in Little League covered much of the same writing basepath, the third proving not much has changed with the NRA and un control in the last 55 years.

The Hill With It—1969

At the age of 10 and as a reward for one of my few good report cards, I was taken from Sycamore into Comiskey Park to see the White Sox face the New York Yankees.

It was then 1952 and the all-powerful Bronx Bombers ripped the White Sox in both ends of a double header to practically cinch another American League pennant.

Playing in center field was the "kid from Commerce, Oklahoma," Mickey Mantle. The "Mick" had a pair of sensational games that day. From then on my fate was sealed. I was going to play center field for the New York Yankees and be just like Mickey Mantle.

Fortunately for professional baseball I have subsequently turned into a hack journalist. But I, like most 10-year-olds, have never forgotten that dream, or the idol that went with it.

Last week, through the courtesy of White Sox public relations man, Don Unfurth, I came as close to that dream as I will ever get. Don sent me a field press pass to the Thursday night White Sox - Yankee game.

SO THERE we were, gathered around the batting cage: Tresh, Pepitone, Ford, Mantle and Hill. With practiced nonchalance, I fumbled with the camera straps, dropped the light meter on the ground and tripped over one of the cords and snapped about 16 out-of-focus pictures.

But the highlight of the pre-game warmup was my conversation with the "Mick." I waited until he was done batting (he put about three in the seats in batting practice), casually sided up to him, took a deep breath and uttered:

"Could you sign this ball, Mickey."

He nodded in the affirmative, then carefully put his signature between the seams of the ball. I mumbled a "thank you" and stuffed the ball in my sweater pocket, with the sweat of a 10-year-old running off my hands and down the back of my neck.

THIS EUPHORIA LASTED until I went up to the press box to watch the game. There I first noticed the "the Mick" was running with a slight limp. Another disturbing item was the day-to-day batting averages that showed Mantle hitting only .226. But this same statistic sheet showed Mantle with 534 career home runs, and said he needed only one more to move into third place on the all-time list. I had a feeling that, somehow, he may just hit that one tonight.

The first time up, he was walked on four straight pitches and I thought, with a feeling of pride, that despite his .226 average the pitchers were still afraid of him.

The second time "the Kid" came up, the score was 0 to 0, the bases were loaded and there were no outs. I leaned over the press box railing and said to myself:

"This is the one, grand slam shot for Mickey's 535th. What a place for it."

Mantle took a called third strike, dropped his bat on the plate, and slowly walked back to the dugout.

The third time he came up, the game was still scoreless and again the 10-year-old's spirit took hold of me. "Maybe this time," I hoped.

MANTLE WENT FOR a pitch that was a foot outside, struck out again and walked back to the dugout like an old man with two bad legs and no real spirit left for the game.

When Mantle came up for the fourth time, I was already on the Edens expressway, gazing at the mournful lights that are Chicago.

I read in a Friday morning paper the Mantle had singled his last time up.

Somehow, it didn't matter so much anymore.

The Hill With It—1969

Spring, the long awaited Spring, releases the myriad of wonders that have lain dormant all winter.

Noteworthy events of this annual re-incarnation are the return of the flowers, the bees, and the Loudmouthus Americanus, i.e., the little league parent.

This latter species is characterized by a flaming red breast, a large, sharp beak, and a reduced cranial cavity.

He can be found periodically fluttering from grandstand to dugout throughout the summer hurling invectives at managers, coaches, ballplayers, and the P.A. announcer. If questioned he will also verbally debate truth, country, and motherhood. Especially motherhood.

My only immediate contact with this all too prolific species was one summer three years ago when I managed a Little League team in Houston, TX.

For clarification I must admit that 99% of all Little League parents do restrain their pride and that Texans are a lovably eccentric lot. But I met the king of all Little League parents that summer.

I had just sent a nine year old, and ten thumbed, little towhead into center field in the late innings of a game in which we were trailing about 17-3.

No sooner had he had gotten into position in center field than I saw Dad leave his seat in the bleachers and head my way.

Fearing the worst I pulled my hat down over my head, but he ignored me with scornful distain and continued toward right field.

Once he left the cover of the bleachers he moved with all the stealth of an Indian; dashing from lightpole to lightpole down the right field line.

This guy was so elusive that by the time he had fought his way to the right field fence everybody in the ballpark was watching him...except...his kid. He was either too nervous or embarrassed to look around.

To complete the picture this tall Texan then dropped to his hands and knees and began to crawl through the tall grass in right field. With the grace and skill of an angry rhino he slithered through the grass to a position directly behind his prodigy.

By this time everybody in the ballpark was rolling on the ground in hysterics. Undaunted, this proud parent remained there for the rest of the game. Once in his place of seclusion he did have enough sense to stay there, but he couldn't resist an occasional peek and periodically his head would loom above the weeds in deep center-field.

After the game I literally ran him down to ask him what he was doing. As it turned out he loved kids and *had just adopted the boy about a month before.*

With a heart-warming tale like that I told him I'd arrange to have a chair set up in deep center field for the next game. He declined.

The Hill With It—1969

The National Rifle Association (NRA) has received much criticism for its stand against gun control legislation and if the latest NRA news is a true reflection of its thinking, it deserves every word of criticism.

The million-member organization has the time and the money to wage strong lobby campaigns in Congress, as well as to flood every paper in the country with propaganda best suited to its interests.

The latest piece of mail to cross my desk was from NRA president Harold W. Glassen, who forecasts a step-by-step legislative campaign to end private ownership of guns by all residents of the United States in the near future. This is, at the least, exaggerated and, at the most, ridiculous!

I own three guns and no one enjoys hunting or just walking along the Kishwaukee plinking tin cans any more than I do. Yet, I cannot understand the thinking of the NRA.

The point it keeps referring to is that the new gun legislation is in direct conflict with the Second Amendment which states "A well regulated militia being necessary to the security of a free state, the right of the people to keep and bear arms shall not be infringed."

THE POINT that is not mentioned is that at the time of the writing of the Constitution most of this country was still fighting off Indians and using guns to put food on the tables. I haven't heard of an Indian attack in DeKalb County in about six weeks.

The original Constitution did not give women the right to vote either, and that has long gone by the wayside.

Glassen's release further states "We are witnessing the strange and masochistic spectacle of tens of thousands of normally proud and level-headed Americans begging the federal government to take from them by force of law one of their civil rights, the right to keep and bear arms."

What I see instead, is tens of thousands of proud and level-headed Americans who are sick of seeing their leaders being cut down in the streets, who are finding it harder and harder to hold back the tears as they see everything this country is supposed to stand for thrown back in their faces by newspapers across the world.

The federal gun legislation that Glassen is so opposed to calls for the licensing of all firearms in the country. The new Illinois legislation that goes into law July 1 will, in effect, license all gun owners.

THIS TIGHTER control should bring about an increased awareness of the responsibility that is involved in gun ownership. It should also chip away at the "frontier justice" attitude that invades every segment of our society because of the availability of firearms. It will also *make it increasingly difficult for the criminal element to carry guns.*

As for the pheasant, rabbit, and deer hunter, I cannot imagine him being legislated from the American scene. For the most part, he is well aware of the responsibility in owning firearms anyway.

But this legislation is necessary to restrict those who are not aware of the responsibility and everyone must do his share. I, as a hunter, am willing to spend the small amount of time and money necessary to register my guns.

I, as an American citizen, am disgusted with Glassen's prediction that there will no longer be private ownership of guns in the near future.

PERHAPS HIS biggest gripe is that the new laws may also ban interstate shipment of guns, of which the NRA has a big and lucrative share.

By sheer size alone, the NRA could be instrumental in effecting strong gun legislation. It's time it quit fighting the gun registration laws and realized how beneficial it will be to the nation.

A LOT OF VERY INTERESTING DEAD PEOPLE

When I went to work for the Rockford newspapers in 1969, they were in the basement of the rather majestic Rockford News Tower built in the 1930s alongside the Rock River. It was modeled after the *Tribune* News Tower in Chicago.

The Rockford papers rather modestly proclaimed: "No better edited newspapers can be found than those published in Rockford with their heritage of serving Rockford and northern Illinois with all the news while it is news." No redundancies there. All the news while it is news. Delivered the following day. Boy, was that about to change.

Working at the Rockford papers wasn't quite a seismic shift, but certainly a jolt. One change was they were an all-union enterprise. I became a member of Local 5 of the American Newspaper Guild, one of the oldest in the country. It was a membership that would have more meaning come a strike vote a year later.

The papers were old school. Very few women were on the reporting staff and none in management. Its core was a chaotic basement newsroom environment combining worn furniture, cigarette smoke, clicking wire-copy machines. Casually dressed people sat at desks shoved closely together banging out stories on paper on ancient, noisy typewriters, heads down, focused, somehow able to ignore each other unless the building caught on fire. Which better not be on deadline.

Others sat in sort of a tight circle at the copy desk correcting with marker pens the stories that had just been banged out on noisy typewriters. Editors wandered around, asking questions. A couple reporters were talking on phones.

To watch the flow of news, none of it made any real sense. It was a land of strict deadlines and sudden downtimes. The marked-up and corrected pages were sent in pneumatic tubes to a big press room out back, where they somehow became the newspaper created by adults to be handed out to kids at 6 a.m. or 5 p.m. to be delivered door-to-door. The dumbest system in the business world—until it worked. Several times a day and night. Seven days a week. Much adrenaline was required. We loved it. It was glorious. It was who we were. Then came computers, digital, company job cuts and working at home away from all that insane fellowship.

My first job in Rockford was as a police reporter—very traditional in the day for new reporters. I worked from a worn desk at the back of the crowded newsroom. The job basically required eight hours a day or night riding around in a cheap, light-blue AMC Rambler. With a police monitor on the dashboard to listen in on all reports from police, fire and occasionally the sheriff's departments. At the end of each round, I would return to the newsroom to write crime stories, with an occasional heart-warming barking-dog-saves-family story.

I had seen very little violence before this, certainly none inflicted on one person by another except for our high school fist fights in the community park. The only dead person I had ever seen was a good friend's mother in a funeral home casket. She was very puffy and pale with a huge goiter on her neck. That image sticks, too.

The police monitor was the best source for stories. The filed police reports waiting in a desk tray were often late, brief, lacking detail and requiring me to hunt down the right cop for more information.

Until they knew you, and trusted you, the right cops were often reluctant to be very forthcoming for numerous reasons, including ongoing investigations and victim safety. Some of it was just bad or incomplete information received, maybe sloppy police work.

My police beat work got off to a slow start. About the first week on the job, I heard police chatter on the monitor about a robbery at a mom-and-pop grocery store. I drove to the scene and waited outside and watched through the window as the police spoke with the old woman who had been robbed. When the cops left, I went inside and introduced myself.

"Hello, I'm Bob Hill with the Rockford Morning Star."

The woman never responded, she just waved her hand and slowly walked bent over behind a curtain at the rear of the store. She returned and put 50 cents in my hand. She thought I was collecting money for a paper route.

A little later I was covering an orchestrated presidential press conference given by Richard Nixon on a Rockford IL airport tarmac. It was one of a half-dozen orchestrated press conferences he held that day, flying to each at taxpayer expense to tout his achievements, his plans to end the war in Vietnam. Pure political theatre with journalists sitting in the audience at every stop to hear the same scripted BS.

I hung around outside for a while, watching all the staging, then went inside to sit with the locals and travelers watching the event on a TV in the bar. It was a much more spontaneous audience with better color and honest quotes—literally inside-out. A large lesson was learned there. A good and different story written: Politics from a bar stool.

The various and sundry dead people on Rockford police beat came soon enough. I was at a funeral home where the body of a man missing for a week had been taken after being pulled from the Rock River. His body was horribly bloated, swollen to almost twice normal size, his face a purplish disfigured mask, his arms and legs blown up like a wrinkled balloon.

I was called to the back yard of a woman who had committed suicide by pouring gasoline over her body and setting herself on fire. Her head was burned bald, her bluish dress burned cinder-black into her body as she lay on her back in her backyard. I stared at her and all I could think about was the pain she had endured, what she had been thinking as she lit the match.

One night I got to the home of a shooting victim before the police arrived. I went inside first—not an especially good idea. The victim had been blasted in the stomach with a shotgun. He was sitting in a chair holding in his stomach with two bloody hands. He was somehow coherent, carefully explained to me what had just happened, naming the man who had shot him even before an ambulance arrived. He died soon after. The assailant was arrested and eventually charged with murder but never went to trial because he had terminal cancer. A trial would have been a waste of money.

Court trials, five-alarm fires, fatal wrecks, gunshots and asking parents for pictures of their dead children became part of the routine, the latter a journalism cliche' at the time. I was witness to a gunfight between police and a mentally ill man barricaded in his house. Wanting to get a better look, I edged up behind a tree, only to realize bullets were flying past just a few feet on the other side of the tree.

One January, on a 20-degree-below-zero night, I was called to a scene where a young man lay face down in the street, red blood leaking from a head wound onto the white snow. He had been sliced open by a pair of scissors. He was clearly dead. The cops standing nearby, talking, trying to stay warm, ignoring the body, the night around them frozen silence.

My lede on that story read, "Torbert Beard lay face down in the snow at 20 below."

═══════

Police reporting came with some of the same problems the police faced. The truth was hard to come by. One night the police beat moved to a crowded tavern where two men had been sliced in a knife fight and not one person saw the incident. That happened a lot. The place looked like it was used for beheading chickens . . . and nobody saw a thing.

A huge man stood at the front door. He dominated the scene. He held an open pocketknife in one hand and he gently moved the blade back and forth across his thumb. He was trying to grow a goatee, he said, but the growth looked tangled and uneven. The police hadn't arrived yet. It was he and I and his knife on the front porch.

"I ain't seen nothing."

All of it material for a crime novel never written. You learn to accept all that, adjust to it. Police, firemen, medical technicians see it every day and still go home to coach Little League, attend their daughter's birthday parties, then go back to work the next day to handle wrecks, fires, dead bodies in the snow. In later years, as more and more instances of police brutality, even murder, went public, automatic respect for police diminished, but that didn't' diminish the daily emotional burdens on the good cops.

I served my traditional year on the police beat and turned the keys of a light blue AMC over to John Bryan. I had been promoted to state editor, the job Rodger Hedges had held when I was hired. I do not remember asking for the job. It meant I would be assigning stories to others that I would rather have written myself. At that stage of my life I felt I had to take the job, but had little interest in climbing the editor ladder. I never did. I just wanted to write.

It was now my turn to make the rounds of those small towns, hire people to call in stories of council meetings and such, with the occasional feature story.

I liked wandering the flat Northern Illinois roads, keeping track of the flow of seasonal crops, hanging out in small stores, and talking to people. It was all practice for a job waiting down the road in Kentucky hanging out in country stores and wandering rural Kentucky finding stories.

I STILL WANT TO WRITE A DAMN COLUMN

Once in Rockford, and even before the state editor job, I constantly agitated for a regular column. I wrote one on request to show management what was possible and nailed it. That led to a regular weekly column, and then goodbye to being state editor with three columns a week, plus occasional features. Bring it on. Keep em' coming.

The low point of that cycle was when I was also asked to review a local stage production. It was a task way above my aesthetic pay grade. Acting somewhat knowledgeable, I criticized one particular actor's skills in the review. After it ran, I learned I had criticized the wrong guy.

Mistakes are inevitable at any paper where reporters crank out stories daily, and as staffing becomes more difficult. Good reporters—and most are—hate to make mistakes in stories. Their names are written on the top of them. Later on, working in Louisville, I saw that all mistakes were instantly corrected, an apology issued in print with reporter's names attached. You don't see that much any more.

My all-time favorite correction, if not one of the best in journalism history, came later in Louisville. It surely led to more discussion than the original mistake, but the Louisville limousine company I had written about insisted on it:

"Because of a reporting error, Bob Hill's Jan. 9 column mistakenly said a Cosmopolitan Limousine customer conceived her second child in a Cosmopolitan limousine. The mother actually said the child was conceived in another company's limousine."

A good copy desk, checking for errors of all types, can prevent such missteps. It saved me from dozens of published errors over the years. Nonetheless, copy desks have now been eliminated in many papers to cut costs. I'm sure readers notice. No one really wins there.

My early Rockford career was interrupted in 1970-71 by a newspaper strike against the Gannett-owned papers. We shut down the company for 69 days, including both Thanksgiving and Christmas of 1970. It was a contentious time, with the Vietnam War raging, tensions high in a very young news staff, and Gannett earning big profits. Our negotiators from Local 5 brought in national members of the American Newspaper Guild to help with, if not lead, the tense negotiations. All the other four unions at the paper honored our strike, the only way it could work.

Internal politics and peer group pressure are always factors in such negotiations. You must appear to be guild-united to get any results, with Gannett on its way to becoming the largest newspaper chain in the United States. Leaning well away from the Republican world of my youth, my basic instincts had become pro-union. Newspaper publishers and owners were making a lot of money. The vote to strike was almost unanimous. Solidarity. Brotherhood and Sisterhood. The few women on our staff raised clenched fists, too.

All guild members walked the picket lines on frozen, occasionally sub-zero, winter nights. The drivers of cars coming past would sometimes honk horns in support. Some raised their middle fingers in apparent opposition. The guild pay for walking was $60 a week, a fraction of the $200 regular pay. I became a guild captain, ensuring others showed up to picket, and later was elected guild vice president, a job with minimal duties and paid trips to annual union rallies in places like Vancouver, B.C.

I walked the lines at night and found day work erecting steel barns at a flat, windy pig farm in frozen January. Other days we worked inside the sheds building hog pens. Another rustic learning experience in the books.

After 10 weeks walking the picket line and being kind to hogs we settled the strike for a $31-a-week pay increase over 30 months, bringing our top pay to $235.50 a week. We had been asking for $255.

A company official said the $31 increase was exactly what it had offered before the strike. All we got for our trouble was a six-month extension on the contract. All of us—management and employees—were happy to get back in the building. Our pro-guild attitude held, but we never talked much about the strike after that.

In early 1973 came one of the great newspaper journeys of my life, a trip to Bratislava, Czechoslovakia, for the World Ice Skating Championships. The reason was Rockford resident Janet Lynn. At 19, she was already the five-time Senior Ladies National Champion and bronze medalist in the 1972 Olympics at Sapporo, Japan. At 5 feet 2 inches, with a carefully crafted mop of blond hair, Lynn was favored to become world champ along with 20-year-old Karen Magnussen of Canada.

Bob Hill and Janet Lynn's father, Florian Nowicki, found it necessary to join a guard outside Zimny Stadium.

The skating championship came with a history lesson. Our chartered plane of reporters landed in Bratislava only about 28 years after the end of World War II. The Iron Curtain with its tall fences, guard towers and ominous bunkers was built a few miles out of town, barely separating it from Austria.

Very curious about all that, I found a taxi driver who spoke almost no English. I offered him a $20 bill—American dollars were of greater value at the time—and gestured I wanted to go see the wall. He was willing and we drove the few miles to the Iron Curtain, passing those incredibly dull, Soviet-era offices, houses and apartments that looked like rows of giant gray boxes.

Driving along the Iron Curtain only 28 years after WWII had ended, looking up at the metal fence with barbed wire at the top and armed guards in towers above, was a little frightening. There it was, the real deal, living history, fodder for hundreds of news stories and analysis. We drove in total silence along the wall for about 15 minutes, the driver very wary, me glancing up, trying not to look like a tourist. We made it back to the hotel. I'll never really know how much danger the driver had been in for his $20. Or what he bought with it.

The ice-skating championship lasted a week, lots of time to walk the streets of Bratislava, wander into shops with long lines and limited goods. I kept my passport with me. Oddly enough, with armed guards at many corners, the streets themselves felt very safe, probably better than some large American cities.

One of the flight attendants on our airplane was a native of Bratislava and she arranged for a meal at her family's home. It was a small wooden house furnished with old tables and chairs, colorful ceramics and wall hangings. So much history here, too. We ate a sumptuous meal from the family's limited supplies, conversed with their daughter translating, smiles all around. The language was no barrier. I have never felt more welcome at any dinner. I suspect that dinner cost her family a lot.

Writing ice skating stories behind the Iron Curtain

also proved interesting. It took a day of wandering to secure my press pass, and then all reporters were set up in the same room behind long rows of typewriters. With a six-hour time difference and the Rockford papers coming out in the morning and evening, I was doing double duty, but without complaints. It actually gave me more time to file stories.

We were all banging out stories on deadline. The problem was all copy was handed off to clerks who took it to another room where it was transcribed and sent to Rockford. Reporters were not allowed back in there. I had no real idea if my stories made it back or were heavily censored by the Communist word police. I eventually called Rockford, and everybody seemed happy.

The ice skating was held in Zimny Stadium, a boxy structure originally built in 1940 and upgraded a little from there. The opening event was a concert held at the Philharmonic of Bratislava, a wonderfully adorned place, a welcome change from parades of flags and a long way from Midwestern corn fields.

The skating was endless, occasionally spectacular, with politics often entering the picture. One couple saw the music for their performance end before it was over. The stoppage was later blamed on the person in charge of the music being from a rival country. The couple kept dancing in a strange silence and were declared winners.

Janet Lynn, a prodigy competing at 19 in the ladies' singles event against the best in the world, had thousands of hours of practice and dozens of competitions before this one. She would later say she was nervous, didn't feel comfortable before her turn in the compulsory free-skating program. She started well, fell, got up, and fell again in the stunned silence in the stadium where she had been a favorite. Five years of practice and competition were suddenly erased in a few minutes.

Lynn hugged her coach as they walked together back to the dressing room in tears. Lynn would finish second best in the world. Karen Magnussen, who later won the title, hugged and cried with Lynn in the dressing room. Everyone in the dressing room was crying.

Soon after that trip to Bratislava another possible life change presented itself. Our Rockford sports editor had moved on. Lew Winkler, one of our top Rockford news editors, called me into his office and made a very surprising offer in his distinct Southern Indiana dialect.

"Heeeel," he asked, "do you want to be sports editor of this damn place?"

That was his total pitch. No warning. The world's shortest job interview. I was caught off guard. It had never been mentioned before. Being sports editor in Rockford would have included a lot of major league sports, with some travel, maybe to the World Series or Super Bowl. The paper still had two company planes left over from previous family ownership. I'd be covering the Cubs, White Sox, Bears and Bulls for sure. A little like being back in the press box with Turner Lake—only with much tighter deadlines.

I'm sure I said "yes" to the possible offer at that time. Take the job and then think it over. What could go wrong with that? I went back out to my office. Winkler never mentioned the job to me again—and I never asked.

I did think it over. Was the offer sincere? Was Winkler thinking it over, too, considering another candidate? But mostly I was about ready to move on from Rockford, try deeper newspaper waters. My ambition, curiosity and Inner Voice nudging me further down the uncertain road. But what would have happened if Winkler had followed through and I had taken the job, or I had pushed a little harder to get it? My entire future would have changed, and not necessarily for the better.

It's always interesting to look back at those moments and wonder where a different decision would have led. Sports had been my early personal life. I probably could have been sold on that sports editor job, the Cubs, White Six, Bears and Bulls. I never thought enough at that time about the travel, the time gone from family, the price I would pay, or that the Rockford papers would also soon face serious financial cutbacks.

The future I did choose—moving on to deeper journalism waters living in an old farm house—turned out to be rich, full and very happy. But maybe it would not have happened had Winkler tried a slightly more subtle sales approach.

NOTHING BEATS THREE FRIENDS AND A GRAIN TRUCK

===

Along with the changes of minds, goals and ambitions came the prerequisite changes of personal addresses—like six of them in six years. It was typical of our 1960s and '70s age group, uncertainties and financial conditions. Many of the moves were made with friends lifting sofas onto family farm trucks, with a little more furniture being hauled at each progressive move.

When Janet and I first moved to Sycamore from Houston in 1965, we lived for a few months in a small, second-story apartment reached on a rickety set of outside stairs. The place had a big window that led out to a porch roof which occasionally seemed like a good place to sit and drink a beer with friends. With the job at Chrysler, we moved the 35 miles to Belvidere to a duplex apartment behind a bowling alley, the requisite entertainment in our automotive social circle, with bar.

When Jennifer was born, we moved to a bigger apartment across town, our home, when the tornado struck. The job at the Sycamore papers led to purchasing a mobile home for $5,000 in a new mobile home park in Sycamore on the edge of town. Home equity began there. Slowly. It was where we lived when Robb was born, a park later abandoned due to constant flooding from a nearby river, then, ironically, was transformed into a city park. Our new mobile home was only purchased when "Tige" Hoffman, Janet's uncle who sold us "Old Green" for $150, co-signed our loan.

The job in Rockford came with a move to a house Janet's father owned in Genoa IL, part-way between Sycamore and Rockford, putting us back in a two-story house, but with inside steps and a big vegetable garden out back. Our sixth move was more pure serendipity. Driving the back country roads from Genoa to Rockford I noticed an old farmhouse perched on a small hill near what was left of Irene IL surrounded by corn fields.

It looked empty, but not abandoned. There was no realtor sign stuck in the yard. On sheer whim I stopped one day and asked a neighbor if the house was for sale. He sent me to a nearby gravel pit whose owner also owned the house.

It turned out the house, a corn crib and an acre of land was for sale for $15,500, with about 25 percent down. After about 10 years of marriage, we had about $1,500 in savings. I cashed in all my U.S. Savings bonds that Chrysler had demanded we buy. A best high school buddy loaned us $2,000 and we had our down payment on a place in the country. He remains a best high school buddy. Equity up.

Irene Illinois residents Bob and Janet Hill with pitchforks.

We lived there for about three years with a big vegetable garden, a grape vine, a hand-planted apple orchard and two beef calves in a converted corn crib. For entertainment we had friends out on beer-soaked hayrides traveling past the nearby general store singing "Irene, Good Night."

Very mild cannabis plants, left over from the WWII and Northern Illinois hemp-raising days, grew wild in nearby roadside ditches. At one party, after the Rockford paper had won some award for a series on the evils of marijuana, we presented the winners with their own home-grown plants in ceramic pots. Standing ovation.

GOOD JOURNALISTS ARE BEST PEOPLE IN THE WORLD

I've always believed good journalists are the best people in the world. They come from many economic, cultural and regional backgrounds. The best are honest, funny, reliable, wanting to write, to explain, to be heard but mostly not seen.

Some are driven to be in the business, others seem a little surprised that's where they landed, perhaps on the way to something else. I could always relate to that. There were also some imposters who disappeared into the business world. And a few good ones went off to become lawyers. We managed to forgive them.

Fun was a prerequisite. For one Rockford story I joined by mail an alleged religious organization called The Missionaries of the New Truth, which sold guaranteed ministerial certificates for $15. With no real legal laws defining a minister, I thus joined the New Truth Church and was able to perform weddings. All that mattered was the couple to be married had completed the state-required marital paperwork. The minister didn't matter.

Not long afterward I was standing on a stump in a beautiful, wooded park not far from the Mississippi River marrying a copy-desk buddy and his bride. Only four of us were there, including Janet.

The ceremonial words were honest, poetic and well-edited. The stump about two feet high. That marriage lasted almost 50 years until he died. In a second marriage ceremony, I very reluctantly performed a paying-gig inside a house with families in attendance. That marriage lasted about two years.

'I pledge peace and love'

Linda and Bob wanted to get married.

At 31 and 26 they had known each other for 2½ years and shared a distaste for bureaucracy tempered with the feeling that some ceremony was needed; a starting point where love and trust come together and the PTA meetings follow.

Bob had traveled a lot and Linda has a six-year-old daughter from another marriage so the starry eyes had long since come in focus, and suggestions of pre-marriage counseling from established ministers left a sour taste.

So they picked a minister with a mail order ordination, a man who had never performed a marriage before, and set their wedding for the front yard of Willow Church near Stockton in a grassy green valley molded by the hills of Jo-Daviess County. A small creek ram-

bles past a few yards away.

The wedding couple, the minister, and two witnesses traveled from Rockford in a yellow van, happily toasting the event and even the Kelly Springfield tire plant from clear plastic glasses along the way.

Gray clouds rode low over the hills as Willow Road turned from asphalt to yellow dust, but the sun slipped free past the clouds' ragged edge as the van pulled into the churchyard.

WILLOW CHURCH is simple and white, but its front porch is a cathedral of oak and the sun slanted through to the minister standing on a low, rough-cut stump and the wedding party standing under two of the cathedral's pillars.

The groom wore new tan harness boots, plaid pants and a green and white striped shirt with a buckskin vest. A bright orange scarf was tied around his neck.

The bride wore a matching long skirt and jacket over a tan sweater. Her shoulder-length hair blew in the wind.

"Linda and Bob have come together here today because there is love, and their love is a wedding at a country church in October where strong winds snap the air clean and life is an empty slate surrounded by promise," the minister said.

The winds snapped a limb from a tree above even as the minister spoke, and ruffled the mane of two horses looking across a sparse wire fence at the ceremony.

A rooster crowed from a faraway farm, and a herd of Holsteins lay sleek and bored on a hill behind the *church. Less bucolic, noise of a rivet gun spattered forth from a nearby body shop.*

"For love is as the wind," the minister said. "It brings gold-flecked sunsets across umbrellas of blue, and it brings dark and thunder shouting across the black ink of night.

"And love is as the green willow tree: it must be free to bloom in these winds, yet it must have deep roots or it will shrivel and die, and the very winds that nurtured it will bring it down.

"And where there is love, there is peace, so let the five diamonds in your rings become your symbol or peace, and of your love, and of your roots."

The minister nervously tugged a ring from its box and gave it to the groom.

The bride handed her bouquet of russet wild flowers laced with bright mums to a witness, and the groom slipped on the ring.

THE MINISTER, *new at the ceremony, gave the groom more words than he could remember easily, and he paused before finishing.*

"I pledge peace and love . . . and this ring is the symbol of our marriage."

The bride was given the pledge more slowly, and she handled it better.

"May your love grow, and peace be with you always," the minister said. "You are now one."

As he finished, a flock of geese beat across the heavens to the south completing the tableau of man, earth and sky.

As their shrill peals died, the sun again slipped behind a ragged edge of a gray cloud and a cool wind blew waves of green grass at the feet of the party.

The mail-order minister turned from the party toward the wind, and its coolness brought moisture to the corners of his eyes.

Reporting always offered a mix of surprising opportunities, both off and on the wall, and a stump. Good journalists rarely talked much about any sort of rarified mission, or even greater good, but it was all about getting out the word as we saw it.

That, of course, was a sometimes-flawed position that met with some opposition from those being written about. Another flaw at the time was the lack of women and minorities in our profession, a dismal gap somewhat closed in more recent years, with much more room for improvement.

Journalism, perhaps more so back then, had its own lifestyles. We all worked together packed in the same room, same ever-moving deadlines depending on editions. I always enjoyed writing on deadlines, head down, alone in a room full of people, focused, intense working in a time bubble, most of the required words showing up, at least after a few years practice,.

With the Rockford morning-paper deadline set at about 12:45 a.m. there was an inevitable rush up the street afterward to the nearby bars with 1 a.m. closing times. Good friends who left the building earlier would have a beer waiting for me . . . or two.

We would discuss the day's work, and what might

come next. That could lead to after-hours parties in someone's house. Which could lead to more beer and, in the 1960s and 1970s, marijuana consumed in tight circles of bodies sitting cross legged on the floor. The inhalers discussing criminal court cases over pot. As God is my witness I never inhaled there. That seating arrangement was too uncomfortable.

If the evening ended in the bar, I would head back to the newspaper to get my car, pausing to grab a morning paper rolling off the thundering presses to delivery drivers.

I loved watching the presses roll. It was magical. Just hours earlier those printed words were a conversation with a politician, some time spent with a circus clown or a desperate farmer, a passionate column about some enduring problem. Now those words, written, edited, packaged and printed, were spilling out the mouth of a huge printing press. I'd grab a paper, see where my story had landed, and take it home. Read it front-to-back later in the morning. Then do it all again the next day.

READY FOR DEEPER WATER BUT UNSURE WHICH RIVER

By the spring of 1975 I was ready to move on from Rockford—precisely to where was another question. Or maybe even why? My personal instincts had always been to settle down somewhere. My professional ones were sending a different message. There's a bigger and better world out there, son.

I had done a little preliminary investigation. The copy-desk guy whose wedding I had officiated while standing on a stump had moved on to the *Chicago Tribune*, commuting 90 miles each way. He did like his cars.

A few other Rockford reporters also had moved on to Chicago papers, so, I thought I would start there to test my future. I

Bob Hill off on his journey across Northern Illinois.

put together a resume, added a few of my columns and features clips and mailed them to a *Chicago Tribune* features editor. I waited a few weeks and got a letter setting up a job interview.

I read it about six times. I was married with two young and growing kids, yet already mulling over commuting the 90 miles to Chicago—or moving into the city—which would have been a stupid idea. We didn't like big cities. Houston had been enough. But Janet and I decided to see where the interview would lead.

I drove the 90 miles to Chicago into heavy commuter traffic, parked and entered the mighty, 463-foot, neo-gothic Tribune Tower near the Chicago River. Looking around, I remember thinking at the time, "*Well, maybe this wouldn't be so bad after all. A few years here and who knows? This is the big time.*"

I was led up to the editor's office, and after a brief wait went inside. He was sitting hunched over a desk covered about six inches deep in notes, old newspapers and various pieces of personal debris. He looked at me, got a puzzled look on his face and uttered the words that all job applicants crave: "*Tell me again why you are here?*"

Call it 90 miles—actually 180 miles—not wasted. We spoke for about 15 minutes about why I was there—not that it mattered. I'm not sure he ever even found my clips in the paper landfill on his desk. His basic response was to forget about that interview-letter thing, we aren't hiring now. Try again in six months. So much for The City of Big Shoulders. Back into the car and the outbound commuter traffic.

Let the record also show that in the subsequent demise of American newspapers the neo-Gothic Tribune Tower was sold for $240 million in 2016 and converted into luxury apartments. The Tribune itself was sold to Alden Global Capital, a hedge fund known for buying and gutting newspapers. As more and more newspaper employees now work from home.

With the *Chicago Tribune* debacle, good luck was again playing me a favor, but I didn't know it at the time. I was too disappointed about the alleged interview. Living in or even near Chicago would have been a bad idea with false promises. We could have adapted, dealt with the traffic, housing and schools in the name of personal progress, or ego. Just testing personal limits, measuring myself against the best. But truly happy? No way.

Still not grasping all that, my Plan B was to send resumes and clips to many of the best papers in the country. Most were in big cities like New York, Washington, even the St. Louis paper at that time. The only response I got was from the *Louisville Courier-Journal & Times*.

The newspaper clips I had sent with my somewhat limited resume included one of my last ventures at the Rockford papers. It was a 10-day journey hitchhiking across Northern Illinois and Southern Wisconsin carrying a 30-pound backpack and bright orange Rockford newspapers carrier bag. Absolutely no agenda. Just go. Thumb out, billfold used if necessary. See where life takes you in small-town rural Illinois. Write about it.

The journey eventually included a sweet, empty

country church near Afolkey and the Blackhawk Hotel in Lena IL, where losing your room key wasn't an issue because all of them were the same. In another adventure, two brothers crammed me into the cab of their hay-laden pickup truck, my backpack included, just because they could.

There was an almost obligatory visit to Durand IL, the self-described Outhouse Capitol of the World in a not particularly crowded field. I attended a goat and antique auction in a two-acre field near Eldena, took in a three-lane bowling alley in West Brooklyn and rode an Amtrak train to Dubuque, IA. For the big finish I bummed a ride on a Mississippi River barge in heavy fog. It was a pretty good dress rehearsal for things to come in Kentucky. I wrote this about part of that journey:

Include riverboat barges among the things that go bump in the night as they skitter and slide down the Mississippi River with bellies full of corn, wheat or fertilizer for Europe and Asia.

They are giant metal boxes pushed by towboats that are tiny by comparison. Upper Mississippi River towboats can push a maximum of 15 barges that jut out almost one-fifth of a mile and have a total weight of 40 million pounds.

Cpt. Pelo Parker, of Grand Junction TN, a man who doesn't weigh 160 pounds, herds them along with a steady crew of two.

One of the fun things in writing this book was re-reading the hundreds of columns written in Rockford more than 50 years ago and learning they still worked, as in "There are no new stories only new reporters" motif. The best of any story is timeless. Human frailties, concerns, tragedies and comedies are inevitable, only the occupants change. My favorite columns have always been about people, places, observations and slices of life. The locations didn't matter. Politicians' rants, lies, bullshit and honest offerings don't change, just the bullhorns. I rarely write about politicians, but such is necessary to do the job, and I would weigh in, two fingers flying, as the bullshit got a little too stinky.

Eventually most of the places and people I wrote about became, as was the title of one collection of columns, "Old Friends"

Six of my favorite Rockford columns, as glued and saved on the slick pages of a very thick wallpaper catalog, bring back forgotten memories, people, places, even co-workers.

There is the small-town dog catcher who drove 27,000 miles in one year to find or rescue 2,600 dogs, taking many home to the 13 kennels she and her husband built. There is the beloved, cigar-smoking mailman who knocked on neighborhood doors to hand over the Social Security checks, and a slice-of-life look at a neighborhood bar that opens at 7 a.m.

A favorite is retired guy who rented a parking lot that holds 17 cars just to stay busy, presenting a good history lesson that reminds us what we can and should be.

Then that story again, told through the hands of a six-year-old girl who became an American citizen. All those stories still alive, well and right here.

Marie's eyes give her away

Marie Collin shuffled across her front yard like Casey Stengel on his way to yank a sore-armed pitcher; tending to her business in white shoes, green socks, blue jeans, red and blue print blouse and blue peaked cap with tufts of short red hair sticking out the sides.

Marie Collin isn't extremely pretty coming at you either. Bulky, with frenches bunched together and a face lined with 50 years of taking care of other people's problems.

When she laughs—which is about every time she puts her cigarette down to tell another story—the room fills with a noise generally associated with auto transmission problems, but don't let Marie Collin fool ya.

Look at her eyes, soft as your mother's lap, and at the corners where the moisture gathers when the stories turn sad.

That's where you see Marie Collin, the best dog-catcher Carroll County has ever had.

In her younger days Marie Collin was a private nurse, but she roared into Mount Carroll about 10 years ago and dogs got a big bite on her life.

She said she has always been dragging animals home, including the time her mother buried the skunk in one hole and Marie's clothes in the other until the air cleared up a little.

IN MOUNT CARROLL she worked at starting up a humane society, but quit after a few years because it had always been her practice to give dogs away and the society wanted to sell them.

The county needed a dogcatcher about then and Marie got the job paws down, and her business has been dogs ever since.

If there's possible trouble her husband Harvey comes along, but when the dog's friendly, so's Marie.

"I just walk up slowly to them," she said. "They're tickled to see me."

For shy males she has a different technique, her little female pet.

You have to hear her laugh to appreciate that technique.

Marie is about as well known in Carroll County as the Mississippi River, but covers more ground.

Last year she drove 27,000 miles to handle almost 2,600 dogs.

But she handles them one at a time.

She and her husband have built 13 kennels on their country acre, and the dogs are fed and their kennels cleaned three times a day.

In fact the dog's life at Marie's shelter is so good one little mutt developed a limp every time Marie gave him away, the new owners kept bringing it back.

"Watch him." Marie told the latest in a series of owners when the supposedly gimpy dog was returned again. "Watch him run to that kennel."

The dog took off like Man O War for his old home, but the game was over and Marie hasn't seen it or the new owner since.

CARROLL COUNTY'S dogcatcher still doesn't sell dogs. She gives them away, hundreds a year, from mutts to pedigreed, S. Bernards to poodles.

But Marie runs a strict adoption agency, and if the dog runs into sub-par housing or battered biscuits she'll go out and fetch it home.

She places hundreds of dogs a month, and generally keeps track of where they go. She only has them killed when they bite or attack animals.

There was a little feud a while back and someone signed a complaint of cruelty to animals against her. Incensed, she represented herself and was giving the prosecutor hell when the case was moved because she had helped the judge find a dog.

The case was moved to another county, but her courtroom manner wasn't tested much there either.

"The judge just winked at me," she said. "I'd gotten him a dog too."

Case dismissed.

Stickling, stogies and the human touch

Don Stickling delivers the mail puffing a cigar you couldn't air mail to Los Angeles for $5 and with a personal touch you couldn't buy for $5 million.

Stickling doesn't just deliver mail, anyway. He starts lawnmowers, gives advice to homeowners on treed racoons and delivers mini-courses on horticulture.

He attends weddings of kids who were born when he started his route, has been pallbearer to one who died, and makes special deliveries to salesmen who need the mail early.

He is friend, confidant, and practically a member of the family to about 300 homeowners on Rockford's northeast side.

"A man," he says, "has to take a little pride in what he does."

Stickling, 55, 927 Kishwaukee St., has become an institution to the residents in his area, bordered by Chelsea Avenue, Rebecca Drive, Burrmont Road and Highcrest Road in the past 18 years.

AFTER STOPPING *at two houses to deliver packages he thinks are important, but which are at the middle of his route, he parks at Chelsea Avenue and Burrmont Road and begins his 15-mile walk.*

It's the day the Social Security checks are delivered, and he taps the doorbell of each recipient.

"That's so they know the checks are there," he said. "They are important to these people."

People who leave the neighborhood may be gone, but are never forgotten by Stickling. He pens little notes to old friends along with the forwarding address. Just as often as he visits them.

Nobody gets by without a comment.

"Harry Truman paid off again," he tells one retiree sitting in his garage waiting for the check.

HE ALSO KNEW *another very important fact. The name*

of the man's barking dog. In fact he also knows the names of all the dogs on his route, barking and otherwise.

His last tangle with a canine was two years ago, and it brought him a new pair of pants from the dog's owner; but Stickling was not injured.

Stickling also knows the names of several grandchildren of route residents, including the grandchild who offered him a pretzel.

He took it. He had no cigar working at the time.

He faults the U.S. Postal Service for its slow service between towns, but has only missed two days of local deliveries in the last 18 years due to weather.

Stickling is a pied piper who picks up kids for a few years until they graduate to chasing girls.

He delivers his day-old sports sections of a Chicago newspaper to a sports fan along the route who is in a wheelchair.

He listens to the birds, digresses on trees, gives directions to passers-by, and once-in-awhile whistles to himself.

ONCE HE WENT *to a sanitarium to shave a former resident who could not shave himself.*

He travels with a postcard showing his last vacation and shares the trip with his friends.

He stops at a lunchroom and he and his wife are invited to a party by a resident.

He spends 10 minutes explaining a postal delay to a worried woman, and spends 10 more with a 100-year-old woman as spry as he is.

In between he bets a hamburger with a teenager the Chicago White Sox will finish higher than the St. Louis Cardinals.

He gives $10 worth of service for a 10-cent stamp.

You gotta believe he runs a first class operation.

Bar opens its doors at break of dawn

Sunlight came streaming through the front door of the Bullroom, 1436 N. Main St., but the flat rays were unable to negotiate the turn into the darker section of the bar.

Instead, they danced with the circles of thin smoke from the hamburger grill as the smoke weaved and whirled toward the air vent.

At 7 a.m. it was the best show in town.

The Bullroom began to open at 7 a.m. two weeks ago to accommodate those who feel they need a drink at 7 a.m.

And if you like exotic dancing with your morning hamburgers, bloody marys and cotton mouth, there is Rose, a platinum blond with a shag hair cut and a china doll complexion.

The bartender is Ann, with short dark hair, dark glasses and the matter-of-fact disposition required to maintain tenure in a horse-shoe office.

The sign on the back door of the Bullroom gets the message across:

Bob Hill

Open at 7 O'clock
In the morning
Mon. thru Fri.
Drink, drink, drink, drink

ANN DIDN'T arrive until 7:06 a.m., but there were no screaming drunks pounding on the door and warning of the penalties of false advertisement.

Only the reporter was there, and Ann admits later she feared he was a robber.

Ann says the bar opens early because there is a need for it. The thought hangs there because people do not drink at 7 a.m. to cure a thirst. By and large, the problem runs deeper.

Rose comes in at 7:40 a.m., snapping on a piece of gum and searching the dim room with tired brown eyes. She is wearing checked hip huggers, a black blouse, a white jacket, gold necklace and triangular gold earrings. She could be 18. She could be 26. She says she is 22.

At 7:50 a.m. a tired looking man with shoulder length red hair walks in and orders a drink. At 8:07 a man named Willie walks in. He is greeted with a shout from Ann. Willie orders a drink.

ANN SAYS once her customers find the morning drinks they almost always come back.

Ann likes to tend bar in the early morning. She says she gets to know her customers better.

She is right. It is the blend of morning numbness and alcohol that keeps the atmosphere low key. There is no frenzy to get smashed and try a backwards flip from the top of the bowling machine. No one is shoving down four martinis for lunch. Everything is mellow.

At 9 a.m. a man wearing grey work clothes and a thoughtful face comes in and asks for a beer.

ROSE HAS changed to her working clothes; a two-piece bathing suit with green fringe she has added. She is busy changing records on the jukebox.

Life is pumped into the Bullroom about 9:30 a.m. when two construction workers rock through the back door.

"Is this where you cure a hangover before you go to court?" the smallest one asks.

He is stocky with a handsome Italian face and even white teeth. He laughs easily, and his laughter drives the bar's intimacy away. Talk of where do you work, and why, is replaced with dirty jokes. Newcomers turn their backs, and talk only to the person on the next stool.

ROSE DANCES at 9:50 a.m. She always calls it dancing. She is not heavy, but complains of gaining too much weight.

She has only been dancing a month. She works four hours at the Bullroom in the morning and five hours in the Blue Garter, 218 E. State St., at night.

At 9:55 a.m. a mailman enters, hands Ann several letters, grabs a quick look at Rose and leaves.

Outside, the yellow sun is pouring down over the tops of sidewalk awnings. Inside men and women are

drinking and telling dirty jokes.
Some look at the dancer. Some stare into their drinks. It is a bar, and it has a dancer.
It doesn't matter what time it is.

He parks 17 cars then goes home

His day is television and small talk and some of his nights are 17 cars long.

He said his name wasn't important because he's parked cars for 35 years and has been called dozens of names.

"Some might call you one and some might call you another," he explained. "It don't matter much. I park 17 cars and I get my butt out of here."

He parks cars in a downtown lot near State Street. Three decades ago he rented the lot and worked all day seven day a week. Now he works the nights he wants to, parks his 17 cars at 35 cents each and goes home.

He splits the 35 cents with the lot owners. He says it's not the best life, but at 78 it's the best life he's got.

His wooden shed isn't much of a refuge from boredom. The fan of the electric space heater scrapes against unyielding metal, competing with football cliches from an old General Electric radio on the upside down fruit crate.

His chair is straightback and hard, made useable with a tattered cushion. There is no such luxury on the visitor's bench along one wall. The shed is maybe six feet square, and its inside walls are bare.

HE TILTS HIS CHAIR back and rests a wet shoe on the door jam and explains why he parks 17 cars on the nights he feels like working.

"The less I have to do the better it suits me. But I've got to get out of the house. You know that. What would a fella do if he can't get out of the house. But if it's a bad night I don't come down. Summertime's I hardly come down at all. People park absolutely free. I just do this to help a friend. A man has to get away from home. You know that.

"I only park 17 cars because that is all the room I have unless people double up. I tell people to lock their cars and take the keys with them. Then they can leave when they want. If I get more than 17 cars then some people are blocked. I'm told this happens sometimes when I'm gone. But I don't stick around to see it. I get 17 cars and I'm gone.

SEVERAL CARS came in and he directed them to open spots. Through the door glass it seemed as though he knew the drivers.

"You know I've been here 35 years and don't know two dozen names. I know a lot of faces, but I don't know the names. I never had a reason to know the names.

"Sometimes I start at 4:30 and sometimes I start at 6:00. There's no definite times. Sometimes I even leave before I get 17 cars. But a guy has to get out. You know that."

He has a son in Seattle, Wash., and a nephew in Washington, D.C. He visits each at least once a year. His wife died 21 years ago Dec. 13. He lives with a niece, and says he does some visiting during the day.

The 16th car came in and he crunched across the snow to meet it. He came back and tilted the chair again.

"One more car for this old boy," he said.

"I got a little garden in the summer. Some tomatoes, onions and radishes. It ain't much, but it's something. A man has to stay busy. You know that. I had a good home, but life's lonely now. You can do what you want, but it's not a good life."

"IT'S NOT REALLY so bad. I enjoy meeting the people. Then I go home, put on my slippers and watch television. In the morning I can get up when I want to."

The 17th car came in, and he moved his car to block the entrance while the last space was filled. He turned out the shed light, and hid the radio behind the metal screen, and locked the door.

Often two cars come together to compete for the last slot, but he sends one away. He parks 17 cars and no one double parks.

Bicentennial justifies U.S. history study

I've expressed before the fear that all thing good about our Bicentennial celebration may disappear under a pile of plastic Minuteman models and Melmac plates portraying Washington crossing the Delaware in shades of pink and blue.

Like the man said: No one has ever gone broke underestimating the taste of the American public.

So I have a suggestion for a Bicentennial present that might, ah, revolutionize the event.

Give a friend a good American History book.

After you have read it yourself.

I know the thought of actually having to read about all the stuff that's happened in the past 200 years doesn't have the historical appeal of a fully illuminated, guaranteed automated, polyethylene, American Flag paperweight, but it could be worthwhile.

You might learn when polyethylene was developed.

I make this lofty suggestion about 450 pages into a 571-page book I am reading on American history. It's taken a month to get that far, so I'm not killing the job.

But I've learned it's a pleasure to read a comprehensive history book at a leisurely pace without having to worry about a final examination.

You even find yourself staying awake.

I'VE NEVER BEEN sure who's at fault, but I came away from my lower level history courses knowing little more than George Washington owned up to cutting down the cherry tree a few years or so before leading the entire country against the hated British.

My more contemporary lessons were not much better. *I can remember being amazed to eventually learn we did not win World War I and World War II all by ourselves.*

John Wayne actually had some help.

It seems many of us hold up for admiration of a history that's one-third fact, one-third patriotic fervor and one-third Hollywood.

The gap between what we are and what we think we are may not be 571 pages wide, but there is room for improvement.

Those who stick with the "Freedom of Worship" founding theory, which is valid as far as it goes, might be interested to know in the Massachusetts Bay Colony the Puritans made strenuous efforts to bar other immigrants who did not agree with their religious beliefs.

Stuff that in your Thanksgiving turkey.

WE SURELY COULD *not have won the Revolutionary War without the aid of France. But there are other interesting statistics.*

At the beginning of the Revolutionary War, there were 2.5 million persons living in the colonies. In 1776, the American Army reached its peak with 90,000 officers and soldiers. This represented one of every eight males old enough to bear arms.

In the latter part of the war, the figure dropped to one man in only 16 of the fighting age actually participating in the war.

The passion for independence was obviously not universal.

All this is not to say that smart aleck kid has read

a mere four-fifths of a history book and has declared himself reigning expert with authority to badmouth all Bicentennial efforts.

On the contrary, I don't think there will ever be more impetus for people to take an honest look at our history, wars and all.

Maybe it will help in this recession to know the country has been suffering them in varying degrees since Ben Franklin first built a stove.

Watergate may have no equal, but there have been incompetent, immoral, inept politicians in this country for 185 years doing whatever and whoever they could.

And that, class, is called taking solace where you find it.

Sonia's as American as her truck-driving dad

Sonia Wiltfang wrapped five tiny fingers around her daddy's thumb and looked shyly around the Winnebago County courtroom through almond eyes.

Her father, Hiram Wiltfang, 50, of Stillman Valley, buried his daughter's fingers in his strong truck driver's hands, but said nothing.

Words might have cluttered up their conversation anyway.

Six-year-old Sonia became an American Tuesday and her mother, father and two of her six brothers and sisters were in Rockford to see it.

So, as Wiltfang pointed out, was a large chunk of Stillman Valley.

The Wiltfangs live in Stillman Valley hard by the creek, as the saying goes, where Chief Blackhawk gave a few Army irregulars a lesson in Indian warfare.

Wiltfang has been driving and unloading trucks for years, and has the strong fingers and the scar tissue to prove it. He wore a dark solid suit. It said a lot about him.

His wife, Marion, 45, cheerful, more brightly dressed, explained why the Wiltfang family adopted Sonia and grew from eight to nine members.

"We talked it over and figured we could support one more," she said. "There are a lot of us to give to her."

THE WILTFANG CHILDREN *now run in age from 26 to 6. Two of the oldest are now married, adding two grandchildren and two sons-in-law to the family visits.*

"When we applied we did not even think we would get a child," Wiltfang said. "We figured the adoption agency would think six was enough."

But number seven, a Korean girl named Dae Soon Park, showed up at O'Hare Airport three years ago. She became Sonia Dae Wiltfang. Nothing is known of her original parents.

The Wiltfangs have so enjoyed the experience that three times last summer they went to O'Hare just to watch as other parents meet their adopted children.

SONIA WAS *enjoying herself Tuesday as her mother explained she was really beginning to feel the excite-*

ment. Sonia spent part of the time autographing the back of Polaroid pictures for the Stillman Valley contingent in the back row.

Today, her first grade class in Stillman Valley is going to give her a party for becoming an American.

That has really got her excited.

There is some gentle irony in the fact persons waiting to become Americans were asked to show up at 8:30 a.m. for a ceremony that began about 9:30 a.m., but not enough to change any minds.

The honorees were also met with a detailed history of our flag before Circuit Court Judge Robert C. Gill welcomed them in what he termed a labor of "pure, unadulterated joy."

TWENTY-SIX PERSONS of varying shades and nationalities joined Sonia near the judge's bench. She was in a red, white and blue pants suit with white shoes and socks. An older sister was wearing the same thing.

Sonia stood in the front row and raised her left hand as the judge asked for the right. She had her right hand buried in her father's at the time. Sheepishly, they both changed, and Sonia stuck her right hand up about half-mast while her dad cupped her shoulder with his left hand.

He stood grinning like a man ready to leave for a six-week vacation.

His wife smiled at the pair from her seat, and the folks from Stillman Valley joined her as Sonia Wiltfang became an American.

ALL I KNEW FOR SURE IS THEY HAVE SOME HORSE RACE

In moving on from my Rockford colleagues and friends, my June, 1975 Louisville interview was with the *Louisville Times*, the much-lessor-known and publicized evening paper to the *Courier-Journal*. I had at least two things going for me in Louisville. Steve Blain, newly hired in the business section for the *Times*, had been a friend and beer-drinking companion in Rockford, and helped push me along in Louisville.

The other plus was Mike Waller, a classic, hard-nosed *Times* editor with a steady hand and wicked sense of humor. He had grown up in Durand IL, about 20 miles from Rockford, although he swore, he knew nothing of its fabled Outhouse Capitol status. The Midwest work-ethic remained part of Mike even as he went on to ever higher newspaper jobs in Kansas City, Hartford and later as publisher of the *Baltimore Sun*.

"You decide how to handle it," Waller would say of a story, "or I'll decide for you."

Waller wrote and edited a book, *"Blood on the Out-Basket - Lessons in Leadership from a Newspaper Junkie."* It was a perfect title, although modern day journalism doesn't have much use or need for copy-filled out basket, bloody or not.

With many contributors, the book dove into ancient, pre-chain-management ideals such as respect employees, communicate, be an agent of change, listen, really listen, take risks, embrace innovation, be tenacious, uphold standards, reward performance and commit to diversity. Waller is photographed in the book in his office in a normal position. He was leaning way back in a chair, feet up on a messy desk, Pulitzer Prize plaque on wall above his head, tie loosened, talking on the telephone. All-in-all, still not that far from Durand.

While interviewing with the *Louisville Times*, I had lunch with two editors in a riverside restaurant and briefly toured the then scrawny, vacant Louisville downtown and wharf area.

I learned of the Bingham family, owners of the newspapers, a television station and huge printing operation all in the same block. I was told of the family's love and respect for good journalism over profit, although their near-monopoly situation was pretty good for business. It was an empire later bitterly divided in a family dispute, all the operations split up and sold, a loss to community and family.

The irony was I was leaving a cost-cutting Gannett newspaper in Rockford in part to escape its relentless profit motives only to see Gannett buy the Louisville papers 12 years later, its heady profit motives intact.

The *Times* executive editor then was Mike Davies, very energetic, still in his 20s and something of a Boy Wonder. He, along with Waller, would later move to Kansas City and then East Coast newspapers.

Davies was leading an upgrade of the *Louisville Times* in the 1970s, hiring many good, experienced journalists. The *Courier-Journal* was always the paper with the national top-ten reputation, its closet filled with Pulitzer Prizes, which was forever an irritant and inspiration to *Times* reporters.

Barry Bingham Jr., the head of both papers, would hand out coffee mugs saying, *"The best thing the Courier-Journal has going for it is the Louisville Times."* We didn't think he was patronizing.

Barry was a slim man with a handlebar mustache and a sincere need to be one of the gang. He lived in a large house above the Ohio River and hosted regular Christmas parties and such. The mansion rooms were often chilly at such parties as the family sought to reduce heating bills to help preserve the environment.

Barry made it a point to personally interview all new reporters in his office, sort of stiffly curious about what brought us to Louisville and what our plans might be. He was very approachable, took some pride in it.

Exhibit A on that trait occurred as the newspapers then held regular meetings to apprise the staff of its plans, a rarity in that corporate world. At one meeting editor Len Pardue was trying to adjust the height of the slide projector and having no luck, shouted out, "Hey Barry, can I borrow your billfold."

On another occasion the newspaper softball team challenged Kentucky Opera to a softball game, figuring an easy win battling the baritones. As it turned out, one member of the opera team, Bob Bernhardt, had been a good enough baseball player to earn a spring training call from the Kansas City Royals. He had a ton of hits in this Newspaper-Opera performance and the opera kicked our bassoons. The only revenge I got was to run the game story in my column in Italian with the help of local Italian restaurateur Vincenzo Gabriele.

The final score was in English.

The better part of that game was Barry Jr., who we doubted had ever played a softball game in his life, wanted to join his company team for the occasion.

Unsure what to do with The Boss, we suggested he play second base. As we took the field for defense, Barry went out and stood atop second base, glove in hand, appearing a little uncertain if that was the correct location. We then had to explain to him when on the field second base is normally played about 15 feet over toward first base.

The most memorable thing about my first Louisville visit was Steve Blain and wife, Kitty, who took me to the late-great Kentucky Fried Chicken Bluegrass Festival then held annually on the Waterfront Belvedere on the Ohio River.

I was somewhat familiar with Bluegrass music, liked what I had heard, but had never heard or seen it live. This was a full immersion including Bill Monroe, Doc Watson, Ralph Stanley, Tony Rice and Mark O'Connor. With Allison Krauss, New Grass Revival,

Seldom Scene and a very happy Czechoslovakian band in future events. I was mesmerized. It was live. It was free. It was Louisville, Kentucky.

THIS IS GOING TO WORK—I HOPE

It was also June 1975, when Mike Davies added me to the list of new *Times* reporters. I needed the traditional two weeks to prepare, explain the move to the family, get us packed and sell the Illinois house. Davies agreed to that, then called and asked if I could start the following Monday. Who could argue?

I still remember that drive down to Louisville leaving the family behind with no real idea what was ahead, but it felt right and Janet, again, was fully on board. As I drove around Indianapolis and headed south, I shook my fist at the big *Louisville* traffic sign overhead, offering an "I got this!" pose.

Not really.

My goodbye party from the Rockford newspapers came with a fitting gift, a genuine, upright, odor-free wooden outhouse placed on the party host's lawn. It had been hauled in from Durand by a grateful group of men for my promotion of their "Out House Capitol of the World." The celebrants had painted "OVER THE HILL WITH BOB HILL" on one side and "GOOD LUCK BOB" on the other. Few journalists have been

The Durand Illinois Outhouse Society offered Bob a fine goodbye gift. He declined.

so honored.

When first hired at the Times, I lived for a few months with Janet's relatives in Louisville. After our family all got together again in Southern Indiana, we briefly returned to Illinois to learn that someone, thinking we had gone for good, had totally stripped our garden of all tomatoes, potatoes and other crops. Nothing was left.

Irene, Good Night.

It would be August before the Illinois house was sold; the family moved south to a new home in Southern Indiana. That purchase involved more luck leaning in on serendipity. We wanted another old house, but with more land. At first, we looked south of Louisville, which would have required driving 15 or 20 miles through traffic each way to get to the downtown *Courier-Journal* building. No way. Our realtor suggested, "Try Indiana." It was just across the Ohio River, and at the time much less settled.

We went to a Hoosier realtor's office. She was not very encouraging, especially in our price range, offering no hope or houses. As we talked, her phone rang. As she answered, Janet picked up the realtor's book of listings and began turning pages. Near the back she saw an old farmhouse near Utica IN with six acres of land. The old, grainy house pictures were not inviting. The possibilities were.

Janet showed the farm listing to the realtor. She said it wasn't her listing, but she would call the right realtor. Twenty minutes later we were in Utica, a small, 200-year-old, almost forgotten town on the Ohio River about eight miles upriver from my new job. Utica was somewhat bigger than Irene, but with a river view and, as would learn, a red-neck reputation. It's Ohio River site would include regular floods, the worst a January 1937 flood with 13 inches of rain in 15 days on frozen ground. The onslaught washed away much of the town, halting what had been promising growth.

Our farmhouse was literally hidden behind rows of old, 20-foot apple trees buried in tent-like honeysuckle vines. We drove past the house the first time, unable to see it from the road. We turned around and pulled into a long, gravel driveway flanked by weeds and a cow pasture.

It got worse. The long, low worn-looking house, built in the 1860s, had a leaky, angled tin roof that badly needed painting. Its clapboard siding was flakey white, the original wood shutters moldy black. An overgrown water maple tree was pushing up through the roof of a breezeway between the house and a summer kitchen. A monster sugar maple lurked over a broad front porch. The back acres of the place were covered in grass, weeds and marauding maple seedlings. The Civil War was alive and well when this house was built.

Reasons for the neglect soon became apparent. The house owners were getting divorced, but still lived there. Their hearts, minds and billfolds were not into upkeep. Their dogs had clawed at the doors and woodwork leaving rivers of scars. All the wallpaper was ancient, faded and needed replacement. Every base board needed to be repainted.

The house had one bathroom. All the plumbing was old and rusty, some once connected to wells dug in the side yards. The wiring was soft, inadequate and not up to code, probably 50 years old. All of it would have to be replaced.

The house had been heated by wood-burning stoves for decades. Its chimneys were packed with creosote, a reality we would learn the hard way when we first started a fire in the fireplace. The creosote caught fire. Flames roared 10 feet into the air, leaping out the top of the old brick chimney like a blow torch. We were too stupid to know just how close we had been to burning a wooden house down. At least the creosote was suddenly removed.

The roof of the dilapidated, one-car garage behind the house had partially collapsed, the job finished when another rotted maple tree fell on it. Our children's bedrooms would need work. The one upstairs had a ceiling so low adults could not stand up in it. The back porch had fallen into ruin, a storage area for firewood.

Someone had dug a musty basement below part of the house, which had no air-conditioning. We lived with that in hot Southern Indiana summers for several years before adding window units, then central air.

So, yeah, of course we bought the place—that same day. It was six acres only eight miles from work for $37,500. It had a good feel, a presence, a benign ghost who hung around with us making the roof creak. We had about $12,000 equity from our previous house. We loved all the possibilities of this old house—the needed realities not so much. It was the beginning of my endless jokes about being 50 years in on a five-year remodeling plan.

The house also served as a marvelous site for some rousing-if-not-legendary newspaper parties, 50 to 60 people crowded in and around, a jukebox in the back room, someone strumming a guitar from the roof of the barn, a live baby pig delivered as a present, a wide front porch for group singing and employee satire. We listed the parties in Roman numeral fashion, UTICA I to the final UTICA VII.

The bigger picture is that house, that place, that land, was eventually filled with flowers, shrubs and trees as we created our own arboretum. We hosted wildflower walks, big garden-art shows and kite-flying contests. For 20 years we operated Hidden Hill from our home, a commercial nursery featuring rare plants and local artists whose employees became close friends. We met hundreds of great gardeners, traveled the country and world looking at rare plants and exotic places. It kept us rooted. It was the center of our happy lives for half a century. Much of it deductible.

How would our lives have been if the realtor's phone had not rung? What if Janet had not picked up the listings book? Where else would we have landed without our six acres?

Serendipity.

I KNOW I AM BETTER THAN THIS

It took me almost a year to feel comfortable in Ohio River Journalism waters. Our two kids were fine, their elementary school now just 45 seconds down the road—and they still got to ride a school bus. Janet was the forever-busy mom, and later a teacher's assistant in elementary schools, wanting to work the same hours as our kids were in school. I had gone from writing columns in Rockford with a mostly relaxed mindset to being back in the reportorial world with editors, quite naturally, calling the shots.

I had no real misgivings about the move to Louisville, our new and needy six-acre estate, or my future. I wasn't thinking that far ahead. But the words I wanted to fulfill my writing obligations still hadn't made the transition south from Illinois. All writers worry. It's part of their internal creative process, but I knew I could do better. My editors were kind, gave me space, but why had they hired me? Was I disappointing them?

Why the worry? Because I had suddenly found myself in a building stuffed with incredible journalism talent in a city that had its problems, but also offered fine arts, good parks, great theatre, Broadway productions, a fine museum, championship college basketball and a free bluegrass festival with Bill Monroe. None of which had been so previously available. All about 20 minutes from home.

The Bingham newspapers of that era had a Washington Bureau and state bureaus in Frankfort and Indianapolis. The two papers combined had regional bureaus in Eastern, Central and Western Kentucky and Southern Indiana, along with metro editions, and separate deadlines for each. With a total circulation pushing 400,000 on Sundays.

It's sports departments routinely covered national and some international sports, while covering Kentucky and Louisville college and high school athletics, with excellent sports reporters and columnists on short deadlines, often only 30 to 45 minutes. Our best sports columnist, Dave Kindred moved on to the Washington Post, the Atlanta Journal-Constitution and The National Sports Daily, covering the sports world, writing books, winning dozens of awards with a spot on 60 Minutes about his newest calling, writing about girls high school basketball in Central Illinois.

Each Bingham paper had television, movie and theater critics, local or state columnists and separate editorial staffs. They had an ombudsman to deal with community newspaper issues, a book critic, education reporters, medical reporters, large general assignment and feature staffs and investigative teams hidden away on other floors.

They had a feisty Saturday *Scene* magazine and fat Sunday magazine with longer in-depth stories done by reporters given time to succeed, and columnist John Ed Pearce, always erudite and eloquent. We had company airplanes and wrote stories from around the nation, and sometimes the world, from Mexico to Cambodia-Thailand.

The dedicated photo staffs were among the best in the nation, then working with film, paper, developer, fixer and rinse. I loved to watch the end of that process, the shadowy images floating up through the chemicals, slowly coming into focus, then frozen in time.

Magic. Often on strict deadlines.

Hovering over all that were large copy desks filled with knowledgeable, occasionally-feisty people who routinely lived on strict publishing deadlines, could spell well and generally hated semi-colons.

In all, the *Courier-Journal* and *Times* would win 11 Pulitzer Prizes including deadline and investigative stories, editorial cartooning, photography and column writing. The winning range would include a spelunker trapped in cave to anti-busing photography to the Beverly Hills nightclub fire to the Carrollton bus crash to gubernatorial issues and damage.

The Pulitzer for writing went to *Courier-Journal* writer *and* photographer John Fetterman. His July 1968, Sunday Magazine story told of the arrival home and funeral of PFC James "Little Duck" Gibson, an Eastern Kentucky native killed in Vietnam.

When at a loss for my words, I would seek out Fetterman's story hanging on a wall outside the Sunday Magazine office, every word perfect, tinged in sadness and mountain community pride. He wrote how the mourners, Knott County friends and neighbors, first gathered in Little Duck's living room, then at a rural cemetery, where James "Little Duck" Gibson was laid beneath "a bit of the land he had died for."

The story began:

"It was late on a Wednesday night and most of the people were asleep in Hindman, the county seat of Knott County, when the body of Private First Class James Thurman "Little Duck" Gibson came home from Vietnam.

It was hot. But as the gray hearse arrived bearing the gray Army coffin, a summer rain began to fall. The flat raindrops glistened on the polished hearse and steamed on the street. Hindman was dark and silent. In the distance down the town's main street, the red sign on the Square Deal Motor Co. flashed on and off."

So, yeah, given all that talent, I was feeling in Louisville a little like the new kid just up to the Big Leagues from AA Irene. There was good reason for that talent, a company mindset willing to invest. The *Louisville Times* and *Courier-Journal's* profit margin at that time was said to be three-to-five percent, but the Bingham family still owned a radio and television station on the same block and a huge printing company next door, so money did not seem a large issue. Quality was. *Courier Journal* and *Times* employees seemed mostly happy in a business where grousing is mandatory. Most stayed with the papers for many years, often whole careers unless drawn to brighter lights in bigger cities.

Meanwhile, reported profit margins for the Gannett newspaper chains were in the 20 to 30 percent range.

Still coming were the massive digital and social media growth that would forever change the business. All that eventually mixed with internal Bingham family issues that would force the 1986 sale of the company to Gannett for $300 million, outbidding the *Washington Post*, the latter a missed sale that could have offered a whole different, much more beneficial journalism outcome. Although the *Washington Post* now has its own problems, too.

In announcing the sale Gannett President Al Neuharth stood on a desk in our newsroom and promised no changes. Gannett closed the afternoon *Louisville Times* a year later, a sign of things to come not only in Louisville, but across the country.

Yet, in many ways lamenting the demise of print newspapers makes as much sense as lamenting the demise of the Pony Express. It is inevitable. But so much else has been lost with the demise of so many small-town papers, including local news, the monitoring of local tax-supported agencies and a sense of community.

NOTHING BEATS ON-THE-JOB TRAINING

My first year in Louisville came with fiery protests and KKK rallies, with the federal court-ordered busing of students in Jefferson County Public Schools, and then a harrowing airplane ride into the Eastern Kentucky mountains to cover a coal mine disaster.

Busing was a totally artificial and eventually failed attempt to cure decades of neighborhood racial segregation in Louisville by putting kids from heavily minority areas with bad neighborhood schools on buses very early in the morning and shipping them across town to better, predominately white schools.

Some white kids also had to be shipped in the other direction for several years of school, but more Black kids than white had to be bused. Students and parents—who also had to reschedule around their jobs—had to get up early to do this and the children got home later. Kids were being abused to solve a long-standing adult racist problem. Fifty years later the Louisville public schools are still dealing with many of the same problems.

Even most Black leaders supported the federal lawsuit to integrate the schools as the best available educational solution at the time. Its need was the result of white flight from West Louisville following the local and nationwide 1960s race riots in protest of generations of segregation and the murder of Dr. Martin Luther King. Red lining in Louisville housing and poorer Blacks being pushed west out of growing downtown areas contributed to the issue.

In Louisville in 1968, a police skirmish over a false arrest of a Black man eventually grew into a full-fledged riot at 28th and Greenwood streets. The protests lasted almost a week. More than 2,000 National Guardsman were ordered to town. Buildings were burned, two teens were killed and 472 people were arrested.

I had started in Louisville in 1975. Two months later, anti-busing protests were held nightly for weeks, with bonfires in South End parking lots. Windows were smashed in the *Courier-Journal* building in one protest march down Broadway. The Louisville papers continued to support the public busing program even as some of its leaders had kids in private schools.

Our reportorial jobs were to nightly drive around Louisville's mostly blue-collar south side, look for protestors, speak with those willing to talk, drive back downtown very early in the morning and write something for our afternoon paper. Some nights I was the only one in the normally hectic newsroom. So quiet. Peaceful. Alone with my notes and the duly-noted shouts and threats of protestors.

Overall, reportorial damage during the riots and

protests were minimal. After dozens of nightly trips, many of the protestors became "regulars." We got to talk about other, more day-to-day things besides school. As often now the case with politics, real bonds were developed as long as you stayed away from the political elephant in the room.

I got sucker-punched in the parking lot of the Kentucky Fair & Exposition Center by a protestor who then took off running between parked cars. We had been ordered by newspaper management to avoid conflict. I let him run.

Several hundred Ku Klux Klan members led by three masked horsemen marched a mile through Okolona, a community south of Louisville that had been a hotbed of anti-busing protests. Sherman Adams, Kentucky Grand Dragon of the United Klans explained the march was only to show support for the United States Constitution and all law enforcement agencies. It said so right there in *"We the people of the United States."*

It was about that time the KKK went on a self-described, three-day promotional campaign in Louisville, Paducah and Harlan County in Eastern Kentucky to sell its virulent, racist, antisemitic and separatist views as a by-God-American religious experience. Their Lord also opposed busing students to achieve integration.

There was then sort of a passive acceptance of that. The KKK was allowed to hold rallies at an East Louisville motel, a Paducah civic center and a lumber mill in Harlan County. They were organized by the Klan's Grand Wizard David Duke, then 25, an articulate college graduate who for a time also taught English for the State Department in Laos. He went on to become an international spokesperson for Holocaust denial. He used the gatherings to recruit new members. The cost was $15 membership and $5 a month dues for Duke's salary.

Louisville Times reporter Ric Manning, photographer Michael Coers and I journeyed into the Eastern Kentucky mountains for the Harlan County KKK rally. It was only about a month after I had joined the paper. It was my first trip to Eastern Kentucky, one I would make dozens of times later for the *Louisville Courier-Journal* as its Kentucky columnist. It was all new to me—Appalachia, myth meeting reality, the coal mines and the culture, the mountains rising low and green, the roads curling through them.

I would later enjoy those trips to the mountains, the people, the kindness and hospitality up front and their suspicions held at bay. Deeper in the mountains, poverty was everywhere, but the old lesson "never judge a book by its cover" was never more true than in Appalachia. I would learn that a lot of wisdom, poetry, kindness and truth lived there, too, along with the need to get out and go north to find work.

The KKK rally was held at a sawmill in Verda in Harlan County just off Jones Creek. It was a poor area in a county once nicknamed "Bloody Harlan" for its 1930s skirmishes, executions and bombings during coal strikes.

I parked among other cars and trucks and watched as a middle-aged man got out of his car next to me. He strapped a pistol to his waist, lifted his white, hooded

KKK robe from its trunk and carefully pulled it over his head. He glanced at me, as if waiting to see my robe, then moved on.

We walked into an open area where some other hooded men, women and children had gathered. A 32-foot wooden cross soaked in kerosene had been set up nearby. Not all the 400 to 500 people milling around on the site seemed that interested in the rally, which felt more like a family reunion. Many were just curious about what was happening.

Several Appalachian towns had been settled by Blacks who had moved north to work in the coal mines, a migration repeated as people moved north to work in Detroit. Harlan County public schools had long been integrated, with an active NAACP chapter. Union coal miners on site declared many of the protesters "scabs."

The socializing mood ended as the KKK members gathered to hear their leader preach hate, their white-cloaked children pulled along. As 22 white-cloaked Klansman rallied, chanted and tossed burning torches onto the base of the cross it caught on fire, the flames roared upward.

When the flames reached the horizontal bar, somehow the cross broke and lurched sideways sending the Klansman below running in panic away from the falling flames, looking up over their shoulders a moment forever captured in a classic Michael Coers photograph.

"I don't know what happened," Grand Wizard Duke told Ric Manning about the crashing cross as the crowd wandered off, grumbling. "They (local Klansman) did it and they didn't do it right," he said.

The following spring, in March 1976, was the Scotia coal mine explosions that killed 15 Eastern Kentucky miners. This was normally *Courier-Journal* territory, but *Times* reporter Ira Simmons and I flew down on a cold, wet night in the company plane. As we neared the mountain airport our pilot pulled out a flashlight and ran the beam along the edge of the wings, checking for icing. He seemed calm about it, just another night in the cockpit. Just a little ice. Maybe. His passengers not so calm.

On the Scotia trip I interviewed those I could outside the fence and well above where the miners had died. Simmons found a way to get inside the building where family members were keeping vigil, scooping the *Courier-Journal* on that one. When we got back several Louisville Times editors invited us to lunch to talk about it.

SO WHEN DO I GET TO WRITE A COLUMN AGAIN

About 1977, I was still thinking column, but the *Louisville Times* already had a local columnist, the very perceptive and funny Richard Des Ruisseaux, also a beer-drinking buddy and co-founder of the National Society of Newspaper Columnists. The only other possible opening for a column was *Scene* magazine, the more hip, timely and fun Saturday read that was open to the 1970s world.

The *Courier-Journal* was the Grande Dame of Kentucky journalism. The *Louisville Times* was her younger, livelier sister. When new ideas were tried, the *Times* usually tried them. And the Saturday *Scene* was one of those ideas.

Back then, the *Times*—which already didn't publish on Sunday—was facing low Saturday circulation, low enough that one possibility was to stop publishing a separate edition on Saturdays, in favor of a "combined edition" like the Sunday newspaper.

But this also was the dawn of city magazines like New York magazine. These magazines covered the cultural revolution that was shaking up America with everything from rock music to miniskirts. Such magazines offered lively writing, lots of opinion, guides to their city's live entertainment and a fresh approach for a younger audience.

Times editors decided to try the same thing: Publish a "city magazine" every week by completely reinventing the Saturday edition. It wouldn't have a traditional newspaper front page with headlines; instead, it would have a full-color cover, like a magazine. It would have stories written with more stylistic flair, like a magazine. It would cover youthful topics, like popular music, restaurants, nightclubs, street fashion and cars. It would be fun, readable and off-the-wall as well as informative.

And it worked.

The Saturday *Scene* became the most popular issue of the *Louisville Times*, often sought out by an additional 20,000 people. These *Scene*-lovers found restaurant reviews, music reviews, lists of live events and a series of eye-popping cover stories.

Its editor was Greg Johnson, a recent Indiana University graduate with a fun and inventive bent—the perfect man for the job. *Scene's* up-front syndicated columnist at that time was—and what manner of fate was this?—Mike Royko, my Chicago urban idol.

I had written a few stories for *Scene* and was doing an often satirical garden column called "Down and Dirty." I suggested to Greg that I'd like try a regular column. Johnson talked it over with management. It was decided local was better. A column was offered, and my urban idol was replaced. By the newbie from corn country. I was back in the column business. More serendipity.

COLUMN WRITING AS A SPORT

Getting back in the column business wasn't all ego, although it's hard to survive in the column business without one. Give or take the occasional political rant, I never was about changing the world overnight. I mostly preferred a sharp needle to a hammer. I just liked to go out and paint pictures, let the moment speak for itself with insight, humor, pathos, satire or some old-fashioned mockery, although sometimes you could be so damn right about something no hammer need apply.

I'd get up about six a.m. and go to work, liking the silence. If I was rolling, I could get out of the office in three or four hours, column done, next case, no editors need apply. Unless I had done an interview the day before, I often had no real idea what I was going to write about as I drove to the office.

That was a good thing. What shows up in print then is the genuine you, not something smothered in thought. Stay out of your own way. I tried to avoid using the first person "I" unless the column was pure opinion. Why should I have to tell someone "I" saw the purple giraffe coming out of the brush." It's an observation. Just describe it.

I had heard of columnists who wrote two or three columns ahead to make up for the inevitable bad days, even vacation, but I never went there. I was a strict adherent to the Columnist's Prayer:

Dear Lord,
I live my life
In mortal dread
Someday I'll die.
One column ahead.

After a while I began to rate each column on a scale of one to 10, very happy to maintain a seven or eight average. Don't sweat the bad columns. Your next one is due tomorrow. Long-time readers will forgive you. There are no 10s in the column business, but you must keep trying.

In writing almost 4,000 columns I rarely went to press conferences, political-stunt sessions or pure media events. Reporters get used enough as it is, and it's getting worse. As learned in Rockford, some days I would just go sit in cafes and bars in different parts of town and listen. My favorite such occasion was with an old woman who sat and talked about her pet chickens and their egg production. Much more fun than a mayor announcing a $300 million shoe factory.

Serendipity was mandatory, especially in my Kentucky columnist days when I would leave home Monday morning in my pickup truck and just cruise around the state for two or three days wondering who or what would show up. My luckiest find was a guy I heard had been divorced six or seven times and lived somewhere on a certain country road. I found him sitting in a chair on his porch like he was waiting for me. We talked of marriage and its issues for an hour, including him placing wife wanted ads in the local paper. None of that had quite worked out.

The Kentucky columnist's job pretty much consisted of wandering the state looking for stories. Like one Ellis Wilson plowing behind a pair of mules. And him giving me a chance to try it.

One of the good things in life—mules

LITTLE STURGEON CREEK, Ky.

Sing out, you poets, of the man with a bull-tongued plow. Shout your message of a job well-done by man and beast harnessed to wood and steel. Ellis Wilson has his cornfield plowed, and he's got his two mules, Kate and Dorie, to thank for that.

"Mules," said Wilson, 66, the son of a mule-driving man, "is something good."

You can take that to the bank. Mules is something good. So is Ellis Wilson and his wife of 45 years, Esther, 65, and their son, Bernard, 31. They're mule people, all of them.

Ellis Wilson's father, John F. Wilson, wore out a shed full of plows following oxen and mules over Owsley County hills and knobs. John Wilson was born in a house on an Owsley County hillside and died 98 years later in his son's house not a half-mile away.

"He was a worker," said Ellis Wilson of his daddy. "He always was saying he never got too far from home."

He was a worker. And so is his son. He's a little man given to mixing his store-bought plug of chewing tobacco with some of his home-grown that he stuffs in a back pocket of his coveralls. His face is tucked back under the bill of a Mack Truck cap. He is one sly and humorous mule man.

"You tell them people," he said, "that the man's so far back in the sticks he never even seen a car."

Ellis Wilson has seen a car or two. He even bought one once and drove it a few times.

"My boys wore it out," he said.

But the man has never plowed a single furrow with a tractor. He plows and disks with mules, mows hay with mules and forks it into the barn; he picks corn by hand and hauls it from the field by wagon.

"I reckon I'm one of those old-timers," he said.

He is an old-timer with a flair. Not 15 seconds after I confess a lifelong desire to plow behind a pair of mules, Wilson is in the barn harnessing up Kate and Dorie. The best offer for permanent farm work is $30 a month, plus room and board.

"We may just keep him at that if he's right good at a plow," Wilson announced to his wife and son.

Mrs. Wilson thought the wages might be a little high.

"When me and him first married 45 years ago," she said, "he worked all day for 65 cents a day. We didn't worry. We didn't have nothin' nobody else had."

Kate and Dorie went along with the program willingly. Wilson hitched them up, linking the bridles, collars, hames, trace chains and butt straps, single trees and double trees until the mules jingled in the harness.

He added the No. 10 Vulcan turning plow, a shiny one-bladed implement used to turn over new ground. Then we marched resolutely up a steep grade toward the angled hillside that passes for Wilson's garden and cornfield.

"Sure, I'll come along," Mrs. Wilson said. "I've only been seeing this for 60 years."

Most of the ground had been plowed already, so we weren't able to break any new sod. Wilson slowly walked the mules across the field; the wet dirt sliding off the plow blade and mounding up along the furrow.

Wilson learned to plow when he was 7. He had to reach up and grab the wooden plow handles while his father worked the mules.

"We all learn't by doing," he said.

Wilson cut four furrows and turned the plow over to the flatland columnist. The columnist was grinning so hard he thought his face would fall off. He could not see—mule plowing being what it is—what kind of expression Kate and Dorie had on their faces.

The plow sliced through the hillside and the dirt tumbled down below it. It was strictly the Kate and Dorie show, with a man to hold the plow. There was little strain on the arms and back, although a long day behind two mules in thick sod would be a different song.

My first furrow looked as if it were cut by a blind wino, but Wilson was encouraging.

"Plowing don't hurt a bit if you understand it," he

said. "But if a man ain't used to plowing it can get him hotter than anything else he ever done."

Normally, the mule reins are knotted and looped around the plowman's back, but Wilson held them for obvious reasons.

"We might never catch up to you again," he said. The flatlander—ever grinning—sliced three more furrows— ever straighter—in the loose ground.

Mules, he's thinking, is something good.

Bob Hill plows some ground with Ellis Wilson, Kate and Dorie.

ENJOY THE PROCESS—YOU COULD HAVE A REAL JOB

Becoming famous will get in the way if you like to just hang out and watch people. Try to settle for "sort of well known." But you will get to meet a lot of famous people, even columnists. At one National Society of Newspaper Columnists Convention in Louisville I was drinking beer with Dave Barry. The late-great Molly Ivins was our guest speaker at a Florida convention the night of the O.J. Simpson "low speed chase." Being columnists, we started a pool to guess how long the chase would last. Molly won.

Make notes about possible column ideas before they disappear. I used to jot them down in pencil on my office walls. Save the best letters from the critics—they are probably right. Accept ideas from editors and co-workers, but always make it clear you have the final say. Most of those ideas are very good.

I remember compliments from readers. One was sincere praise from the guy riding on the back of the garbage truck picking up trash on a Monday morning. The other was from a guy sitting at the bar at Teek's World Famous Bar and Grill, a favorite newspaper watering hole.

He was sitting at the bar, head down staring at a beer He looked up at me and said, "Hill, you can make do where there ain't no do."

Then he went back to his beer.

That *Scene* job worked well. I was doing a mix of *Louisville Times* features and *Scene* columns, when another opportunity showed up. Mike Davies had moved from Times managing editor to the same position with the *Courier-Journal.*

Then, Billy Reed, the *Courier-Journal* "Kentucky columnist," became the *Courier-Journal's* sports editor. The job had been an almost sacred position in which the author would roam the state's 120-counties seeking out hidden places, local color, fine characters and interesting observation. The King of Bluegrass Journalism had been Joe Creason, a Kentucky journalist so popular Louisville named a park after him.

Davies, a little bit like Lew Winkler had done with the sports editor job in Rockford, called me in as a surprise and offered the Kentucky columnist job. Only Davies was serious. I was perhaps the only Hoosier in history to be asked.

But he wanted me to travel the state's 379 miles in length and 170 miles in width and write *four* columns a week, up from the previous three. Also included were some ventures into the more bucolic areas of Southern Indiana, the two regions together given the somewhat forced label "Kentuckiana." I didn't give it five minutes thought. Sure. Deal. Why not? Back to full-time column writing.

At that time, save my two trips into the mountains for a KKK rally and coal mine disaster, I had barely been into Kentucky. I would come to find that a good thing. It was all new to me. I had to learn the truths for myself.

The job required new transportation, a shiny-new and very basic 1977 Chevrolet pickup truck costing $4,000 and purchased from the manager of a local dealership whose kid I coached in Little League. The truck basically rusted in place, but lasted long enough to crisscross Kentucky and southern Indiana a few years. Company mileage—something like 17 cents a mile—helped make the payments.

That truck and I went to a lot of interesting places. Being gone a couple days a week in it would be a burden for Janet with the two kids. But Davies did give me two weeks to learn the turf, to travel the state, one week in each direction with Janet and the kids coming along, also getting a sense of the state, although I suspect their favorite times came in motel swimming pools.

My co-workers at the *Times*, feeling slightly betrayed as I headed over to the rival turf, threw cream pies in my face in the *Times* newsroom. Tough love. I still ate lunch with them when possible. Then I was off on a new Kentucky adventure.

FROM HICKMAN TO GRAVEL SWITCH TO BUTCHER HOLLOW

As the following columns will indicate, the Kentucky columnist's job was fun, always educational and, at times, inspiring. History lived out there in the Bluegrass and beyond.

Learning of Daniel Boone and early settlers pushing through the Cumberland Gap into Kentucky, seeing the still-rutted tracks of the Wilderness Trail, the sad Trail of Tears of the Cherokee Nation and other tribes being pushed out of their Georgia homeland and across Kentucky to Oklahoma.

The Mississippi River site where Confederates had placed a long chair across the Mississippi River to stop Union gun boats.

The Jefferson Davis Memorial rising up above Kentucky farm fields only two hours' drive from where Abraham Lincoln was born.

In a way, everywhere I had even been in life, the rural landscapes and small-town places I had lived, the neighbors, the culture, the sense of place prepared me for the Kentucky columnist job. Actually, given its place in *Courier-Journal* history, it was more of a mission.

Kentucky is a state of distinct areas, and, in a sense, cultures, not counting the universality of its University of Kentucky basketball. The Eastern Kentucky mountains had its early role in American history, mountain communities, boom-and-bust coal mines and companies, immigrant miners, historic names.

Central Kentucky had its lakes, tourist caves and farmlands. Western Kentucky had its farmlands and huge strip-mining operations. Northern Kentucky had its beautiful knobby hills and towns up along the Ohio River.

Louisville was a separate place unto itself, much more crowded, not quite southern or midwestern with its more diverse and often segregated residents, much stronger arts than many outsiders expected, urban issues, Democratic base and, yes, University of Louisville basketball.

I tried to make my ignorance of all that an asset, particularly Eastern Kentucky. I didn't know all the old stories. I didn't know any of the stories. I had learned to wander and listen, but the most important thing this time around was not to be judgmental, to avoid or accept mountain cliches and rural, small-town ways of life. That was my background, too, just from a different part of the country.

Loyal Jones, a retired director of Berea College Appalachian Center, summed up the mountain culture the best. He said people who live in Appalachia have something most other people lack: a strong sense of place and feeling of belonging. Appalachia, he said, should be judged by its own values—family, land, traditionalism—rather than the mainstream values of accumulation, wealth and power.

I didn't have any real sources for stories when I started, and I was writing four regular columns a week and a garden column. At first my columns were stories I saw out the truck window, read in a local paper or just hanging out in busy places.

Once into the Kentucky travel a year, or so, and I hit all 120 counties, I'd get some letters and phone calls about persons and places of interest. Once out there the best way to a good story was often to look, listen and shut up when someone else was talking.

Often in my Kentucky travels I was aware of being watched as much as I was watching. I was the stranger sitting around a pot-bellied stove in a general store listening to local life stories. Good stories. Fun stories. Interesting stories. Told by the world's best, home-grown story tellers. Then get back in the truck and find another story. And I was getting paid to do it.

My Kentucky travels would include meeting 94-year-old Claudius Greeenwade, the son of a slave, just by knocking on the door of his ancient home. Meeting a couple married 80 years came through a story in a weekly paper. Country Songwriter Louise Cox was so proud when she got to hear one of her songs played on the radio she had to tell me.

I was sitting around a country store in Clover Bottom as the locals had a little fun with the visiting journalist. Almost in that same vein, what woman celebrating her 104th birthday wouldn't want to do it with free oysters?

An absolute favorite was an evening spent drinking moonshine with Herman Webb, Loretta Lynn's brother, up in Butcher Hollow, KY.

Nature erasing only log of life for son of slaves

ROARING SPRING, Ky.—The woods are so thick, the rutted road so steep and the journey so difficult that Claudius Greenwade rarely visits his parents' graves anymore.

His parents were slaves, buried in one of the hundreds of desolate, forgotten cemeteries of rural Kentucky. Their graves are marked with plain gray stones. They lived, raised a family and died, leaving no pictures, no mementos their children can touch or feel, nothing.

"I was mighty young when my daddy died," Greenwade said. "I never did get to learn the flavor of him,"

Greenwade is 94. His surname is that of the man who owned his father. He lives on his 50-acre farm in southern Trigg County, barely two miles from where he was born. He splits his time between a small, heated trailer and an old, gray crumbling house with buckled floors, warped walls and a patched roof.

"My house got old," he said.

He is the last of his family. He outlived three wives and one son. There may be a brother somewhere, but Greenwade isn't sure. A nephew farms the 50 acres.

Bob Hill

Greenwade still tends a garden, a backyard patch of corn, tomatoes and melons. He lives on $170 a month in Social Security, plus what little the farm brings.

"They may know me down in Louisville in the agriculture office," he said. "I gives them a report on the farm here about once a month. They like to check on what we're doing."

He is a small man with big, strong hands. As a youth and man, he worked hard. He has always worked. He likes to be near work, around it, getting his pleasure, if not his groceries, from it.

"I worked on a farm where they had 13 men, and they always paid me last," he said. "The boss always waited to deal with me. He said he had men who could pick me up and throw me away, but I was the man he needed. . . . I was the man he needed."

The dirt road up to his parents' cemetery crosses a dry creek bed, then cuts across a hill where dry corn rustles in the field. It is a lonely place, overgrown with underbrush, yellowing grass and thickets of trees tinged in scarlet and gold.

Claudius Greenwade

Greenwade walks erect, but with a wooden cane. The hilltop is so overgrown that he cannot find the gravesites. He walks off the road into the woods, pulls up short, then looks around.

"My daddy had mighty modest white people that was over him," he said.

The cemetery is found farther up the hill and around a curve. Only one or two of the graves are marked. The rest are just rocks, placed in even rows, most of them nearly buried in ferns, honeysuckle and scrubby cedar trees. Unless you knew exactly where to look, the graves could never be seen from the road.

Greenwade climbed through a deep gash at the edge of the road, crossed a rusted fence and began searching.

"My mother made us children go to grammar school," he said. "Then we tried to teach mother her ABCs. She worked for people in town, and they was always paying her in change. She hated that. She'd rush home to the children so we could count it for her."

He walked past the stones, searching for his parents', but he could not tell one from the other.

"I got uncles and aunts in here, too," he said. "I dug the grave for one of them. We had to dig our own graves in those days."

He walked over to one stone, looked at it, but said he could never be sure if it was one of those that marked his parents' graves.

"I'm just not for certain," he said, "and most of my acquaintances is dead."

80 years isn't a piece of (wedding) cake

DENNISTON, Ky.—Lord, they have been married 80 years.

They slipped past those early paper, cotton and leather anniversaries in a log cabin and celebrated their 30th anniversary in their Possum Hollow home surrounded by their children.

They swept past sapphire, gold, emerald and finally, after 60 years, enjoyed their diamond anniversary.

Then they went off the anniversary gift chart. Its makers didn't allow for gifts for any marriage time served past 60 years.

The pessimists.

The anniversary celebrations were noticeably short on precious stones and long on family. Lydia Wells insisted on cooking for each of them, and the 80th, held last Sunday, was no different.

Her husband, Lynn, might get a little rowdy at the affairs and tell some stories on his wife. Like their wedding night, July 25, 1898, when they slept in a bed in her parent's two-room cabin with her mother in another bed a few feet away.

Her mother, as was her habit when her daughter slept in the bed alone, placed a small candle at the foot of the bed. Lynn wanted to put it out. Lydia wouldn't let him.

"Momma always does that," the 14-year-old bride told her 17-year-old husband.

Their marriage recovered. They eventually had 13 children, 47 grandchildren, 87 great-grandchildren and 35 great-great-grandchildren.

The optimists.

The Guinness Book of World Records lists the longest known marriage at 86 years, but that was between two cousins in India, and they were each 5 when their arranged wedding took place.

The American record is listed at 83 years, and that wedding also took place in Kentucky.

Maybe it's something in the water.

Anniversary stories such as these tend to scurry past the bad in married life and to polish the good. They shouldn't. There is too much of both. Especially after eight decades.

Lydia and Lynn Wells (1978)

The Wellses lost two children when they were babies and lost three more in accidents when they were adults. They have been burned out twice, losing everything they owned, including their $4,000 life savings and their marriage license. As a child, Mrs. Wells wasn't able to go to school much. Her father needed her at home. Often at the opposite end of a crosscut saw.

Wells worked as a Menifee County farmer, and they have stayed in that section of the Eastern Kentucky hills all their lives.

He told his relatives early that he had his eye on that Lydia Rupe and would marry her if she'd have him.

They finally met at a corn husking and quilting bee at Uncle Dan Wells' place. They went to a little party *and played together that night.*

"They had a lot of kissing there and they wanted me to join, but I wouldn't," she said.

A year later, during a pouring rainstorm, his uncle, the Rev. Raney Wells, married them in her parents' house.

"No, I didn't think I was too young at first," she said. "But then I figured I was too young after I studied the thing over."

But you had to walk a far piece in those days to find a professional marriage counselor. The first baby came 13 months after they were married, and the next 79 years—good and bad—flowed right behind it.

"When the family was all well, we was happy," she said, "and when they was sick or anything we was unhappy."

It would be good to report that both are in good health, but that's not the case.

Lynn Wells, 97, spends most of his time in bed, which he leaves only to eat the meals his wife still cooks for him.

Lydia Wells, 94, has slowed. But she still works her garden, cans and freezes its offerings and cares for her husband.

They moved in with their son after their second fire, in November 1977, but Lydia Wells wouldn't stay there. They were set in their ways and wanted a home of their own. They moved to a trailer next door to their son.

She says their marriage survived because they treated each other as they wanted to be treated. That's a start, but it seems to gloss over the love, pride, pain, work, disappointment and plain cussed stubbornness that went with it.

Not to mention fixing a hot breakfast every morning for 80 years.

What's it like to hear your song on the radio? Ask Louise Cox

The words and rhymes—those classic, unpatronizing, unapologetic, country-and-Western words and rhymes—always have lined up in Louise Cox's head, and then pretty much on cue.

Sure, the Muse hands those lines out to people to be used at various levels of sophistication. We all get the same 26 letters to work with, although the finished products might not reflect it.

But Louise Cox can do it. She can flat pound out a country-and-Western refrain in 30 seconds, and every element in its place. There's not a self-conscious word in it. Take her song, "The Postman" . . .

> Please give me the address to heaven.
> I'm sending this letter up there.
> I'm writin' it to my daddy.
> He's in heaven somewhere.
>
> Or this line about a wayward young father, a neglected wife and their

child:
. . . her bottles were always
empty,
and yours were never dry . . . .

Louise Cox was 11 years old when she began writing country songs. She was sitting in school in study hall when the Muse started handing out messages in meter. The first song this grade-school kid wrote had these lines:

Although, my dear, I love you yet,
My wife and two little kids, I can't forget.

She's written hundreds since, most that got no farther than her spiral notebook. In fact, none of them escaped her spiral notebook, save occasional airings in a family band, until a few months ago. That was when Louise Cox went to Nashville to cut a record.

There was nothing special about the method. You and a neighbor could take a three-string ukelele and a washboard to Nashville and cut a record if you had the money. There are studios all over town just waiting to oblige.

But this was different. Louise Cox is now 52. She has been writing her songs for 41 years. She wanted some hot wax of her own. She wanted to hear one of her songs on the radio.

There had been some musicians in the family. One of her daughters, Linda Allbritton, sings in a band in Florida. Another daughter, Terri Jennings, of Bullitt County, sings with a local band called Honky Tonk Heroes.

So Louise Cox selected two songs, picked up her Bullitt County daughter, and headed to Nashville to make a record. It cost about $425, which included studio time, the actual engineering and mixing of the record and 500 copies, with labels.

The studio band included a steel guitar, piano, drums and a lead guitar. The band listened to a tape of the songs about three times, picked up the melody, and was ready to go. Terri Jennings climbed into a recording booth about the size of a shower stall, went through both numbers about three times, and a record was born.

> Put yourself in my shoes
> And wear them for a while.
> You'll find you're getting lonely
> Just to see somebody smile.

The finished record arrived a few weeks later. One side was clean, and pretty much true. The flip side included a separate, higher-pitched voice that was mixed into the final product.

"This was my dream of 40 years," said Louise Cox. "I always wanted to do a record, my daughter got to do it, and I wanted to hear it on the radio."

The world's bandstands and radio stations are overrun with frustrated singers and songwriters, so the air time took a little doing, but Louise Cox did it. She had grown up in Shelbyville, still has family there, and had once cut some commercials for its radio station.

Her sister knew some of the present management and took Louise Cox and her record to station WCND,

940 on your AM dial. The station agreed to play—on request—"Put Yourself in My Shoes" and the flip side, "I'm Going Out."

Through some coincidence, there have been several requests for both sides of late.

WCND—on request—played "Put Yourself in My Shoes" about 9:16 a.m. Thursday morning. Louise Cox listened to it sitting in a big recliner in her den, surrounded by pictures of her family, a spiral notebook full of songs in her lap.

She looked off across the room, her eyes focused on whatever it is eyes focus on when one of your songs is being played on the radio.

"If this goes," she said, "if we can get a big push with it, well, you just never know what might happen."

Knife trader nicks stranger's wallet

CLOVER BOTTOM, Ky.—Once upon a time a small bunch of the boys were sitting around Billy Brumagen's General Store in Clover Bottom talking about the weather, taxes and how many ticks can balance on the head of a coon dog.

Brumagen allowed as how his store was the oldest in Jackson County, with the rest being either torn down, blown down or burned down.

Brumagen was sitting on a chair, except when he had to leave to answer the phone. Mike Richardson, 16, and Darryl Miles, 25, were sitting on old boxes and *pop cases. Leonard Abrams, 77, a retired farmer, was speaking his piece from an old wooden stool.*

The boys were all saying there wasn't much to do in Clover Bottom, and Abrams said, quiet as you please, " 'Cept trade pocketknives."

The thought kinda lay there in the air a few seconds as the boys waited to see if the stranger would take the bait.

He did.

"Pocketknives?" repeats the stranger, and no sooner are the words spoken than Abrams starts gently reeling him in.

"Yep, we trade and sell pocketknives," says Abrams. "Bin doing it about 15 years and ain't made any money yet."

"OK, let's see what you got."

Abrams reaches his right hand behind his bib overalls and pulls out a small can of oil. It was a definite sign the man had come to deal. Some pool hustlers carry their own breakdown cues; Abrams had his own oil can.

"Use it to oil the blades," he explains.

The right hand again drops behind the front of his bib overalls and here comes a pocketknife, a Schrade Walden redwood-handled model 175. There is the kind of silence in the store that is usually filled by a low whistle of appreciation, but the other boys remain silent.

"Hit's a good one," Abrams says.

The stranger is familiar with pocketknives and has seen them traded before, but doesn't really know the model numbers from left center field.

He pleads ignorance.

Abrams doesn't have any trouble believing it. "Hit's a good knife," he says again.

The stranger wants to see a little more merchandise. Abrams drops his left hand behind the front of his bib overalls. Here comes a smaller Schrade Walden model, this time with a swirled handle the boys later describe as butter and molasses.

"Them's both good knives," Abrams says.

The stranger checks the merchandise. The first model has one blade. The second model is a little older and more rusty, but has two blades.

"I've lost money on about every knife I ever sold," Abrams says.

The stranger could use a pocketknife. Life on the road is tough. A man could always use a knife to plunge into the top of a recalcitrant pop can.

The negotiations begin. Abrams sits on his chair mopping his brow with a red bandanna.

"I got to have $6 for that first knife and $5 for the other."

The stranger holds a knife in each hand, wishing somewhere along the line he had picked up a course in Knife Swapping With the Locals.

"I'll sell them both for $10."

"I don't need two knives."

"I got to have $6 for the first and $5 for the second. That's a fair price."

The boys on the boxes and pop cases nod in agreement. Brumagen's not talking.

"I haven't heard no offer from you," Abrams says.

"Five dollars for the first knife."

"Got to have six."

"Five-fifty."

"You're a good boy. You got it for five-fifty."

The stranger puts the knife in his pocket. Abrams puts the $5.50 in a brown purse.

"How much did you really make on this deal?" the stranger asks.

"About $10," Abrams says.

Silence.

"I'm only kidding," Abrams says.

The boys on the boxes and pop cases say he's only kidding.

For Edith Kast, 104, free oysters were a sure bet

Edith Kast was having some fun—you could tell that. Not that she wanted the fun to show too much—a 104-year-old woman does have her dignity to protect—but her sense of humor will get the best of her on occasion.

"You're not going to put all of this in the paper, are you?" she asked, giggling just a little bit.

You'll also have to credit Greg Haner, the manager of Mazzoni's restaurant, 2804 Taylorsville Road, for some of the fun. He's the guy who put up the sign near the restaurant door that said, "Free oysters to anyone 80 years old accompanied by their parent."

Haner did it mostly as a joke, but Mazzoni's is such a Louisville institution—it has been in business for 108 years—that he knew he might have to pay off someday.

"When you get as many generations of Louisvillians as I do," he said, "you know it's in the realm of possibility."

Actually, anything seems possible with Edith Kast. She was born in Iowa on Feb. 16, 1888, one of eight children— four boys and four girls. Her father was a farmer and surveyor, traveling around Illinois, Iowa, Minnesota, Tennessee and Kentucky laying out many of the roads we use today. The entire Kast family—parents and children—traveled from Minnesota to Tennessee in a covered wagon.

Edith Kast and her son Merl (Photo by Larry Spitzer)

"But don't put that in the paper," she said, giggling again.

At 21, she married Joe Kast, another name that has been known in Louisville for almost 100 years, a family of bookbinders practicing a craft nearly as forgotten as the covered wagon.

"We've carried that on a long time," said Edith Kast.

She was married to Joe Kast 61 years. They had two children, Conrad, 77, and Merl, 83. Her health—and she has always eaten anything she wanted when she wanted it—has remained remarkably good. She cares for herself, walks very well but with a cane, and does not need a hearing aid.

She had cataract surgery a few years ago, but she still reads anything she wants, with glasses.

"I'm the wellest person you know," she said. "Everything is still under control. . . . I drove a car until I got to be 100, but then I thought my eyesight was beginning to get a little bit bad, and I better quit."

She doesn't like television. "All you see are those young girls jumping in and out of bed with men," she said. "I don't like that."

Conrad Kast lives in St. Louis. When he was in town a few weeks ago, he had an urge to make a pilgrimage to Mazzoni's for oysters—and he took his mother with him. It was then that Edith Kast saw the sign about the free meal—and thought it would be fun to come back.

"They asked Conrad if he qualified," she said. "He told them no but he had a brother at home who did."

On Tuesday afternoon Merl and Edith Kast went to vote—she never misses—then headed over to Mazzoni's about 4 p.m. for a very senior citizens' meal. It was, in many ways, a convergence of wonderful Louisville institutions.

"They said they'd come for the free oysters," said Haner. "I knew it had to happen some day."

The Kasts got more than oysters; they each added a bowl of chowder and kale greens, two other Mazzoni specialities.

"We didn't bother to check their identification," said Haner.

"I like good food," said Edith Kast. "I don't like that slipshod stuff . . . but you're not going to put that in the paper, are you?"

Butcher Hollow, Moonshine and a place in time

I didn't expect to find a band playing in Webb's Grocery up near the top of a crease in Butcher Hollow. I didn't know what to expect. I was up there because Lorette Lynn was born and raised up there and my journey came with the territory—Loretta's and mine.

Most of the fun in being the Kentucky Columnist for the Courier-Journal came with the mandatory wandering. The Appalachian Mountains included a whole lot of up and over and around and down. In towns below the hollows—or even up in them—coal was king. It made millionaires of distant owners, gave the miners a survival wage along with black lung, and destroyed the landscape. Those towns were mostly rows of small, cheap houses built by the coal companies where the miners lived, paying forever rent to management and buying food on forever credit at the company store.

The miners "owed their souls" to those company stores, as "Tennessee" Ernie Ford opined in the 1950s in a song actually written by Merle Travis, a Rosewood, KY. native, in 1946.

Some of those coal camps remained in surprisingly good shape, the often immigrant miners or their families eventually buying them and repairing any damage. Others were rotting in place, porches sagging, weathered siding a streaked and dirty gray and brown. Many more were just torn down, nothing left but ghosts.

Driving uphill into the hollows produced an uneven mix of small, rectangular houses with front porches pushing out from sloping, wooded hillsides, old barns perched behind them. In between were sloping pastures carved from the woods, some with livestock, others barren. The scenery repeated itself all the way up to Webb's General Store in Van Lear, a town created by the Consolidated Coal Company in 1909. It opened five mines, digging for coal around the clock, until shutting down in 1946, leaving the damage behind.

Thirty years later the band in Webb's store was offering a lot of country classics and some bluegrass. Once the coal camp store offered some food for the locals and Loretta Lynn souvenirs for the tourists drawn there by the name.

Herman Webb, Loretta's brother and one of seven siblings, offered a handshake and then a trip a few hundred yards up a hill to an old homegrown, tin-roofed house with a wide porch and swing where most of the family, including Loretta, had once lived. It's interior, as expected in a living museum, came with washboard, quilted-covered bed, old hand-hewn furniture, rocking chair and curtains. Outhouse out back.

Webb, a handsome, white-haired tour guide told stories with the easy charm of a man with some practice. We wandered the house, Loretta's music accompanying us, and then Webb made an offer to seal the deal:

"Would you like a taste of moonshine?"

"Well, sure."

He made his way to a back room and returned with a clear bottle of the home-brewed. He offered no explanation for its source, and I didn't ask. He twisted off the top and offered me a taste.

This was not your coddled, well-aged Kentucky bourbon from a barrel. No water or crackers were offered to cleanse the palette. No sniffing of the bottle to test moonshine aroma. No swishing it around in the mouth to build excitement. Sip away and swallow.

The instant taste was liquor-strong, angry, and harsh, with little after-taste. Not that one was wanted or expected. Different parts of my tongue were not seeking different flavors. I resisted the urge to cough, took another slightly larger swig to be polite, gulped, and handed him back the bottle. I couldn't imagine drinking enough of that stuff to even get a mild buzz, much less howling at the moon. Webb looked at me and smiled. Mountain hospitality was in the room.

The night got better from there. As we talked, he said most tourists were happy to just visit the house where Loretta and family had lived as a child, but she was actually born in a much smaller house further up Butcher Hollow. Would I be interested in seeing it?

He took me out to the front porch and pointed to a small road, not much more than a path, the wandered along a creek going further up into Butcher Hollow.

It was close to dusk when I started, following the creek until the path diverged, heading more uphill into the hollow. I walked along in growing darkness, unable to see very far behind me or in front.

Loretta Lynn's parents, Clara Marie Ramey Webb and Melvin Theodore Webb had lived in that very small house somewhere ahead. He would die of a stroke at age 52 after battling black lung disease. Loretta Lynn was born in the house in 1932 before the family moved to the Van Lear home. She got married at 15, had six children with her husband Oliver "Doolittle" Lynn, got her first guitar and started singing. She would become the most awarded female country artist in history, including releasing "Coal Miner's Daughter" in 1970.

And here I was walking up into Butcher Hollow about 10 years later to visit her birthplace. The path leveled off a little and I could see the house, not much bigger than a cabin, in a flat opening ahead.

Old Kentucky home
A few still recall the birthplace of the 'Coal Miner's Daughter'

It sat below what looked to be a mountain of mine waste rising behind in the darkness behind it. I walked slowly toward the house, sure it was deserted, but then not so sure it was deserted. It all felt a bit spooky, totally alone with Loretta Lynn's original family house way up a path into Butcher Hollow.

I walked forward and nervously peered into the windows. No one home. That thought echoed with me. No one home. When was the last time anyone was home here? Mountains looming in the distance. Night closing in. How does one get from this distant, desolate place to world-wide fame, a coal miner's daughter?

I walked back in the dark toward Herman Webb's store, silently thinking the day over, moonshine and an *empty house. The band was still playing as I left.*

Some columns just came from stopping by two men sitting under a shade tree. One of them made a little extra money picking up discarded aluminum cans. Being paid by the pound, he had become convinced the cans weighed more when crushed by his feet. Physics in the least expected place.

I picked up a father and his seven-year-old son hitchhiking along a busy I-71 and heard a sad tale of sad lives. Watching an estate auction in Southern Indiana brought a little more hope of family endurance, some valued possessions passed on to the next generation.

W.P. "Possum Gleason" was found in a cemetery near Wolf Creek, KY, where at 87 he sold and erected tombstones, including his own. A father-and-son duo in Morehead, KY. ran a taxi service, their company sign, and telephone nailed to a tree in the side yard.

It's crushing if Jesse Harris gets his can

BIG CLIFTY, Ky.—So here we have two good men, Jesse Harris, 63, and Russell Witten, 56, sitting under several shade trees, pondering why it is the Laws of Physics have packed their bags and fled Grayson County.

Harris is a man who adds to his retirement income

by picking up discarded aluminum cans and selling them. He is paid 17 cents a pound, plus all the cans he can eat.

Witten is a tobacco, corn, cow, chicken, hog and cucumber farmer. With all of the above hoeing and hauling, he earns 17 cents a hour, plus pickles.

The Law of Physics under moderate debate between the two men was: Which weighs more, a pound of crushed aluminum cans, or a pound of uncrushed aluminum cans?

Harris, a serious and reasonable man, said he noticed that if he mashes the cans with his right foot, as he has been doing for years, there are 20 cans to the pound. He says if he doesn't mash the cans, it takes 25 to make a pound.

"I know it doesn't make any sense," Harris said, "but I've weighed them and it makes the cans heavier if you crush them."

You can bet your last case of no-deposit, no-return bottles that Harris crushes every aluminum can he can get his foot over.

"He don't miss either," says Witten.

Witten, too, shakes his head over the crushed-can findings, but he has a theory on why it works.

"The only thing I can figure is the air gets trapped inside somehow and makes the crushed cans heavier," he said.

The way in which Jesse Harris gets his can is a story in itself. When he first started 10 or 12 years ago, he was a pop-bottle man, but the deposit was only two cents each, and he couldn't find enough to pay for his shoe leather.

"Now they're up to a nickel, but you still can't get ahold of them. There's too many other people out looking too."

So a few years ago Harris jumped to the aluminum-can league.

"I've seen him many a time walking along the road with a sack of cans," Witten says.

Time was, Harris said, he would walk along the road almost every day picking up cans. Then the competition got stiff again.

"There's a man over to Summit goes out looking for cans in his car," Harris said. "Him and his wife, and his three boys help too. Now everybody's picking up cans."

But rather than see Harris abandon the aluminum-can business too, the good people of Big Clifty have rallied to help him. They know Harris makes the half-mile walk from his house to town almost every morning, so many of them leave their aluminum cans in their front yards. Harris goes by Pence's Grocery, Wade's Grocery, Witten's Variety Store, and will make a run past the post office in stoop-shouldered pursuit of aluminum.

The local beer drinkers—be it out of charity or just general slovenliness—are also a big source of aluminum.

"A few of the boys sit uptown almost every night drinking beer," Witten said. "They just throw the cans out of the car. They know Jesse will be by in the morning."

"Once in awhile I find a full one," Harris says, adding he knows how to empty a beer can as well as crush it.

Though he has quit walking the highways, Harris will still collect 200 pounds of cans a month. He has them stacked in cardboard boxes behind his house. He hires someone to take them to an aluminum recycler in Elizabethtown every two or three weeks. In his good years, he could earn $50 a month. He makes less now.

After Harris and Witten finished filling in the history of the business, conversation drifted back to the weight of crushed vs. uncrushed cans.

Harris confesses he will occasionally use his left foot, but his right remains the big hammer. Witten reaffirms that Harris doesn't miss. Harris leads the party to the rear of the house where his cans are stored. He is a little embarrassed about being interviewed on crushing aluminum cans. His cans are stacked about five feet high. Every one is crushed. That makes them 20 to the pound.

"It MUST be something to do with the air," Witten says.

For father and son, it's a rough road

JELLICO, Tenn.—*Chances are the man was doing some lying, but he seemed willing to trade at least part of his life's story for a free cup of coffee for himself and a hamburger for his boy.*

The pair had been hitchhiking along I-75 just above Williamsburg, KY. The rain had stopped, and the boy, being 7, insisted on sloshing through every puddle he could find. His dad carried a plaid cloth suitcase. He was a little man and he carried the suitcase easily, so it couldn't have weighed too much. He accepted the free food with a little reluctance and the ride to the Tennessee border with the matter-of-factness of a man who has been there before.

Mostly, he looked straight ahead when he talked. He and his son had sat out the rainstorm in a woods, apparently under a leaky tree, and their clothes had drip-dried to parts of their skin. The man wore a cheap, bright gaudy shirt that looked as though it had been made in Nashville and decorated in Honolulu.

His boy was a different story. He would look you in the eyes when he answered a question, and would look at you out of the corner of his eyes when he didn't.

The eyes were blue, the hair blond, his T-shirt exposed a little more of his flesh than the manufacturer had intended, and maybe it was his haircut, but it seemed as though his ears were a little too big for his head.

The pair had been on the road two days, heading south from Kokomo, IN, to their home in Tennessee. They had spent two days going north to Kokomo, spent one night at a relative's house, then headed south again.

"Why didn't you stay longer?"

"They don't like me around."

"Why did you go up there then?"

"I have to wander around."

"Why do you take the boy?"

"I don't like to leave him home. I want to take him

with me. It's pretty tough. . . . Sometimes I get rides easier when the boy's with me.

"I can't stay around home. There's some guys I've been fighting with said they'd kill me if I stayed around home."

The father is 27. He said his wife had been running around on him, so he divorced her. She had custody of their two other children, a boy, 5, and a 15-month-old girl.

The man rested a hand on his son's shoulder for part of the ride. It was obvious that his feelings for the boy went beyond being a pawn in a hitchhiker's world.

"I don't want him living with her," he said.

The boy has been hitchhiking with his father since he was 4. He has been to Kokomo twice and to Florida once.

"I just like to lay on the beach and take it easy," the man said.

"All I see is cars," his boy said.

The father hitchhiked to Texas with his other son when he was 4. They got to Fort Worth, turned around, and came back to Tennessee.

"I want to take the little girl with me," the father said. "I want to take all three of them, but my wife won't let me."

When I picked up father and son, they had spent one night in a woods along the road in Indiana, and the second night in a woods above Corbin.

The man said later that another driver had bought them breakfast just before I picked them up. The boy didn't eat the hamburger I bought him. He saved it in a white paper bag to be eaten on the road.

His father had left for Kokomo with $20. He had $3 left, and was 60 miles from home at the Tennessee border near Jellico.

He said he had been hurt in a car accident and suffered blackouts and internal bleeding. He said he can't work.

"I can't even read," he blurted out.

The Interstate highways all look the same. The son was convinced he was heading north again.

"Daddy, I want to go to Grandma's," *the boy said over and over.*

"We are," *his father said.*

"No we're not," *the boy answered.*

The boy was to start school soon after he returned to Tennessee. He said he wanted to be home, yet he wanted to be with his father. He doesn't like hitchhiking, but he doesn't like school either.

He seemed to understand that he would eventually travel the same road as his father. He had his life's philosophy worked out at 7 years of age.

"I'll be here and there," *the boy said.*

Mementos of a lifetime bought, sold, paid for

The auction was in Indiana, one of a half-dozen listed in the paper for that day.

The goods to be sold were laid out in a long L-shaped

line along the back of the house, stretching from the back door to the front sidewalk.

I don't know how long the couple that owned the house had lived there, but someone said they had been married for 50 years. They were giving up the house and moving to a small apartment.

And their life's surplus was to be divided among 100 strangers at cut-rate prices in a few hours on a Saturday morning.

Much of the surplus could be labeled vintage attic castaway. But the better items told something of the old couple and the way they lived.

The man had once owned a hardware store. He was obviously a tinkerer, a fixer of things gone wrong, an old-school plumber, electrician, carpenter and mechanic.

Dozens of boxes of nails, plumbing fittings, tightly wound spools of wire, insulators, chisels, hammers, cabinet hinges, saws, hasps, files, wire cutters, nuts, bolts and washers were stacked at the head of the line. The tools were clean and in good condition, as solid as the man who had used them.

The woman had gone through her household goods carefully, keeping the best, putting the odds and ends of her dishes, sewing goods, Christmas decorations, dated kitchen appliances, small tables, mirrors and extra bedding on the auction block.

The auctioneer stood on a crate under a tree in the neatly trimmed back yard and announced the terms of the sale. He said he was glad to be back among country people and emphasized his point by removing his clip-on tie.

His hair was short enough to guarantee he could become president of any VFW post in America. He had a voice that would carry through a six-foot brick wall.

"Stick around," he told the buyers, "I'm gonna tell my newest Dolly Parton joke in another hour."

The old couple stayed in the background as the selling began. Soon the auction became theater at two levels: the pitchman on the crate and the underlying sadness of the couple watching their belongings go off in a dozen directions.

The buyers pressed around the auctioneer. One heavy-set man found his view blocked by a small tree, so he snapped off the tree's biggest limb.

The tools and garden equipment went first. A young, blond boy, identified as the old couple's grandson, bought many of the tools. He stood on the back steps of the house, bidding shyly, steadily collecting a pile of his grandfather's things.

The old man's lawn mower went next. The model was so old it had to be started with a separate starter rope wrapped around the crankshaft. The old man had made the task easier by welding a pulley to the side of the engine.

But the machine was in excellent condition.

"It's guaranteed to start with the first pull," the auctioneer said.

The old man eased through the crowd, wrapped the rope around the crankshaft and pulled. The engine ran so quietly it could barely be heard 10 feet away. It sold for $26.

The crowd worked its way down the line toward the Christmas decorations and furniture. The couple stayed in the background. The grandson continued to bid, adding a few old picture frames to his pile.

There was a small traffic jam in the road along the house as people leaving—boxes and bags in hand— ran into late arrivals.

The best of what was left was an old wooden trunk. It was a work of art, with neatly dovetailed corners and lined in paper decorated with red roses. It had been made with wood from the Black Forest in Germany. It had a fat metal lock—a lock to be closed with a heavy metal key. All morning people had been looking at the trunk, rubbing its grain with their fingers and testing its lock.

But when the strangers had finished bidding, a young, blond boy went home with a big pile of tools, a few picture frames and his grandparents' old trunk.

Possum's life is a monument to work

WOLF CREEK, Ky.—Even Possum Gleason's mother said Possum wouldn't live a long life, that the croup would squeeze the life from his frail lungs. But she poured spoonfuls of medicinal coal oil down his throat, and so far her prediction has been off by 87 years.

Her boy never did grow up big, but he grew up honest, and you only have to look at the man's hands to know he has worked for a living.

W. P. "Possum" Gleason has worked on farms, in

rock quarries and in sawmills since he was 10 years old, but his real story is that he has been a tombstone salesman for 50 years.

"I sold my first one to Willie Kendall in 1918," he said, "and I've sold six more to the family since then.

"When I first started, I walked everywhere I went. I didn't have nothing. Then I got a Model-T Ford and I can remember many a time I got hung up in the mud and had to push her out.

"I didn't have no education because I left school in the fifth grade. Right at first I was afraid to go to the homes of the really educated people, but after I dealt with them I found out they were the best ones to go to.

W.P. "Possum" Gleason

"When I first started selling monuments I was told to be honest above all things. I got through all right. I didn't make a lot of money, but I got through. I only got beat out of $14.20 in all those years, and I think that's pretty good."

Gleason is 5 foot 3 and weighs 110 pounds. There is a dignity to the man that goes beyond anything medicinal coal oil had to offer. He wears work shoes, work clothes and a straw hat that says "Let's go fishing."

He often takes that advice; his usual companion is his 1952 pickup truck.

"I'm getting old too," he says, *"so what's the need to get a new truck?"*

Gleason has sold monuments all over the Wolf Creek area in Meade County, and his sales have stretched from Eddyville, Ky., to Mattoon, Ill., and Missouri. When he sold, he usually contracted to set up the monuments in the cemetery, too.

He has set up hundreds of monuments, first digging a hole, then pouring in wheelbarrows of cement to form a solid base.

"It all has to be done just right," he said. *"You have rock and dirt, rock and dirt, and then cement.*

"I don't think I ever set a monument without wondering if the people underneath me didn't wonder what I was doing. I was always careful to set it just like they was there to help me."

For many years Gleason's wife, Grace, helped him. She was used to work. It took a little work for them to get married.

He wasn't quite 19 at the time. She lacked a little of being 17. They had set a wedding date in July, but didn't tell anyone.

In the meantime, Grace's mother, fearing her young daughter was getting too serious about Possum, asked him to quit coming around.

"He'll quit coming around this Sunday, Momma," Grace told her.

That Wednesday night, they eloped.

"Her mother shoulda known we was gonna do it," Gleason said.

They eloped on Christmas Eve. Taking an uncle and a cousin along as witnesses, they went by horse and *buggy to Stephensport, Ky., and then took a river boat to Cannelton, Ind., to the preacher.*

"That was the slowest team of horses I ever saw," Gleason says.

The wedding trip took two nights and one day. The marriage lasted 60 years and 10 days, until Grace died in 1969. The union produced six children. Possum and Grace shared a wedding cake baked by the hospital staff for their 60th wedding anniversary.

"You don't really miss them till they're gone," Gleason says.

Grace Gleason is buried in the Parr Cemetery south of Wolf Creek. Gleason was its caretaker for almost 40 years. He worked thousands of hours to keep it green, neatly clipped and gently sloped.

He has erected almost 150 monuments in the cemetery.

He runs off the names and the history of the families, including his grandfather, his mother, his uncle and a little brother. He points out the red granite monument where his wife is buried, the monument he will share with her when he dies. There is a wedding bell carved on the monument, with their wedding date engraved inside.

Gleason erected this monument, too.

"I did it extra right, same as I did the rest of them," he says, "I never did hold out on the concrete."

The fun begins when the cab leaves Morehead

MOREHEAD, Ky.—This is to present Sherman and Sonny Conn, father and son, 68 and 33, the once and present owners of Morehead's White Top Taxi service, the original Conn act, who will tell you of driving taxis in the hills of northeast Kentucky.

For openers, the White Top Taxi extension phone is outside the office under a maple tree. The phone sits on a yellow plywood box nailed to a fence post. The taxi drivers don't go in the office. They pull up under the tree and wait for the phone to ring.

The White Top Taxi fleet includes two full-sized 1968 Chevrolets and a 1964 Chevelle. The trip rate is $1 anywhere inside Morehead, but most of the fun begins when the company takes passengers outside Morehead. A lot of passengers travel amazing distances from Morehead by taxi because of a lack of other transportation.

Sherman and Sonny Conn

Sonny Conn, who bought out his dad in 1969, tells of the time he had just hired a new driver and repeatedly warned the man not to take anyone out of town unless the passenger paid *first.*

"*I don't know how many times I told him that,*" Conn said.

So the first thing the new driver does is take a woman passenger about 150 miles out of town to her home. They get there and the woman doesn't have any money. Neither does the driver.

"*The guy was trying to sell his spare tire to get gas,*" Conn said.

The driver refuses to leave without the money. The woman said she couldn't pay until her welfare check came in. So the woman and her family invite the driver to live with them until the check arrives.

"*They cooked for him, give him a bed, everything,*" Conn says.

Three days later the check comes in, the driver gets his $45 fare, and he finally gets back to Morehead.

"*Had another passenger that swam the Licking River in the dead of winter to try to beat paying a fare,*" Sherman Conn says. "*The driver took off after him. They both swam the river, but the driver got his man. Said if he7d had a club he would have killed him.*"

Sherman Conn smokes cigars that look like Louisville Sluggers. He was in the taxi business 43 years before selling out. He went through four wives in the process.

"*When I taxied, I taxied,*" he says.

His taxi stories roll out between puffs on his cigar.

"*Son, I had one fella come in about eight one night and said he wanted to go to Ashland. I took him to Ashland, and he wanted to go to Charleston, West Virginia. I took him to Charleston and he wanted to* go to Crab Orchard, West Virginia. When we got there he gave me a $50 tip and I was so far from home he bought me a motel room. He said he was going to the lobby for a minute so I went to sleep.

"I slept all night, and I never did see him again. I got back to Morehead and there was police all over the place. They said he robbed a bank in Chicago and had been riding taxis ever since,"

The stories continue.

"One time I was taking a bunch of preachers to Anderson, Indiana, and the cops pulled us over in Cincinnati. He's holding us with a submachine gun. He tells us to get our hands up. We musta had our hands up for 30 minutes, and there wasn't even a pocketknife in our whole crowd.

"Finally the cop tells me they're holding us for killing two clerks and robbing a grocery store in Rowan County. Someone had tipped the cops that I was taking people out of state and they thought I had the killers. They held us in Cincinnati 15 hours before we got out."

Conn can't remember how many times he has been robbed.

"Son, one time a guy robbed me of $5 and I gave him a hard-luck story and he gave me the money back."

Conn once took a group of people to a Canadian border town and stayed awake in their desolate motel all night because he was convinced Indians would rob and murder them. He took a man bear hunting in North Carolina and had to wait with him for two weeks until they got a bear. One of his drivers ran out of gas after taking a passenger out of town and was arrested for stealing the taxi.

A woman had a baby in the back seat of a brand new taxi.

"Ruint the whole seat," he says.

Another time Conn took a woman from the Morehead bus station to a house in the hills of Fleming County. The woman asked him to wait, went into the house, grabbed a child and started to leave. A man came roaring out of the house, grabbed the child back, beat the woman to the ground and leveled a shotgun at Conn.

He got out of the jam with the only line he could think of.

"Lord, God, don't kill me," Conn pleaded, "I'm just driving a taxi."

Serendipity is mandatory in any successful column-writing venture. I happened to be at the Abraham Lincoln Birthplace National Historic Park the day the "Boundary Oak'" the 350-year-old white oak that once defined the original Lincoln property, was cut down after its death. It didn't surrender willingly.

Politicians exist to be lampooned, and three-time-failed gubernatorial candidate Larry Forgy got some well-deserved flack for his opposition to the Kentucky Education Reform Act, a much needed state venture.

On the best days you can find columns and essays without ever leaving home. I wrote of a quiet moment of my life in our yard at 4:45 a.m., and offered a slice of slightly larger life in our small town of Utica Indiana huddled up against the Ohio River.

Then, for a Big Finish, is a story of a visit to the then very quaint Elvis Presley Birthplace Park in, where else, Tupelo, MS., with the locals very much in charge of the show.

Budging the Boundary Oak wasn't easy

HODGENVILLE, Ky.—Let it be said the Boundary Oak went out with a fight.

The ancient white oak began growing about 350 years ago, give or take a half-century. Historians believe it spent its formative years alone in an open clearing, a "wolf" tree they called it. It stretched 90 majestic feet into the sky, and its limbs spread a little more than that.

In time it became a landmark, and if the settlers didn't call it the Boundary Oak, the historians who followed did. It did serve as a boundary for Tom Lincoln's farm near Hodgenville, and maybe his boy Abe did play underneath it; we'll never know.

The oak survived a lot in those 350 years: lightning, beetles, bad drainage and what proved to be harmful attempts by man to preserve it, but it died two years ago. And this week, because the National Park Service feared the weakened limbs might be dangerous to tourists at Lincoln's birthplace, men with chain saws came to trim it back.

Or so they thought. The plan was to cut off those wonderful angular limbs and leave a mammoth stump about 25 feet high, and then inject preservative into the trunk to save it.

This, of course, required that something akin to a historical environmental impact statement be sent to the park service regional office. It went from there to a state preservation officer in Frankfort. Then to a review board in Washington, D.C. Then back to the preservation office. With side trips back to the regional office between each step.

This Wednesday, some three months after the paperwork started flowing, the tree limbs came down without much protest, and some of the wood is being saved by Nick Eason, superintendent of the national historic site. But trimming back the trunk proved to be another matter.

A man with a 30-inch chain saw began biting into the trunk about 25 feet above the ground. The 10-to-15-foot section to be removed towered above him. The upper section was attached by nylon rope to another tree and a portable hand-operated winch.

The saw couldn't begin to cut all the way through the thick trunk, so one worker winched while the other cut. They couldn't budge the upper section. They moved the winch twice and cut a little more, but they couldn't topple the section. In one final try, the winch broke.

Plan B was to attach the rope to the worker's truck and pull at the section. No luck. The rope broke.

Enter the beginnings of Plan C, some helpers from a young adult work program. They used an Army surplus truck with a power winch and a 1/2-inch steel cable. Terrain logistics dictated that the cable be looped around a small tree and then angled up toward the trunk.

They winched. The rope broke. Then the cable broke.

Plan D called for a strange assortment of vehicles and bindings. The tree trimmers' truck was attached to the Army surplus truck with a logging chain. The Army truck's front wheels were blocked with wood. Its cable was looped around a tree and was tied to the 1/2-inch nylon rope that ran to the remains of the Boundary Oak.

In successive order: the rope snapped again, the small tree was pulled from the ground, the cable broke again, the workers did a little more sawing, one pounded wedges into the chain-saw cut, and the rope broke again.

By then there was less than 6 inches remaining to be cut in the 40-inch diameter stump, and even the tourists, Bermuda shorts, Instamatics and all, were beginning to wonder what was holding the top up.

"Habit" was the best answer one could give.

Plan E involved a little more sawing, driving wedges into the cut and another tug with the winch. The upper trunk section, almost perfectly balanced, stood firm, as resilient as Abe himself.

Five hours after they started, the workers sawed through all but a few inches of the tree. Again the wedges were pounded into the cut. The winch was tightened, and the top section leaned slightly forward. The cable snapped again, and the section rocked backward, dancing 25 feet above the ground.

Then it slid sideways, made a slow turn and gracefully dropped over the tree, smashing, in one last act of defiance, a small section of the concrete wall everyone had worked so hard to protect.

Portfolios are nonsense up with which he will not put

Bob Hill

To: My Kentuckians Fellow.
From: Larry Forgy.
(AS WRITTEN BY BOB HILL)
Subject: Reform educational.

Much lately has been made of my criticism of the Kentucky Education Reform Act, the part about writing portfolios especially. Some Kentuckians—mostly Democrats—are complaining that pandering I am to the common denominator lowest while wanting your governor to become. Please clarify let me this.

I believe that writing well important is. As we used to say when I was back growing up in Logan County: "The key of knowledge the door of success unlocks."

Having that said, let me explain my position further. Times these are when the basics of life are fast escaping us while our educational system has become down mired in teacher paper-pushing and little children portfolios writing.

Our teachers need time to more better the alphabet teach. We need to the basic skills return. Proper expression and syntax we can later teach with these building blocks in place fully.

Like my basketball coach used to say back at Lewisburg High School: "Larry, your pants you gotta put on one leg at a time."

Along with the basics of education, discipline to the schools we must restore. When governor I am elected I will personally each school principal a letter write outlining my program for in-class-room calm restoring. Each principal I will direct to write me with the results. Orders—summarily executed—these students and principals will be on behalf of everyone.

Discipline I know. When I was a student undergraduate at George Washington University, my job it was 48 hours a week directing traffic in the nation's capital. Stood there I did, at waving automobiles from 50 states and sometimes drivers Canadian. There I learned all and for once that order from chaos must come. There I learned a structure you cannot build without infrastructure solid first having. There I learned the prime rule of education: Stupid, simple keep it!

Examine let us these fangled-new KERA writing portfolios a little closer. Do sentences clean and thoughts clear we really want? Is there merit any in asking little children to essays write, poems pen, short stories attempt? Ask—I must—if well expressing oneself is that important?

So subjective this is. Poor teachers overburdened already must read now the essays, poems and stories of these children little. Poor teachers overburdened already must into tiny minds peer to see inside what is at home. Poor teachers overburdened already must a grade place on a story short, a poem incomplete. Too much educational envelope-pushing, all that is.

Remind me, it does, of an old saying I first heard while five years on the state Council on Higher Education serving: Why fool with a new tractor when the old mule paid for is?

My educational fears and concerns, sincere and genuine they are. Long-suffered Kentucky has with a school system that worthy is not of the people of this state fine. Understand your worries, I do. Writing well and expression thoughtful may appeal to pin-heads intellectual and editorial writers crazed, but give Larry

Forgy a chance at real educational reform in Kentucky.

Leave you let me with this message. Heard let it be from Hickman to Hindman, in every school and polling place loudly. Heard let it be by every parent teacher and school administrator unwilling to change give a real chance:

> *Red are roses*
> *Violets be blue.*
> *To become your governor*
> *Anything I'll do.*

Sometimes the world pauses to let you catch up

You can't pick the moments. They are dealt out at random by an unseen hand. They just step out softly in front of you, hold still for a few seconds, then slip away on rubber-soled feet.

And try as you might, you can't bring them back.

I felt the moment when I walked outside early this morning to go to work. There was no noise; no car wheels crunching on the gravel road, no towboat whine drifting up from the river, no distant yapping of nervous dogs.

It was absolutely quiet.

Think about that a little bit. It doesn't happen much anymore. The world was absolutely quiet. My side yard was striped in deep shadows thrown by the hard light. One of our cats was perched sphinx-like on the top rung of a stepladder, its ears perked against the morning.

Normally, the cats and I are reluctant friends. They belong to my children. I love my children. They love their cats. So we all work at getting along.

But this morning the cat carefully arched its head in anticipation of getting its neck rubbed, an invitation it had never bothered to extend to me before.

I obliged, and the cat and I parted friends.

For the moment.

My dog had temporarily abandoned its night guard duty to run the fields. He often doesn't come home again until after sunup, his coppery red flanks wet with dew, his matted hair littered with pieces of weed and wildflowers.

I often wonder where these silent runs take him, how many rabbits or birds he has startled into fearful flight in the deep grass, but that's all between him and a higher authority-

I could smell the purple morning in our lilac bush, a favorite among the row of trees, bushes and flowers that rim the house. The yard light filtered through the flowering peach tree, dulling its pink blooms. The long, lean shadows of the board fence chased one another quietly through the side yard.

Louisville was a splash of impressionistic light in the distance. The moon made a cameo appearance from a hole in the sky, then pulled in behind its cloud cover. A solitary bird, hidden in black woods far away, broke the silence, singing its three-note song, happily unaware of any audience.

And how many of us are willing to sing without an audience?

I didn't move for a few minutes. I was enveloped in the moment. This is the busiest season of the year for me and my family. The apple and peach trees have yet to be pruned. The gladiolus and cannas haven't been planted. The daffodils that circle the driveway must be dug up, divided and replanted.

There is school and work and baseball and track meets. I could spend every day for a month at home and still not catch up on the work.

And there are times when I don't feel like writing a word, times when I feel newspapers are little more than the sincerest forms of futility, times when I just don't care if they come out every day or not.

But the moment took care of much of that. I became a born-again lilac lover. My family was safe in our house behind me.

I was on speaking terms with at least one cat and my dog was off doing what dogs do best.

My son went to bed last night excited about going on a fishing trip with a youthful buddy. My daughter is excited about basketball, track and an honor-student program she will take this summer.

And my wife was probably looking out our bedroom window wondering why I was talking to our lilac bush at 4:45 in the morning.

I never told her it was going to be easy.

Time, like cars, sometimes stops in a small town

I live in a very small town that is huddled tightly against the Ohio River.

The town is one of the oldest in Indiana, having survived almost 200 years of floods and Democratic politics, but success has never gone to its head.

It remains as close-knit as steel wool. I am prone to joke that the town is one of the very few in America bounded on two sides by gravel pits, but I have grown very fond of the place, close-minded as it is.

It is home, and nothing more need be said on the subject.

The town was apparently incorporated a century or so ago, but the incorporation somehow lapsed, leaving the townspeople to get by on their own devices.

The notion that a small band of people can survive without entangling financial alliances with its state and federal government seems clearly un-American now. In fact, we are hard-pressed to remember that the central webbing of this nation was constructed by people who preferred to get by on their own devices.

But the town survived through thick and thin, living on its wits and its closeness. It was generally able to pull together when something was needed for its grade school or volunteer fire department.

At other times, it drifted along with the human tides. The town neither prospered nor died; it just ran in place as the rest of the world sprinted off in new directions, not all of them worthy.

In time, such close-knit isolation caused problems. As nearby communities became striped with sidewalks and dotted with streetlights, a few townspeople began to see merit in such urban trinkets.

Because of the nature of the town's soil, and its closeness to the river, the disposal of sewage became a constant problem that literally bubbled to the surface after a heavy rain.

Some townspeople began to talk about better police protection, a library and a town community center. They discussed incorporating the town again.

Those opposed to incorporation—and a great many people were opposed—argued strongly against it and the accompanying taxes. But progress had begun to peek out from under the blanket.

All this, of course, occurred over a period of decades. Two years ago an attempt to incorporate was swatted down in imperious self-interest by the Jeffersonville City Council, which under state law had to give its blessing before a small neighboring town could incorporate.

Last year, through some magical waving of political wands that has never been fully explained, the town was allowed to re-incorporate along its century-old boundaries.

Within a few months a town board was elected, the township trustees' request for federal funds was being discussed, a part-time policeman was hired and two stop signs were erected along the main street.

It is these stop signs that have caused the most

comment. As far as I can determine, there has not been a stop sign along the main road in town for almost 200 years. Oxen, horse, mule, wagon and automobile have traveled that route for almost two centuries, from mud lane to asphalt strip, without any official eight-sided request to stop.

So there is some feeling in the town that after 200 years of such glorious and unrestricted travel, perhaps two stop signs is a bit of overkill.

There is some feeling that maybe the town board should have put up just one stop sign on the main road this year, and then maybe have waited 50 years or so to put up the second.

I am of mixed feelings on the matter. The pace of automobile traffic through town has been too fast and dangerous, particularly in the summer when the tourists are scurrying upriver toward their boats.

But I do hate to see 200 years of linear open spaces intersected twice by stop signs a mere 100 yards apart.

At any rate, our policeman has been on the job. I've seen the blue lights on his police car leap to life a half-dozen times as he pursued those who ignored the new signs, or the accompanying 20mph speed limit.

Indeed, my wife was nailed for failure to come to a full stop before one sign. The policeman—as has been his wont—warned her, alerted her to his continuing presence and sent her home without a ticket, a sadder and wiser woman.

I don't know the circumstances, but about a week ago I found one of the new signs lying flat on its back along the road, either the victim of an accident or vandalism.

But even with the sign temporarily missing, I have continued to stop at the corner. Even in absentia, the sign's form and function have become a part of my trip home.

I am a changed man. And so is my town.

An Elvis Presley pilgrimage

A steady, sullen rain is falling on northeastern Mississippi, gouging new rivulets in the thick, reddish-brown farmlands, misting up around green cedar trees and winter-browned kudzu vines, drumming against the pale concrete of the Elvis Aron Presley Memorial Highway.

The highway eases into Tupelo, population 25,000, the seat of Lee County, the town where Elvis was born to a dirt-poor farmhand and his dark-eyed wife in a two-room shotgun house on Jan. 8, 1935—45 years ago Tuesday.

Tupelo, a few miles from the Alabama border, is bigger and more prosperous looking than the Elvis legend would have it. And save the Elvis Presley Heights Handy-Pak store, the only such listing in the telephone book, it seems to have avoided the commercial Elvis hysteria its native son visited on the outside world.

The tourists are led to Elvis' birthplace by small, almost inadequate signs placed at irregular intervals along the main highways, the last of which fronts a yellow brick building, apparently the home of a reduc-

ing salon, which advertises: "Lose Weight Our Weigh."

The house in which Elvis was born is now the frontispiece of the 15-acre Elvis Presley Park. Elvis and his parents lived in the house for three years—and in Tupelo for 13 years—before the search for work pushed his father about 100 miles northwest to Memphis, Term.

When Elvis was born in the home's front room—a twin brother, Jesse, died shortly after his birth—the white, clapboard home was one of a clutch of similiar shotgun houses spread along a dirt road in East Tupelo, the poorest section of a town in one of the poorest states in the union.

The other houses have since been bulldozed, and the ground where they stood has been landscaped. The Elvis Presley Youth Center, a red brick and yellow metal building, was built behind the Presley home.

Flanking the youth center is the Elvis Presley Chapel, a strange blend of brick and colored glass, the same mixture of simplicity and wretched excess that marked Elvis' path through life and death, all of it fronted with a $20,000 stained-glass window.

The chapel was built with donations from across the world. Its entrance is marked with an inscription in gold: "With Special Thanks—The Colonel."

Elvis donated the first $20,000 for his park in 1957, proceeds from an appearance at the Mississippi-Alabama Fair and Dairy Show. Original plans called for tennis courts, a picnic area, the youth center and a new, guitar-shaped swimming pool. The dream has not worked out. The old, overcrowded, rectangular pool is still in use, the tennis courts need work, and the youth center has only intermittent use. But there is the Elvis

Presley a Man and His Music Nature Trail.

The old house and its grounds have been sanitized, remodeled, sodded and landscaped to the point where little of the early truth is left. A fine brick church has been built across the street. The old dirt road has long since been paved and is anchored with big, new houses.

The small, white Presley house looks conspicuous and well-scrubbed in the clearing. It rests firmly on brick and block, its front porch two feet above the ground. It can be bathed in electric light at night, when once it had no electricity or water. Neat walkways parade around its edges, leading to new front steps. The house has been repainted and its roof repaired. It has a new rough-wood ceiling, new walls and new flower-print wallpaper inside.

None of the furniture now inside the house belonged to the Presley family. One story has it that Jesse Presley was placed in a tiny casket on an old trunk for a period of mourning, but the old trunk has disappeared, or was sold at the courthouse steps at auction.

The poverty and bitter taste of it all has been washed away in the flood of repairs. It is difficult to stand in an asphalt parking lot and conjure up images of a baby Elvis playing outside under the oak and sweetgum trees or crawling onto the hardpan beneath his front porch to chase a kitten.

But the legend began here, and the thousands of pilgrims who visit the home each month want to touch more than an old family dresser.

"It don't even bother me anymore when people come in here and cry," says Essie Clayton, who has worked in the Presley home almost five years. "I'm just used to

it by now."

Essie Clayton stands firm as both guard and guide just inside the front door in the room where Elvis was born. A thin rope shepherds the tourists through the front room into the back and then out a rear door toward the youth center, its souvenir stand and the chapel.

The house is owned by the city of Tupelo but is operated with firmness and a certain innocence by the ladies of the East Heights Garden Club. The garden club took over the house in 1971 and furnished it by advertising on the radio for old furniture.

Before Elvis died, the house was open a few hours a day for three summer months. Now it is open every day except Christmas from 10 a.m. to 5 p.m., and more than 100,000 people have been through it since he died Aug. 16, 1977.

The house is roughly 15 by 30 feet. Its two rooms are about 15 feet square—five big steps in each direction. The ceilings are barely eight feet high, and look new. The front room contains an old metal bed covered with a white bedspread, a dresser, three small windows with thin lace curtains and an old radio on a square table. Miss Clayton's rocking chair sits between the bed and the window. Parts of the original pine floor peek out around the edges of a 9-by-12 piece of linoleum on the floor.

The tourists put their money in a small fishbowl on an old treadle sewing machine on the table just to the right of the door: $1 for adults, 50 cents for children under 12.

The back room is a repeat of the one in front. It is dominated by an old, black cook stove, and a battered *green kitchen table and chairs. The furniture is mismatched, crude and functional, a perfect if unconscious representation of the way things were.*

The two rooms share a common red-brick chimney built into the wall between them. A brown, wooden mantle hugs the top of the black fireplace in the front room. Above the mantle hangs a picture of the baby Elvis flanked by his parents, Vernon and Gladys Presley.

Gladys Presley's hair is pulled back severely behind her ears. Vernon is wearing a dark hat with a wide brim. His lips are pressed tightly together. Elvis is wearing overalls, a shirt with cuffs, and a small soft-looking hat. All three are looking to their left, off camera. There is an uncertainty in their faces, the smoldering, suspicious look of Henry Fonda in "The Grapes of Wrath."

Even at age 3, Elvis had his lip curled in his sneer.

Miss Clayton talks with the flat monotone of someone who must repeat herself 100 times a day, five to seven days a week. Her words are coupled, one barely ahead of the next.

"This is the original location of Elvis' house. His daddy and granddaddy borrowed $180 to build it . . . lived here three years and lost it . . . they wasn't able to keep up the payments and lost the whole thing . . . I don't reckon on how much the payments was . . . they was hard times back then."

She will fill in the gaps with some prodding, but does not suffer fools or excessive questions gladly. She explains that Elvis' grandparents lived up the hill when the house was built. When the family lost the home, it was rented to others off and on until about 1958. From 1958 until 1971, it was used to store lumber.

"You can just imagine what kind of shape it was in when the ladies took it over," she says.

Miss Clayton knows the name of the man who foreclosed on the Presleys' $180 note. But the secret is safe with her. This is small-town Mississippi. The man's daughter lives and teaches in Tupelo.

"She thinks a lot of Elvis," Miss Clayton explained. "I'm not going to tell on her daddy."

She says the day Elvis died hundreds of floral arrangements—many in the shape of guitars—were sent to the house. The next day mourners were lined up for 50 to 100 yards outside the front door. They still receive wreaths on the anniversary of his birth, and death, and expect to receive a few Tuesday. More than 130 fans from England toured the home last Aug. 16.

"I had an old man last year, a real old man, and he cried so much we had to walk him through and set him down in a chair," Miss Clayton says. "The people come in here and they like to touch the walls. The big, little, old and young, they cry like a baby . . . A lot of people do their crying in here, but they don't know why"

The steady rain slows the tourist business. The few that do arrive don't ask many questions. They are just happy to be in the room where Elvis was born, to absorb its smallness, to come close to him, to be born again.

One is Patsy Griggs. She is small, delicate, well-formed and polite in exaggerated Southern belle fashion. She is an illustrator for a company that makes reclining chairs. She has lived within 30 miles of Tupelo *all her life, but has never visited Elvis' house.*

"To start so small," she says, "and end up so big."

Wesley and Carolyn Wood and their daughter, Leslie, are from Dallas. They are on their way to Arkansas by way of Tupelo, a 600-mile detour. They played Elvis tapes all the way, shutting out the rain, letting the mood engulf them.

They enter the house slowly, staring at the walls, saying little. Wood unfolds a Polaroid camera. Mother and daughter argue over who will be in the pictures.

"I didn't come this far not to get in a picture," Carolyn Wood says.

She gets in a picture, but her head is cut off, showing more of the chimney than her.

"I don't care," she says.

She says they will also drive past Graceland, the Presley mansion in Memphis.

"I've had tears in my eyes since I got here," she says.

They are followed through by a young couple in matching checked shirts. They had been there once before, on their honeymoon.

The tourist line includes three elderly couples from Illinois and a man and his wife from Houston, Texas. The man looks prosperous and well-dressed. His wife has the fading good looks of a beauty queen approaching middle age.

"She wanted to see the place," the man says.

A young man walks through alone. He is 22, pale and slim. His brown, effeminate eyes shine with an open and religious innocence. He says he is a singer and a writer, and he is getting ready to tour with Mr.

Bob Russell, *"who's known all over."*

The young man says he is from Johnson City, Tenn. He says he'd sold everything he owned the night before and began hitchhiking to Tupelo to see Elvis' house.

*"*Me and Elvis have a lot in common,*"* he says. *"*We each have a lot of love and warmth inside. I just had to start here. It seems funny to be standing in his house.*"*

He says he is on a hot streak. He says a truck driver picked him up in Nashville and happened to be driving to Tupelo. He says the truck driver happened to be a friend of Mr. Bob Russell, and Mr. Bob Russell gave him a job.

*"*Music is my life,*"* the young man says.

He says the truck driver also gave him a ride to Elvis' house and is waiting for him outside.

*"*It's funny*"* the young man says, *"*I don't even know his last name.*"*

NOT EXACTLY FULL CIRCLE BUT CLOSE ENOUGH

As I grew a little weary of the Kentucky columnist job, the travel, the continual need to find stories out the window of my pickup truck, the *Courier-Journal* "metro" columnist job opened up. Best I remember, again Mike Davies called me in to see if I was interested. The short answer was "yes."

I didn't like being on the road that much, even though it was through some of the most beautiful scenery in the country. I also had the vague notion that a native Kentuckian should have the job, and it went to Kentuckian Byron Crawford, who moved it into Joe Creason's fabled footsteps.

I had no complaints. I often used to joke that I worked for the Louisville newspapers for 33 years and only had maybe three bad days. That was a lie. I had maybe four or five bad working days. And even they were educational. Even my fault. Bad column. Missed meeting. Management offering/promoting a job to return to the newsroom. No thank you, Been there. Done that.

Column writing mostly felt like working as a free-lance writer on a salary, with benefits, vacation, a 401 (K) and pension. The ball was usually in my court, where I wanted it. The pace was to my liking.

Being in Louisville offered so many opportunities to have fun and get paid for it. A dream realized that covered both was taking batting practice with the then AAA Louisville Redbirds, my best shot at that centerfield wish.

I was given uniform for the day, a bat and there I was standing at home plate as a one coach threw pitches as another offered hitting instructions. Like actually hit the ball. Physically it did not go well. The pitched balls were on me, then past me, and here comes another one, although I did manage to push one ball down the right field line that actually rolled to the fence. Mentally, I was in heaven. Which seemed pretty close to center field.

Bob Hill on deck.

I have often thought about writing plays, a concept that always appealed to me. It just seemed like a lot more work than cranking out columns. Its possibilities became clear when an exploratory group of Actors Theatre of Louisville many years ago created a play based on people I had written about in my newspaper columns.

The production was in a small upstairs theatre. It was just fun to see column-characters live again, talking and moving around on stage from life to book to life. I forgot which columns were used, and it all ran in one weekend, but it was a whole new world. Alas, Broadway never called.

After that I did write a play for Actors. It was some sort of offering they made for rookie playwrights—and why isn't that playwrites? I also forget the participants I created in that play, but they were real in my mind and fun to write. Actors never used it, but I did get $100. I'm sure a lot of playwrights get nothing.

But there is another possible play I still think about constantly but will never write. Others are welcome to give it a shot. Please. It's all about the live, childish, political theater of politicians. Its actors would have to all be short people or very good youngsters, opening the door to their opportunities.

The play would be centered around a presidential race, anything similar in real life or politics where adults are childish idiots. The actors, dressed like children, would toss a stream of lies, invective and insults at each other, ignoring the real issues.

They would strut, pout, grimace, and moan, one manchild constantly complaining about an opponent he was sure to beat had dropped out of the race leaving him vulnerable to a much younger woman. In the right hands it could even be a satirical comedy. Possibly believable. Title it "Small Talk."

I never took an official paid sick day at the papers—

although there were days I couldn't be found. All I ever wanted was to do was my job, find stories, write well and be left alone, and that was mostly what I got. Speak to editors only when spoken to. Look around and see what the rest of the newsroom—if not the world—was putting up with as the business went digital, changed, shrunk and struggled to find answers to the gnawing effects of social media. All I had to do was write another column.

Both our kids were off on interesting journeys in life. Jennifer, with two Ivy league degrees to be elected a state representative in Michigan, and Robb, an Indiana University graduate and world traveler off on a free-lance photographer career that included a lot of work for the Washington Post. Janet continued to hold us all together living out here.

———

Being metro columnist was also a job that mixed with other *Courier-Journal* writing opportunities. More unexpected stuff. One was a chance to watch the U.S. Supreme Court in action, or at least in thoughtful conversation over a brutal murder which would initiate national debate on juvenile death sentencing for more than 40 years.

The details were horrifying, beyond anything I had covered as a police reporter. The case was that of Kevin Stanford, who on Jan. 7, 1981, at age 17, along with David Buchanan, age 16, took turns for 45 minutes sodomizing and raping Baerbel Poore, 20, a single mother, who was working alone at a Cheker Oil Co. station at 4501 Cane Run Road.

Stanford then drove Poore a few blocks away in her mother's 1973 Chevrolet Impala, fired two shots from a .38-caliber pistol into her head and face, leaving her half-naked body in the back seat. Then he returned to the station, stealing 300 cartons of cigarettes and $143.

After the resulting trial, Buchanan was sentenced to life in prison. Stanford, at 17, was sentenced to death by then Circuit Judge Charles Leibson, saying he knew of no other case in which a defenseless victim had been so abused, humiliated and terrorized.

On March 28, 1989, eight years, two months and 20 days after that sentencing, and hundreds of hours of legal arguments over sentencing juveniles to death, members of the Poore family were seated in the solemn U.S. Supreme Court, the words above its columned front proclaiming "EQUAL JUSTICE UNDER LAW," listening intently to every word where the sentence would be argued.

The inside of the Supreme Court is ringed in massive columns, the seating lined up facing the bench, all in all a little like being in the First Church of Judiciary. The names of the justices seated above were from the history books; Burger, White, Marshal, Brennan, Renquist, Scalia, Stevens and O'Connor among them.

Sitting there before them was the wider America they were supposed to represent, never imagining they would be there. That included Bob Poore, Baerbel's father, an over-the-road truck driver whose job was to haul Martha White Flour to Memphis.

"We still care," he said of the family's continuing support of the death penalty for Stanford, "At least we can say we have been to the very top of the hill. I don't want people saying, 'Hey, Bob Poore said the hell with it. Do you know what I mean?"

Seated next to him was Mona Mills, Baerbel's sister, a married, part-time clerk at a convenience store and guardian of nine-year-old Stephanie Poore, Baerbel's daughter. Mona, still dealing with post-murder depression, was having recurring dreams of Stephanie clinging to a vine stretched between two tall buildings, the dream always ending with Mona screaming, "Hang on Stephanie, hang on."

"What I am waiting for is it to finally be over," Mills said, "and then I can go on. You think justice is served and then it goes on and on and on. I was 17 once, too. You don't have to tell me you don't know murder is wrong at 17."

Mills' on and on would continue for 30 more years. And counting. The U.S Supreme Court upheld the death conviction in the hearing the Poore's attended, a decision a later Supreme Court would overturn. In 2003, Kentucky Gov. Paul Patton, saying 17 was too young for a death sentence, commuted Stanford's penalty to life without parole. In 2021, a civil rights attorney for Stanford argued he was a changed man, he should be released from prison. Release was denied. Mona Mills, 40 years after her sister's murder and still thinking of her every day, testified against the release. EQUAL JUSTICE UNDER LAW—depending on where you sit—can also be blind.

═══════

My normal three-times-a-week metro column path

would be happily interrupted every few months with longer feature stories.

One day I found myself in a hollowed-out airplane filled with very expensive thoroughbred horses being flown from Lexington KY to a California racetrack. The high point of the trip was our pilot detouring a few miles to fly over the Grand Canyon after I mentioned I had never seen it. It was also my first trip to California, so photographer Stewart Bowman and I rented a car and drove up the California coast to see what the fuss was all about before flying home in an empty airplane.

Another random journey involved flying to Florida to watch a very religious Kentucky guy push a cross on wheels across the Everglades—apparently another way to get to heaven.

A different kind of trip that could have been dangerous was riding along with a truck driver from Louisville to Atlanta during prolonged and bitter union negotiations to determine how safe such a journey would be.

It was a different world looking down from the cab of an 18-wheeler, a shotgun seat more comfortable and quieter than imagined. We saw or heard no problems during the one-day, 400-mile journey, but never quite relaxed either. I got to fly home.

There would be more trauma, disasters and tornados, along with Kentucky coal mine disasters and a mass shooting in which eight people were murdered in a building one wall over from where I was sitting in the Courier-Journal writing a column.

A warning came over our security system: *"There*

is a man in the building with a gun. Exit by using the stairs."

We all fled outside and watched from across the street as police rushed in. The shooter, Joseph Wesbecker, had killed himself. One of his victims was shown sprawled out on his back in a front-page picture of the next day's Courier-Journal, a placement that came only after serious editorial debate. The final decision had been to show the horror.

The day of the shooting we stood on the street in shocked silence and watched bodies being carried out of the building on stretchers. Mass shootings were not the norm then. Such horror still seemed impossible. Afterward *Courier-Journal* managing editor George Gill walked slowly across the street toward us, and, speaking of Wesbecker, looked at us and said, "The son-of-a-bitch is dead."

AND SOME DAYS THERE IS NO EQUAL JUSTICE

The one book that perhaps tied all 33 years of my journalism career together—reporting, writing, research, serendipity and murder—was "Double Jeopardy," a story about a Louisville man who did get away with murder.

The story was complicated, hurtful and sad. It is a book about a woman named Brenda Schaefer, who in 1988, at age 36, was tied up on a table, raped, then murdered by her fiancé, Mel Ignatow. She was buried in a pre-dug grave behind the Louisville home of Mary Ann Shore, a former Ignatow girlfriend, who witnessed the murder and burial at her home, and took pictures of the crime.

Due to enormous pre-trial publicity, the murder trial was moved in late December 1989 to Kenton

County, KY. Shore, ill-prepared and wearing a miniskirt pulled up to her thighs, was such a bad witness the majority of the jurors did not believe her story. Ignatow was found innocent. The first vote for acquittal was eight to four, with the other four jurors falling in line, one later telling me he thought Ignatow guilty but wanted to get home for Christmas.

Community outrage in Louisville was palpable. Six months later a man laying carpet in Ignatow's home found the still undeveloped film taken of the murder in a heat duct in Ignatow's house, which had been sold to pay his legal expenses. Ignatow was quickly arrested, pleaded guilty and was sentenced to nine years in prison for perjury for lying to a grand jury during the process. Ignatow did not have to go before that grand jury. He volunteered. Had he stayed away he would have walked away from a murder. In his guilty plea testimony, he said Brenda Schaefer had died "peacefully."

I had never met any of the Schaefer family. Brenda's two brothers, Tom and Mike, who said they had read my column for years and were besieged by authors wanting to write the story, contacted me through an agent to write a book for the then William Morrow Publishing, now Harper Collins.

The brothers and I bonded over the book. Their family already knew tragedy. A younger brother, John Schaefer, 28, a Louisville Police officer, had been shot and killed on May 2, 1971, while arresting two men during a burglary.

That Schaefer family trust in me was extended to others. The Louisville police, in particular Jim Wesley and Lou Sharber, who despised the smirking Ignatow and were certain he was guilty, gave me full access. Roy Hazelwood, the FBI agent involved in the case was also very cooperative, a rarity with that unit. His expertise was criminal sexual sadism. I met with him at FBI headquarters in Quantico VA to get a better sense of Ignatow's sadism, why sadists need photos of their conquests, which ultimately got Ignatow in jail.

The book got wide local and national coverage, including true crime television shows. The Schaefers and I had a very uncomfortable interview on "Geraldo," where promises of a serious conversation about the entire story melted into soap opera, as feared.

Mary Ann Shore, who for a time was in prison while Ignatow was free, died in 2004 of a heart condition. If there is such a thing as a perfect death, Mel Ignatow got one. In 2008, after serving nine years for perjury, he fell onto a glass-top table in his apartment and bled to death.

Bob Hill on Geraldo.

I still get a Christmas card from Mike Schaefer every year.

My most recent book, released in October 2023, is "Always Moving Forward," the story of Humana co-founder and Louisville philanthropist David A. Jones. It's the life-story of a man who grew up in blue-collar West Louisville—one of five children whose mother worked nights in a bakery while his father was unemployed. Jones went on to incredible financial success.

In short, Jones and his partner, Wendell Cherry, who rose up from Horse Cave, KY to become a world art collector, each borrowed $1,000 to form a group to build a nursing home in Louisville. Through many twists, turns, up and downs, but always moving forward, the men grew what became Humana grow into the largest nursing home and then hospital chain in the country before turning to insurance with sales of $90 billion.

Jones then donated hundreds of millions of dollars to create thousands of college scholarships, medical programs, civic programs, the Kentucky Center for the Arts, and many local parks, including the 4,000-acre Parklands of Floyds Fork.

It was a good book put together by a team of very good people—publishing, editing, layout and design. It won several national awards, including a first place and gold star at the 2024 International Independent Press Awards in Newark N.J. But in my mind it had disappointing national sales, being one of the most successful business stories in American history, all of that with a rare family and humanitarian touch the business world could use.

SO YOU WANT TO BE A COLUMNIST. NO PROBLEM

=====

Along the way with the many books, I happily wrote a mixed bag of several thousand Louisville-based columns for the Courier-Journal over my final 20 years.

My column-writing technique was self-taught but hardly unique, perhaps dating back to Aesop and the hammer-and-chisel school of the business:

Write a first sentence. Stare at it. Let it fester in place, even stare back at you. See where it leads. Follow that lead. Like that first sentence. OK, don't like it. Start over again until it—or something else - feels good. If it doesn't, rinse and repeat. Keep staring. Stare a little more. Oh yeah, you've got a deadline. Get typing. Or chiseling.

But a likeable first sentence can show up. Then a second. Maybe even a third. Feel free to call such stone-cold-progress a paragraph. So then read the entire paragraph over three, four, five times, word by word, making some changes until it feels right. On the really good days, it. all. just. works.

Then you begin the second paragraph. You might,

but not always, have a little flow going. You finish that second paragraph. Then you go back and read the first paragraph and link it up to the second paragraph. Read both again. Make some changes. Begin a third paragraph. Picking up steam. Finish it. Make some changes. Go back up and read the first, second and third paragraphs. Read again.

In cranking out a thoughtful column you will read over the first paragraph approximately ten million times, moving down the list to the second, third, fourth, etc., over and over, feeling your words sing to the band, and a few good days conducting a full orchestra, lining up to say what you want to say, or at least what your fingers want to say. The mind no longer matters. Just write.

The exception to this process, as mentioned earlier, are the columnists on deadline. Sports columnists, movie and theatre critics, political geeks and such. They often have like 25 minutes between the final out, encore or nomination to a deadline. Just write the damn thing. Something will show up. It's your job.

Another issue with columnists is they can be easily bored. Survival for them—and the reader—depends on a mixed bag of timing, ideas, sources and even mood. They must deal with the world's tragedy, success, failure, humor as it comes. Avoid a rut. Some days you will write a bad column. No fresh ideas. Heartburn. Personal problems. The dog ate your homework. Deal with it and move on. You got this.

Next up will be columns written as long as 45 years ago. They still work because life is ever ongoing even as its occupants change. Humans come and go, but their various trials and tribulations, and stories, remain the same and easily identifiable.

In my case a tip from a reader led to a column about the Louisville Street Department issuing a citation to tear down a doghouse. Thumbing through a magazine offered solid evidence that the mixed aroma of pumpkin pie combined with lavender can create an erection. Where and how is your problem.

A neighborhood walk led to a proud gardener, Mertha Mae Hines, and her prized, back-yard tomatoes. Being part of the consequences resulted in a column about the merger of the staffs of *Louisville Times* and *Courier-Journal* after years of feisty competition. Another living legend came my way while listening to Louisville homebody Pee Wee Reese talk baseball and giving back. And how about famed author John Updike talking golf.

City wants house razed, but one wag is howling

The truth be known, Lula Mae Clark's little doghouse is taking on water. The thing is held together with rusty staples and old duct tape. Its roofing looks like a kin-

dergarten project done on the last day of school. If its plywood walls were any thinner, you could throw a can of dog food through them. The name over the door must have been done by a giddy barn painter.

But it's home. Not necessarily a castle—not even a stable—but a place to flee to in a world too much with us.

At least it was until Lula Mae Clark—half pit bull, half Jack Russell terrier—received notice by registered mail from the City of Louisville's Department of Inspections, Permits & Licenses "concerning the need for the immediate demolition of the structure and all appurtenances located at 602 Caldwell Street, Louisville, Kentucky."

Oh, boy. At first glance it seemed as if the City of Louisville wanted to take out a doghouse.

But there was one large problem with the demolition notice: the canine Lula Mae Clark lives with her owners, Terry and Larry Clark, at 2809 Jomarie Court, miles away from Caldwell Street.

Still, as the Clarks' mailman told them as he delivered the notice, "I don't know how to tell you this, but I've got a certified letter for your dog."

Larry Clark, a man of considerable humor, read the letter, understood an honest mistake had been made, and did not let that deter him from some honest fun.

"I called the inspections department," he said. "I told a woman there I knew Lula Mae's house needed painting, her roof leaked and I'd had to tear out the carpet, but I couldn't believe the city was going to come out and tear it down."

"Did Lula Mae sign for the letter?" the woman asked.

"No," Clark answered, "I had to sign for her."
"Why?"
"She can't read or write."
"That's a shame."
"Well, what do you expect from a dog?"

The mailing included a card asking that properly owners who shared a common name with the owners of property to be demolished—and who received the notice in error—please sign the card and return it.

First Larry Clark wrote on the notifying letter: "Lula Mae Clark is our 3-year-old dog . . . she can't read or write yet." Then he found a red ink pad, slapped Lula Mae Clark's paw print on letter and card and sent them back to the city.

"I don't understand any of it," he said.

The truth is understandable, but not quite as much fun. The canine Lula Mae Clark got her name from the Clarks' daughter, Stacey. The other Lula Mae Clark lived at 602 Caldwell St. in a house the city now finds worthy of demolition—but no trace of her can be found.

To fulfill its legal obligation, the city sent registered letters to anyone whose name was even close to Lula Mae Clark—including people listed in the phone book as "L. Clark." By sheer coincidence, one of those L .Clarks had a dog named Lula Mae.

Clark said Lula Mae is very upset by all this. In fact, protest signs are being hand-pawed in Clark's office:

"We're Not Going to Sit for This One!"
"They Wouldn't Do This to Lassie!"
"Go Fetch, Yourself!"
"Dogs are People Too!"

Even worse, Lula Mae may soon be putting the bite

on people for protest money. Another fine kennel of fish we've gotten ourselves into.

For a proper Thanksgiving dinner, don't light the lavender-scented candles

Here—presented strictly as a public service—is news that could produce some interesting moments over the Thanksgiving holiday.

The Smell & Taste Treatment and Research Foundation in Chicago has determined that the aroma of pumpkin pie combined with lavender can best stimulate an erection. (This according to an article in the November issue of New Choices: Living Even Better After 50 magazine.)

OK, sure, I'll be happy to pause a few seconds here to allow several thousand of you to go out and rummage around the kitchen. While you're out there, be sure to check out the breadbox and candy jar because the No. 2 stimulant on the list is doughnuts and black licorice. No. 3 is doughnuts and pumpkin pie. Is it any wonder we all like the smell of a bakery?

The man behind the pumpkin-and-lavender plan is Dr. Alan R. Hirsch, neurological director of the 10-year-old foundation. Its basic purpose is honorable: the treatment of patients with smell and taste disorders. It investigates how odors can affect mood, behavior, *learning ability, migraine headaches and exercise strength.*

In the latter category, for instance, its tests determined that the aromas of strawberry and hot buttered popcorn can have the greatest positive impact on strength and endurance. Think that over the next time you sit down to $12 worth of hot-buttered theater popcorn.

"We'd also learned that people who lose their sense of smell due to head trauma often gain 10 to 20 pounds," he said, "so we decided to see if we gave them an extra sense of smell, would they lose weight?"

And that led the foundation folks directly to sex. Their studies had shown that 90 percent of people who suffered loss of smell also became sexually dysfunctional. The initial tests were conducted on male medical students who had blood-pressure cuffs placed on their arms; and smaller, specially designed cuffs on their penis-es. As they lay on tables, partially clothed, surgical masks coated with various odors were placed over their faces. Brave and selfless as this might seem, please hold your applause until you hear the whole story.

"One student," said Hirsch, mentioning a pioneer thousands of women may relate to, "slept through the whole thing."

Others, including 31 off-the-street males of all ages, did not. They lay there, profoundly plugged into medical science, as dozens of odors were paraded past their nostrils. With each test, the doctors would check readings, take measurements. The masks would be worn for a minute, then the participants would be al-

lowed a three-minute cool-down period before the next odor was brought in.

"The most surprising thing was traditional perfumes had only a 3 percent effect on penile blood flow," Hirsch said. "A cheese pizza had 5 percent, buttered popcorn 9 percent and lavender 40 percent."

Various odors were tried individually, then in combination. Older men were most responsive to vanilla. Medical students were very partial to cinnamon buns.

Allow me to confess here a certain inability to fully picture this event. I shall, however, long regret not being present in this libido laboratory for that magical moment when somebody stood up and announced: "OK, BRING IN THE PUMPKIN PIE AND LAVENDER!"

Actually, Hirsch had to take credit for that bit of bizarre olfactory inspiration.

"I just suggested combining results of the pilot studies," he said.

She has tomatoes in her garden, poetry in her soul

It is the music of spoken language we are dealing with here, the sweet rhythm and poetry of common language made uncommon: The Happy Confessions of a Novice Gardener.

The gardener is Mertha Mae Hines. Her garden is no bigger than the top of your kitchen table. Its fruits may be no larger than the ones you grow.

But we want to talk about quality of life here, not quantity of tomatoes.

She calls it her "proud garden."

A thousand poets with all their subtle shadings of thought and imagery couldn't improve on that.

Mertha Mae Hines lives in a big, solid brick house at 4319 Hale Ave. She lives there with Perry Hines, her husband of 67 years. He is 89. He is a big, though aging man, with big hands, hands that swallow others' in a handshake, hands that spread out like meaty shovels across his knees.

Mertha Mae Hines is past 80 and holding. She is a tiny woman, the daughter of a midwife and a Civil War soldier and preacher named Jacob. She is the last survivor of a family of 12 brothers and sisters. Her voice is a musical instrument, rising and falling in accompaniment to her words.

She grew her first garden this year. She had wanted it to be a tiny square, but her husband made it a small oval instead. Then he went back inside to let his wife tend it. A niece brought her four tomato slips, and she bought five more wilted plants at a sale for $1.

But listen. Let her tell about it.

"... So I took the five plants and put 'em under my arm and brought them home. I knew nothing about a garden. Never had a garden in my life ... and me past 80. ...

"I brought 'em home and I didn't feel too good, but I went around and stuck holes and put them in the ground. I took a box and sat on it and just dragged it around. That's how I planted it.

"I put tomatoes, I put onion sets down in the ground

I didn't know how to dig, and I put potato eyes in the ground....

"A neighbor gave me some beans—white beans, navy beans—and I planted them. I never knew a navy bean would grow 'cause I never knew nothing about a garden. Then the tomatoes come up and I got hold and measured them and they is just as high as I am tall.

"A few weeks ago my nephew looked and saw this great big tomato at the end of the garden. I went and plucked it because it was so close to the gate and I was afraid somebody would pass along and pick it up.

"It was so heavy, I said 'I believe I'll measure this tomato.'

"I got a string and put it around it. And I measured the string and it was 15 1/2 inches around the tomato. I said that was a mighty lot of inches."

Later on, "I went to the senior citizens (center) and they marveled at it. And then I went and got on the bus and went to town. The storekeeper come up and said it's too heavy to weigh on his scales. He looked right at me and said it was too heavy. I left the tomato there and come straight home and kept tying up, tying up (tomatoes) 'cause they getting so heavy."

She's past 80, and holding, and her voice sings.

"I was born first day of May, my mother loved flowers and I do love flowers today. She was in the flower garden when that time came, least that's what they claim, and they nicknamed me Mae, born first day of May.

"My husband brought the soil here. He enriched the land . . . married 67 years . . . I read the Bible in my kitchen right over my table . . . I read the Bible every day . . . I start the day with the Lord.

"We never had any children for our own, but I helped to raise my sisters' and brothers' children . . . more than 100 still living . . . no end to the generations.

"Had one nephew from here in this house and left here and gone to Racine, Wisconsin. He helps make cars in Wisconsin. His own mother is still living, but he gets here to see me before he sees his mother . . . I'd taken care of him so you know he must love me."

And her being past 80. And there's her proud garden.

"See these tomatoes . .. I've tied and tied and tied them . . . and I have lots of small ones coming up. I was marveled. I didn't think those things was any good . . . they was wilted . . . five for a dollar.

Merger musings: It is the end of an era . . .

―――――

Although you will not notice much immediate change in the product, the news from the more corporate end of this business is that—effective tomorrow, Sunday, Dec. 1—all news staffs of The Courier-Journal and The Louisville Times will be merged.

There still will be two newspapers, but after competing journalistically with each other for 101 years, nearly half as long as this country is old, the two staffs are going to join up in the interest of better papers and economic necessity. The bottom line says you can't have one without the other.

Very few reporters, photographers or even mid-level editors are bottom-line people. Many of us are even uncomfortable with the notion that newspapers are a business. We would just prefer to wander around in unfettered pursuit of truth, justice and man-bites-dog epics while people working one or two floors below us go through that awful process of having to sell advertising to pay the bills.

I think what I dislike the most about this merger is that it is such a reminder that we are a business, that the sanctity of the First Amendment isn't worth much unless we can come up with about $70 million for new color printing presses to remain economically competitive.

What's most odd about the merger is that so many people seem to think we've had only one staff all along, anyway. If I had a dime for every time I've had to explain to people that I worked for The Louisville Times and not The Courier-Journal, I could buy out Sallie Bingham and purchase the new printing press.

But it's true, folks.

For all those years, reporters from The Louisville Times and The Courier-Journal have been in separate pursuit of news to fill the white space around the grocery ads.

For all those years, and that would include thousands of reporters and editors, one paper has been looking over the other's shoulder, although not always willing to admit it.

There always has been that little "high" attached to not only getting a good story, but getting it first.

But after today, symbolically if not officially, it won't be that way anymore.

I've had a sense of loss about this all week, but partly because there will still be two newspapers and partly because the changes will come gradually, I find it hard to put into words.

Maybe it's because the very first paper I worked for—a biweekly in the town where I grew up—tried to expand too quickly into a daily. The move—abrupt, poorly planned and underfinanced—was a disaster. The newspaper eventually folded.

The second newspaper I worked for was purchased by the Gannett newspaper chain. It cut the staff by about 40 percent, folded the afternoon paper and bled all the money it could from the news operation.

Some fun company, that Gannett.

After those experiences, the Bingham companies seemed about 72 percent heaven, a place that seemed removed from all those ugly business decisions, a paper that for all its faults has always been a good place to work. Now—not quite suddenly—all those bottom-line considerations are popping up again.

All this, of course, clashes directly with my rather archaic view that the whole function of newspapers is to print the news and raise hell, not advertising rates.

I have been thinking all week that today is the last Louisville Times in 101 years that will be put out exactly in this manner, and something profound need be said about that.

Or at least readable.

And nothing will kill a columnist quicker than trying to be profound.

My first thought upon learning of the merger was that the staffs of both papers had shrunk so much that something had to be done—and the merger, if done right, could be a very good thing. I still feel that way.

But I've also been thinking of all the people who have worked for the Times, who enjoyed the competition, who feel a closeness for each other and the paper we put out, who sense the same loss I feel without being able to put just the right typewriter key on it.

Don't make too much fuss over Pee Wee Reese

Pee Wee Reese was marching around the lunchroom of the Audubon Country Club imitating the rolling, jingling, leather-heavy gait of a fully equipped South Central Bell telephone-line repairman.

As Reese explained it, his promising Louisville career as an apprentice telephone-line splicer was cut short about 1938 by a professional baseball career that landed him in the Baseball Hall of Fame, placed him in a national TV booth with Dizzy Dean and made him a legend to every little kid who ever picked up a Louisville Slugger.

But here's the thing about Pee Wee: He remains so doggone unassuming you might have thought he remained in telephone-line splicing. At 74, a little gimpy around the knees but still an occasional threat on the golf course, he knows who he is but never lets it get in the way of what he is—a tough, proud, likable hometown boy who never forgot where he came from.

No fussing over him—please.

"I try to avoid things," Reese said. "When I came back from the Hall of Fame, I was asked to be grand marshal of the Pegasus Parade, but I thought . . . man . . . I don't want to sit up there with all those people watching me.

"When I play in the Foster Brooks golf tournament, a lot of my friends will be out there, and they'll shout at me . . . 'Hey, Pee Wee, who's the celebrity in your foursome?'"

With many of our heroes, those words would ring phony. With Reese, they are as genuine as a Don Newcombe fastball.

Pee Wee Reese and Bob Hill talk baseball.

Reese was one of six children born into a farm family near Ekron, Ky., in Meade County. He was about 7 when his family moved to Louisville's Portland neighborhood. He lived there two years, then grew up around Central Park. During the Depression, his father was often unemployed; Reese's sisters found work; Pee Wee worked for a sandwich company, selling lunches to L&N Railroad workers from 6 to 7 a.m. and bringing home $1.50 a week.

He graduated from duPont Manual High School in the class of 1935 1/2, playing only five baseball games his senior year because of a hand injury. He was 5-foot-5 and weighed about 110 pounds—the physique of a natural born telephone-line splicer, a job he did hold during the 1937 flood.

Except Pee Wee was also back playing baseball.

"We won the city church championship and played the industrial league champions out at Parkway Field," he said. "We got beat 2 to 1, but I hit one off the outfield wall.

"A guy named Cap Neal came over and asked if I had ever thought about professional baseball. . . . I said, no, I hadn't—and I really hadn't."

Reese signed for $150 a month—with a $200 signing bonus—to play for the AAA Louisville Colonels. By 1940 he was playing shortstop for the Brooklyn Dodgers. In 1941—"155 pounds of cold, rolled steel"—he was playing in the World Series against the Yankees.

"I'm four years off a utility pole," Reese said.

"I'm in Yankee Stadium, and I look around and I say, "What the hell am I doing here?"

After World War II—when Reese served in the Navy—he came back to be captain of the Brooklyn team, playing in every World Series game it later played against the hated Yankees and befriending Jackie Robinson in 1947 during those very difficult days of baseball integration.

Reese always kept his Louisville roots. After retirement, one request he couldn't avoid—"somebody talked me into it"—was lending his name to the Pee Wee Reese Cystic Fibrosis Celebrity Dinner Party. The an-

nual dinner-dance began in the 1960s with about 60 people in Bernie's Back Room, 4023 S. Third St. It now draws about 600 people to the Gait House.

The dinner-dances and auctions of celebrity-donated items have raised more man $1 million for cystic fibrosis. The fun part is that many Louisville personalities—sports figures, politicians, disc jockeys and media types (even your humble correspondent)—serve the food, occasionally toward the floor.

This year's dinner is special because, after 25 years as host, Pee Wee Reese will hang it up. He'll be taking his golf game to Florida next winter. University of Louisville basketball coach Denny Crum will lead the event next year.

Pee Wee will be honored by the home folks about 8:30 p.m.

Don't expect too much of a fuss.

For duffer/author John Updike, the pen isn't always mightier than the sword

John Updike has the laugh of an 18-handicap golfer: delivered easily and well, with full measure of required self-effacement, but hinting at a deeper, more brooding side.

Bogey golf will do that to a man. Or a woman.

Updike, the Jack Nicklaus of fiction, poetry and criticism, will be in Louisville Feb. 25 at the Kentucky Author Forum evening honoring Wilson W. Wyatt Sr. Updike will sign books, be interviewed by National Public Radio's Robert Siegel, perhaps demonstrate the delicate art of smashing a three-wood from a sidehill lie to a terraced green 210 yards away.

Updike first took up golf when he was 25, an age when most golfers have already hurled a half-dozen nine-irons deep into nearby lakes. He's been at the game almost 40 years and still struggles to break 90; a beneficent God ensures that genius does not automatically carry over from the pen to the putter.

Updike has chronicled his golf agony and ecstasy in 30 lyrical essays and stories nicely packaged in one small book, "Golf Dreams" (Alfred A. Knopf, $23). He will discuss that book—among others things—with Siegel.

"I prefer to write in the mornings," he said by phone from his home in Massachusetts. "I do sometimes feel guilty when I'm out on the course instead of writing, but from noon on I can live with that guilt."

Updike won two Pulitzer Prizes writing the life of Harry "Rabbit" Angstrom, basketball star turned car salesman. Reading the preface of "Golf Dreams" leaves the impression that Updike was all but ready to abandon golf for weekends more productively spent selling Volvos.

He came to those feelings when he learned during a routine visit to a doctor that he had shrunk a half-inch in height at the same time he had lost 10 yards distance with his five-irons. This was life—and death.

"My image of myself," he wrote, "was that of a 6-foot

man who could hit a five-iron 150 yards. In all dimensions, I was shrinking.

"My love of golf had been of its generous measurements—its momentary amplification of myself within a realm larger than life. If my golf was to shrink, as I had seen it shrink for others, to a mingy, pokey business of arthritic shoulder-turns and low, hippi-ty-hopping drives that merely nibbled at the yardage, I would rather not tee up."

Yeah, well, golfers revel in whiny worry, self-pity and doubt. They are always either quitting the game or heading out for more lessons, or both. Those moves—and moods—are interchangeable. Updike teed it up last summer, last fall, and will tee it up this winter.

"I was feeling gloomy when I wrote that introduction," he said. "I'm playing a bit better now. I'm looking forward to playing a little in Florida. It's the very nature of the foolish sport that we keep trying."

His 200-page book is thick with observations about golf as life, his most-quoted one providing some sort of a recurring virginity: "When you stand up on the first tee it is there, the possibility of a round without a speck of bad in it."

As a writer, he is always caught between trying to concentrate on his game while observing the humor and angst in the larger surroundings. He offers these brief pronouncements on the latter:

GOLF RELATIONSHIPS: Many men are more faithful to their golf partners than to their wives.

THE GIMMIE GAME: A unique and universally accepted form of cheating.

GOLF CADDIES: The fact is, most Americans are

uneasy with servants.

GOLF WISDOM: Golf is life, and life is lessons.

GOLF HOPE: The thought that if we have one good shot in us, we must have thousands more.

Updike recorded "Golf Dreams" on cassette tape. It's the perfect traveling companion for anyone driving to Florida or South Carolina for a few weeks of certain frustration on foreign links. He sees many parallels between golf and writing; each must be polished with patience and practice, practice, practice.

"Both offer spurts of ecstasy," he said. "A really good shot speaks for itself. It comes from somewhere else."

COLUMNS CAN FIND YOU

In many ways, if you pay attention, columns find you.

For years I had driven past a man sitting in a lawn chair on Louisville's River Road whose mission in life was to wave to people. Who then waved back. A nice moment in anybody's day. The man's name was Jimmy Myers. Later stricken with cancer, I wrote a column about him and his absence along River Road that brought 175 cards and letters. And much more.

I once visited former Miss America and television personality Phyllis George Brown at her Texas home for a feature story, We got along very well. She was easy to like. I later became very irritated with her when she espoused to be a true journalist. No way. It takes way more than fame.

Well-aged Louisville legend Muhammad Ali was sadly whipped in a fight by Larry Homes in a fight witnessed at a closed-circuit fight in Louisville's Freedom Hall. The locals were very disappointed, but no one booed him.

After 103 years the *Louisville Times*, my early alma mater, was shut down by chain-newspaper economics. I attended the newsroom funeral, wrote a final deadline column about it. But refusing to go out with it's head bowed, the staff hired a Dixieland Band to march around the newsroom and into the street after a final deadline.

In one of the most tragic, sad, arrogant and sick power moves in Louisville history, thousands of blue-collar residents were illegally tossed out of their homes for an airport expansion. The sad truth came years later from the Kentucky Supreme Court decision long after the homeowners were booted out.

In perhaps the most poignant column I ever wrote, a couple married two years were in a serious car wreck. She was in a coma for more than a year. There was no medical hope, so her husband, who found another relationship, divorced her, then adopted her until her death.

Jimmy welcomed our waves

Your cards and letters to Jimmy Myers covered a 12-foot section of wall at the Neurath & Underwood Funeral Home on Thursday. They were the "thank yous" that had given him joy and satisfaction as he lay dying and will be a source of pride and comfort to his family for as long as he is remembered.

For years Myers, unable to work, had sat in a lawn chair in a shaded place along River Road and waved at passing drivers. He did it because he liked to wave. Last November, stricken with emphysema, then can-

cer, he had to stop.

The news of his imminent death in a previous column brought him more than 175 cards and letters. They came from Indianapolis and Paoli in Indiana, Hopkinsville and Murray in Western Kentucky, the mountain communities of Eastern Kentucky and people who drive along River Road.

Pam Holzknecht of Louisville was thoughtful enough to include a Polaroid photo of herself sitting in her van waving, just so Myers would recognize her:

"Dear Mr. Myers . . . I want you to know that your wave started my day out with such positiveness and contemplation. . . . I also thought you were smiling because you weren't fighting the Rat Race anymore. . . .

"I lost my mother to cancer two years ago. I cared for her the last six weeks. I then realized how important it is to tell people how they have influenced lives. I want to thank you for all those waves and smiles. Many of my friends appreciated your waves as well. You made a difference. Truly."

Holzknecht was one of the regular wavers, a diverse group of people who had a common bond in an everyday man:

"Mr. Myers. I just wanted you to know God and I are thinking of you today. I miss you on River Road. The White Cadillac Man." . . .

"Jimmy, I drive a gold Mercedes and met you at Christmas 1995, when I stopped and gave you a box of candy. My best to you and your wife. Allen Corbin." . . .

"Jimmy, I would wave at you on River Road going to and coming from Nugent Sand. I drive a '92 Ford dump truck, number 104. I enjoyed waving at you. I wish you good health and happiness. Ray Moore."

One of Myers' favorite letters came from two brothers, ages 9 and 10, who live in Pleasure Ridge Park, but would travel down River Road about once a month: "We are so sorry to hear of your illness and want you to know we love you and miss you and will pray for your strength and also for your family. You are our hero. . . . God bless you. . . . Brandon Wyatt-Farris and Garrett Farris."

Myers' wife, Juanita, said family members would take turns reading letters to Jimmy until the day he died. They were thankful for the mail, the many prayers. The letters were spread around his room at Hospice of Louisville, then taken to the funeral home where Jimmy's sister, Hallie Calvert, lovingly placed them on flat boards, the wall, the carpeted floor.

Many cards had a waving hand drawn on them. Employees at Kentucky Connection, a carpet-binding company, went one step further, sending an elaborate, home-made pop-out card: "Jimmy, A friendly wave makes a person feel special at any time of the day. We at the Kentucky Connection send back to you a wave today."

Melody Knopf of Eastwood said she was a "fellow-waver," but traveled her neighborhood on foot. Her letter was friendly, chatty, as if from an old friend, with a little bit of waving travails included: "I've been training people how to respond to a wave. When I first began walking and waving, a lot of people were perplexed and didn't know how to respond. Now some of them wave first. What progress."

Paoli (Ind.) Police Chief Ronald Shrout wrote, "We need more people like you. Wishing you well." John and Fay Ray of Murray, Ky, said their Sinking Spring Baptist Church had placed Myers on its prayer list and wanted to share its love.

An entire second-grade class at Jacob Elementary School sent Myers letters: "I try to instill in my students the value of small kindnesses," wrote teacher Debbie Powell, "and I used your story as a legacy to them, and others."

Jimmy Myers was buried in Evergreen Cemetery yesterday. He wasn't looking to leave a legacy, but he did: Be kind, be thoughtful, wave. He was faithful to himself right to the end, waving to other patients from his hospital bed as they passed his door.

He couldn't help it. He just liked to wave.

Setting the record straight about who is a journalist and what he/she does

I noticed that Phyllis George Brown was giving journalism lessons the other day. Speaking "as a former journalist," she criticized some reporter for making too much of Lt. Gov. Steve Beshear's comments on her husband's long-distance telephone habits.

I spent a full day with Phyllis George Brown several years ago while working on a magazine profile. She is likable, hard-working, vulnerable and cares about how people perceive her.

She also has, in the naive and money-protected way of people who have been out of the real world for a long time, the irritating habit of unintentionally saying things that offend people.

Because if Phyllis George Brown was ever a journalist, then Jimmy the Greek is next in line for a Peabody Award for investigative reporting.

People like them tend to equate television celebrity with journalism. The former has always had a lot more to it than announcing point spreads, running slow-motion stories about overpaid jocks to the strains of "The Battle Hymn of the Republic" and being beautiful at 7 a.m.

Phyllis George Brown, of all people, should know that by now.

I began in journalism, as many have, bringing home about $4,500 a year from a small weekly paper in my hometown. I had no experience. That was my journalism market value, take it or leave it. The toughest decision I had to make all year was whether to endorse my former Little League coach for mayor. He was one of four candidates. We endorsed him. He finished fourth. Good lesson, that.

Yet I still believe a good weekly newspaper will always have a much greater impact on its community than a Courier-Journal can have in Louisville or a Washington Post can have in the nation's capital.

A good weekly hits home. But $4,500 a year gets old.

I've never felt noble about being a journalist. I don't

like posturing newspaper editors who go around beating their breasts about the importance of the First Amendment and our sacred duty to feed you the truth.

I just like the business. I like and respect many of the people in it. I like the profession's basic ground rules: Write as fairly, accurately and honestly as you can in the time you've got.

They're nice rules to live by. People who hire agents and publicists to deal only in sunshine while screening out the bad and the ugly can't possibly understand journalism. It's not a question of paying dues, either. Television celebrities do that too. It's more a matter of where and how.

In the years I worked for a weekly, I wrote stories, took and developed pictures seven days a week, delivered newspapers, sold advertising and mopped the floor. When I first went to a daily I wrote obituaries and cruised the police beat. The first night on the job I was called to a garage where an old woman had poured gasoline over herself and lit a match.

I was asked to go into homes of children who had drowned and ask their parents for school pictures. I once beat the police and the ambulance to the home of a man wounded by a shotgun and interviewed him while he was holding in his intestines. I watched the snow melt beneath the still-warm victim of a trailer fire. I spent many hours waiting outside the home of a councilman whose son had been abducted, molested and murdered.

I dressed up as a clown for a circus story, talked with astronauts, traveled to Czechoslovakia, went trick-or-treating with a 4-year-old and hitchhiked the state, writing all the way.

I covered the courts, investigated officials, witnessed elections, watched presidents from afar, ate close-up with governors, wrote about pumpkins, reviewed plays and went to 6,000 high school football, baseball and basketball games. The first night I covered a school board, 800 teachers went out on strike.

I wasn't proud of all those moments. It's not easy to ask tough questions. I made mistakes. At times I felt like what I was, a ghoul waiting out people so I could put their words in a newspaper. But the man was a city councilman. I was a journalist. His son's murder was news.

The business works that way. Journalists gather experiences like barnacles. A lot of it is gritty stuff. Some can break your heart. Most of it is very repetitive. A lot of it is fun.

And we who have done it a long time tend to resent those who, for one reason or another, got to start pretty close to the top without having to ask grieving parents for pictures of their dead children.

We don't consider those people journalists. I hope you can understand that.

On closed circuit, faithful stunned by Ali's demise

They came to Freedom Hall last night to praise Muhammad Ali, not to bury him.

But it still came to $20 a head admission for the wake.

Somewhere between 6,000 and 7,000 people pushed into the hall hoping to cheer for a medical miracle, an Ali victory over Larry Holmes. Instead they sat on their hands in depressed silence as Ali did a perfect imitation of an old man waiting to get run over by a bus.

The Last Hurrah became The Last Harrumph. The Louisville Lip went out before the home folks on his posterior, and with his mouth shut.

The Lip is dead. Long live the Lip.

The Ali faithful began gathering by 8 p.m., almost 3 1/2 hours before show time. Milton Chwaski, the main body counter for Butch Lewis, who staged the closed-circuit-television show in Freedom Hall, said the advance ticket sales had been about 3,200, and he expected that to double by fight time.

It was a crowd well-mixed with blue- and white-collar types and little of the flashy fashions often found in a fight crowd. There was the little matter of the maroon over tan Rolls-Royce with the Texas license plates and white sidewall tires being parked in the "handicapped only" section, but Fairgrounds officials had it moved.

The chauffeur explained that the car's owner was handicapped.

It was a crowd long on enthusiasm and beer lines. Guards were searching everyone that came through the door for contraband liquor and/or smokes. The search was obviously the first of its kind for many of the better-dressed types who apparently had never been to a rock concert or a wrestling match.

About 3,000 seats had been set up on the floor of Freedom Hall facing four 10-by-14-foot television screens. The screens were set up in box-like fashion in the center of the chairs, giving everyone a view of at least one screen, with people sitting at the box "corners" getting to view two screens, making the Ali debacle doubly hard to take.

The closed-circuit viewing came with three announcers and/or color men, including that well-known boxing commentator Kris Kristofferson.

Early in the evening, boxing promoter Don King, one of the three announcers, told the faithful that the telecast was "the largest television crowd in the history of television."

Thank you, thank you. Don Don King King.

It turned out the two televised preliminary fights, including a victory by heavyweight Leon Spinks for gap-toothed people everywhere, contained 95 percent of the solid punches that would be thrown all evening.

The audience, which spilled up in all directions from the packed mass on the floor, observed the fights fitfully.

But Ali, as usual, stirred them up. As he struggled through the crowd toward the ring, the faithful in Louisville picked up the chant of the faithful in Las Vegas. "Ahlee! Ahlee! Ahlee!"

When Ali was announced as being from Louisville, thunder rolled through the aisles. As he taunted Holmes in the last bluff of his distinguished career, the audience cheered him, encouraged him, took him again into their hearts and minds, and chanted "Ahlee! Ahlee."

When Ali danced a brief lick in the first round, the crowd was with him, waiting for those flicking left jabs and follow-up combinations.

For the next few rounds Ali kept his gloves to himself, assuming the pugilistic stance of a man trying to push a bedroom window up and open.

The crowd waited in silence for him to open up. It never happened. When Ali clowned, the faithful were with him, but his lack of fighting left them cold. Ali was old. Ali was slow. Ali was finished.

It ended suddenly, with Ali's trainer throwing in the towel. Stunned, the crowd left the scene of the crime in a hurry. A few looked back over their shoulders on the way out like die-hard football fans getting one last hopeful glimpse of a 72-0 rout.

"Ali threw the fight," one of the faithful said. "He must have thrown the fight."

"Something must have been wrong with him," said another. "When he fights like that, then something's wrong."

"I lost $900 on this fight," said a third, "and I haven't worked in nine months. I'd like to fight that SOB myself."

But for whatever it's worth, not one of the faithful booed him.

All that's left is a century of ghosts

I am sitting here in the newsroom at 5:18 a.m. today writing the final deadline column that will ever appear in The Louisville Times.

The ghosts of almost 103 years' worth of journalists

are looking over my shoulder, and a maintenance lady is pushing her vacuum cleaner past my desk in short, even strokes.

I sure hope at least one of them can spell.

I feel nervous writing this column, more nervous than I ever thought I would be. There is a magic to being able to have thoughts come out of the ends of your fingers and reappear hours later in newspaper ink, but it is a fragile magic, easily bruised, and the resulting ink is not always something to be proud of.

Yet the Louisville Times was often a deadline newspaper. Its reporters often crammed into some distant telephone booth with barely 10 minutes to spare, shouting hastily constructed sentences to rewrite men who could repair them on the fly, then ship them to the copy desk for final polishing.

We did it all the time. We did it for more than a century. We were The Louisville Times.

Over the years, and by a long parade of editors, many who didn't stay, the Times was praised for being feisty, readable, fun, irreverent and a paper for the people.

This was always in understood contrast to our big brother, The Courier-Journal, the more serious and much-better-known flagship of the fleet.

Then, because of economic circumstances beyond anyone's control, The Louisville Times was asked to leave the journalistic stage.

Forever.

We didn't even get to keep our name.

If you worked on the Times, you eventually developed a toughness about things like that, along with some gallows humor, cynicism, and yes, in the intimate moments in the back of the bar, a touch of bitterness.

But more important, there developed a feeling of family among us, a closeness for each other that only the perpetual underdog can understand. A lot of us thought, at least in The Louisville Times' heyday, that we already had one great newspaper.

It is now about 6:30 a.m. and the cleaning lady is still at work, but now in a distant corner of the newsroom. The photo editor is looking over a selection of pictures for today's paper, and the copy editors, that anonymous army that continually sits between us writers and grammatical embarrassment, is already at work on the day's final stories.

Essentially, a good newsroom looks like an insurance office for slobs. It is filled with desks that are littered with reference materials, press releases and old notes that reporters will never use but are afraid to throw away.

We don't use typewriters. We all write on ugly, black video terminals and dispatch our copy electronically into computers that sometimes turn our words into newspaper ink and sometimes send them—irretrievably—to Poughkeepsie.

We also usually hang irrelevant messages on our walls, the occasional basketball goal and maybe even a sincere and thoughtful letter from Oral Roberts.

That's the way we like to work on the outside. But inside, there's an undercurrent of sadness here this morning that irreverence can't hide. We just don't have the time to dwell on it until after we get the copy out.

The ghosts are no help. They all live downstairs in

our library clips and on rolls of microfilm. It is always surprising, and more than a little humbling, to research Louisville Times stories written 20, 30 or 40 years ago and see the bylines of journalists long forgotten, journalists who worked as hard and loved the Times as much as we did.

They're all trying to get into my fingers now. Names such as Marion "Aunt Jane" Green, Harry Bloom, A.Y. Aronson and Bess Conkwright and so many more.

They want to shout, "We were here, too, Louisville! We were here!"

They want to tell me how they crammed into phone booths, shouted their sentences to rewrite men, and complained, sometimes bitterly, about The Courier-Journal in the intimate moments in the back of the bar.

"We were here!" they are all screaming. "How can you forget us? We were here for 103 years!"

It is now about 7:24 a.m. and photographers are coming around taking pictures of the people who are putting out the last Louisville Times. I am still as nervous as I was when I started this column. There is still so much to say, and barely 15 minutes left to say it.

I can hear the computer keys clattering on the copy desk, and editors discussing where to play today's stories. The ghosts are quieter now. The room is curiously silent, almost peaceful.

It's time, and besides, the cleaning lady is gone, too.

Supreme Court ruling merely stated the obvious

It didn't really require a decision from the Kentucky Supreme Court to settle the issue of "blight" in the three neighborhoods around Standiford Field. It didn't require seven jurists in black robes poring over legal briefs to render a just and fair decision.

It was obvious from Day One that Highland Park, Prestonia and Standiford were not blighted. It was obvious that the attempts to grab those neighborhoods under the powers of urban renewal were ill-conceived, arrogant and wrong, and that the entire episode was one of the most shameful in Louisville history.

You could have made the decision yourself. All you had to do was look at the brick homes, the neat lawns and the flower gardens. All you had to do was listen to the people—even those who lived in the older, frame homes— who had been neighbors for 40 years.

Yes, many of them did sell. Yes, many of them wanted out. But in the process the city created its own blight. It pushed a lot of very old, very frightened people out of their homes by creating the impression they had little choice, that the legal forces against them were too strong, that they were no longer wanted or needed in a neighborhood where many of them had spent most of their lives.

The Kentucky Supreme Court's ruling was stunningly simple and succinct. It said the city had tried "to declare an apple to be orange" so it could use its urban renewal powers to acquire the property. It rejected the notion that the neighborhoods were blighted by noise and congestion. It called the city's land grab *"repugnant to our constitutional protections"*—words those who lived in the neighborhoods had long wanted to hear but had never really expected.

The city is not alone in sharing the blame. There's a long, long list of community leaders and organizations who were just as eager to push those people out of their homes. They were more than willing to let a few people pay the price—no matter how unfairly—so the community as a whole could benefit.

Unfortunately, the effect of the ruling at this stage of the game is about like having Three Mile Island declared a nuclear-free zone. Much of the damage has been done. Most of the houses, churches and businesses that make up a neighborhood have been sold. Any return to real life would be difficult, if not impossible. Even those who rejoice in the victory know a lot of people—taxpayers—will be paying for the mountain of lawsuits and legal remedies it will take to settle this mess.

The Biggest Lie in this whole rat's nest of lies has been the steady contention by local planners that the airport expansion and adjacent urban renewal programs were totally separate but just happened to occur at the same time. That's always been impossible for me to accept, especially since all plans were developed secretly, then released behind a tidal wave of carefully timed public relations and arm-twisting.

Now they have all been caught in their lies. The Kentucky Supreme Court has seen the obvious truth. The airport promoters are still wearing their game faces. But somebody—temporarily, at least—turned out the lights late in the third quarter.

Mayor Jerry Abramson, a good mayor who has been terribly wrong about the methods used in this fiasco, may finally see a sizable dent in his popularity ratings, and a little humility at this point wouldn't hurt.

The real lack of understanding of what the people in the neighborhoods were going through has always bothered me. They were being pushed out of their homes only because they were in the way. It hurt. They cried, and their families cried with them.

Now they have won, but what's left? They may get a little more money. But the neighborhood is gone. Their friends are gone. And the new house will probably take the extra money.

The city, in a faltering fashion, tried to hire people to come in and smooth the transition. But you can't hire people to replace friends and neighbors. You can't ask the guy in the 9 a.m. to 5 p.m. relocation office to water the flowers or feed the cat for a week.

The airport promoters were wrong. The Kentucky Supreme Court said so. But the official position remains to regroup, rearm and bulldoze it through from a different angle.

Their arrogance remains. The only change will be in group tactics. I just wish someone would admit the damage. I just wish someone would stand up and say, "Yes, we were wrong, terribly wrong, and I'm sorry."

Love—'In sickness and in health'

She has been in a coma since February 1977, when her car spun around on the ice just east of downtown Louisville and smashed into a light pole.

They had been married almost two years at the time. He was refereeing a basketball game and received word his wife's leg had been broken in the accident. He arrived at General Hospital to find that a priest had been called for the last rites, and the left side of his wife's skull had been removed to relieve the pressure on her brain. She still suffered permanent brain damage.

She is 22 now. He is 25. They had no children. She had been an honor student at the University of Louisville. She had been in love with life, celebrating its good and bad moments in poetry from the time she was a little girl.

> There are times I wish
> I could reach and touch a warm body,
> or feel the morning, or
> knead the sun with my hands
> but all I pull back to me
> is the empty air, or memories,
> or Ferdinand, a green frog,
> from the floor.
> And I still believe in love.

She was in the operating room for eight hours. The doctors gave her a 5 to 10 percent chance of living. She stayed in General Hospital five days after the surgery and was then moved to Norton's.

He was told the space was needed at General Hospital for people who had a chance to live.

She stayed at Norton's for two months. She lived on a respirator for a month. Since then, she has lived on tubes that carry food into her body and the wastes out.

Her weight dropped from 130 pounds to 70 pounds. Her legs and arms have curled up in the fetal position. There has never been even the slightest indication that she has recognized anyone or anything since the accident.

> *There are minutes I wish I could*
> *hold a piece of yesterday*
> *and then turn it over again*
> *till it came into focus and being*
> *but all that I hold*
> *is nothingness*
> *because only fools have yesterdays*
> *in their jeans pockets.*
> *And I still believe in love.*

In April she was moved to a nursing home. She went back to the hospital briefly in May, September, October and November. He tried to get in touch with neurosurgeons in New York, California and Japan, but no one could or would help him.

He worked nights at Ford. Weekdays he worked 9 p.m. to 5:30 a.m., slept until noon and spent the rest of the day with his wife. He spent almost every weekend day at his vigil. His wife's family joined him.

For six months, he visited the nursing home every day. His wife's condition never changed. She never knew he was there.

The following July she went back to Norton's for the last time. The doctors said she was beyond any help. She went back to the nursing home to stay. Her weight went back up to over 100 pounds, but she stayed in the coma.

"It was hard to begin a new life when I had an old life like that," he said. "I'd go out once in a while and get drunk, but it didn't really matter. I couldn't forget. I'd always go visit her the next day. . . . I remember being young once, but now I don't feel too young anymore."

He stayed close to his wife's family. His mother-in-law suggested about a year ago that he get a divorce and try to begin a new life, but he was reluctant. Then his father-in-law died, making a divorce even harder for the family to deal with.

He still visited his wife two or three times a week. The almost $250,000 in medical bills were covered by Ford's insurance. The current $2,000-to-$3,000-a-month bill is being paid by Medicaid and disability income.

In time, he began to date again. But he still routinely checked on his wife's condition. He said he still loved her for what she was and all that she wanted to be. And he wanted to care for her as long as she needed it.

So he decided to divorce his wife, and then adopt her. "That way if things were not done right, I would be *there to get things done right," he said.*

With the help of attorney Stuart Lyon, he divorced his wife two weeks ago. Then, last Wednesday, he adopted her.

"It was something that I had to do," he said.

He has not visited his wife for several months but still calls to check on her. He has begun his new life. He may marry again in a few months. And they will have their own house, and maybe children to fill it. And they will share their own dreams and their own moments of triumph, joy and despair.

> *There are days I'd like*
> *to spend at zoos*
> *eating life, tasting every last*
> *bite until I knew exactly what it was,*
> *but all that I taste is the bitterness*
> *of salty tears,*
> *the cold chill of emptiness,*
> *the icy stare of a polar bear*
> *behind bars.*
> *And still I believe in love.*
> *Do you?*

MORE COLUMNS FROM THE LOUISVILLE DAYS

I wrote often of cemeteries, funerals and the dearly departed. Maybe some of that came from growing up near a cemetery as a kid, playing in it, but mostly chasing gophers. A column below is about a woman who made hundreds of visits to a cemetery where her daughter was buried.

Ann Goodykoontz was a lady who liked to write personal letters, an art now lost in our social media world. Who saves letters any written on Outlook and keeps them in a box in the closet?

What has come to be considered all too common was still very rare on Sept. 14, 1989 when Joseph Wesbecker went on a shooting rampage with an AK-47 at Louisville's Standard Gravure printing company, killing seven people and wounding 13 more. The *Courier-Journal* was right next door. We fled and stood along the street as the bodies were carried out.

Another column told of a mentally ill woman standing screaming on the steps of the old post office building next door, and how the passing world reacted.

Leavening that bread a little bit came a column

about a semi-scientific test to fully determine if 100 yards of dental floss could actually be contained in such a small, plastic container.

The last column in this bunch is about a young man with a troubled life, and a sense of honor and pride, was being paid $3.17 an hour by Pinkerton's to guard millions of dollars' worth of horses at Churchill Downs.

Two strangers passing in a cemetery

The woman didn't want me to leave. As I backed away, seeking a graceful exit, she would follow just a little, holding me with the urgency of her words.

We were at a cemetery, she out of love and grief, me partially out of a sense of guilt over missing a funeral I should have attended.

She had stopped to arrange a few flowers for her relative, then made her way around to other graves, picking up flowers and straightening wreaths. She did it as an artist might hang his works, fussing with the edges, pushing them just so, then stepping back to take in the whole effect.

She obviously hadn't planned to stay long because she'd left her car engine running, and the front door on the driver's side was open. She said she was just in the neighborhood and wanted one more time to stop at the place where her daughter was buried.

There was the sense that she had made this trip hundreds of times and that she would make hundreds more, brief stops to fix the flowers, to check on the neighborhood, to see if everything was all right—even for just a few minutes while the car's engine was running.

She had been there so often that she had met many of the other people who came to her place, people who also had lost loved ones, the people who had left the flowers she was tending and rearranging.

They had met often on holidays, on birthdays, on anniversary dates, on those special occasions when people who do not want to forget go to cemeteries to mourn and remember.

So she had come to know their stories, to share their grief and—when the others were not there to do it—to rearrange their flowers.

"That story there is particularly sad," the woman said, pointing to some gold-leaf lettering on marble that said February - August 1973. "That little girl was the first girl anyone could ever remember being born in the family. The first one ever . . ."

Tiny yellow-and-white plastic flowers had been stuck in the even cracks in the marble near some of the names. A few feet away, someone had left a brief prayer to a loved one, a prayer punched out on blue, adhesive-backed plastic and fixed to the marble above a gold-leaf name.

The cemetery was one of those places tucked in behind a shopping center and flanked by an expressway, but it still managed to breathe tranquility and a sense of peace.

It was early in the spring, and the rich, April-green grass was the perfect setting for white marble and pink granite. The tree limbs, only partially budded, were black and clean in the morning sun. The blue sky had been blown clear by a crisp west wind.

"It took those people a long, long time to get over the death of that little girl," the woman said. "The first one ever in the family . . ."

In time, we made our way past a half-dozen wreaths or bouquets of flowers. She had the urge to talk, and I had the need to be there, and we both felt better for the experience.

"There was a party," the woman said, pointing out a grave but not making it clear whom she was discussing. "One of them got mad and took off, driving real fast. . . There was a bad accident."

She said she had come to like the cemetery. She had been to others more secluded, cemeteries that were more famous or ones that might have had bigger trees, but she was more than satisfied with this one.

"This is such a friendly place," she said. "I like the people you meet here. It always feels so good to come out here."

We never talked much about her daughter. The information came unsolicited, in bits and pieces and so melded into the other stories that, unless your mind was on her alone, it became indiscernible from the rest.

She just kept moving around, fixing the flowers, talking about the people who brought them, not really wanting to leave—even though the morning was growing late and the engine in her car was still running.

Letters are records to be treasured, rediscovered

Almost every morning, seated in the warm glow of her kitchen, Ann Goodykoontz writes letters. Picture her there, a handsome woman with silvered hair and wire glasses, her dress a robin's-egg blue, her necklace a deeper blue, a content figure bent over a kitchen table in the liquid light of morning, writing letters.

On the good days—and she is very busy with other things—Ann Goodykoontz will write letters in her southern Jefferson County home from about 9 a.m. until noon. She uses white, unlined paper, always writing in blue ink with a soft-tipped Bic pen. She writes to her friends and her old grade-school chums. She writes to authors of books she enjoys. She writes to manufacturers of products that do not work. She writes to her children, and to their children. She writes seven to 10 letters a week, every week, and has done so for more than 30 years.

"I've always liked to write," said Goodykoontz, 78. "I've always treasured my family and friends. I like the idea of holding on to friends, and letters are one way of doing it."

Her letters, written in her cramped, flat, horizontal style, can be difficult to read. Her friends do not always reply. Her family rarely answers; they are close, but they are not letter writers. Occasionally, because Goodykoontz's letters are so regular, because their *content may be so familiar, her letters may sit a day or two before being opened. It doesn't matter. Ann Goodykoontz does not expect answers. She is a giver of news, not a taker.*

At year's end she may have received one letter for every seven mailed. She knows people are too busy to write letters. Letter writing is such a chore. The telephone is easier. There are so few people left who care about writing letters or saving them. Ann Goodykoontz is one of them.

"I've saved letters all over the place," she said. "I just can't throw them out, at least not right away. I have a lot of them marked to be thrown away, but I just can't. The longer you keep them, the harder it is to part with them.

"I've got a friend that's an excellent letter writer, and I save all her letters. A while back she wanted some information from a certain time in her life, and I had it because I had all her letters,"

That's the beauty of letters; they are recorded history. A telephone call is made, then it is gone. Letters can be saved, treasured and rediscovered. Most of us would delight in coming across a family letter written 25, 50 or 75 years ago. The young rarely ask questions of the old until it is too late. But to have letters from the past, letters from a parent or grandparent long gone, even the most mundane of letters that told of life back then, now that would be history.

On Mondays Ann Goodykoontz writes to a daughter in Dallas. On Tuesdays she writes her grandchildren in Rome, N.Y. Their mother was killed in a highway accident two years ago. On Wednesday she writes to a son in West Virginia. On Thursdays she writes a daughter in Lexington, Ky.

She's done that every week since her children left college, got married and began their own lives. Thousands and thousands of letters. "When I write my 5-year-old granddaughter in New York," she said, "I often say something about her mom. I want to keep her memory alive, and the grandchildren are so very dear to us."

Between Thanksgiving and Christmas, Ann Goodykoontz and her husband, Jack, a retired Presbyterian minister, send out 300 Christmas cards, most with handwritten notes. She'll send out more than 100 birthday cards a year. She does it joyfully, unselfishly and lovingly.

"I enjoy thinking about the people I am writing to," she said. "It seems like I can't go a day or two without getting hunches or nudges, then I need to write to get in touch with somebody. And when I do, it seems as if something has always happened, that there's been a reason for the letter, that it was the right thing to do."

Community's compassion is one comfort in the face of tragedy

I have never been very good at accepting things on faith. I tend to look for answers where there are none. I want to know why things happen. I want it explained.

But there are no answers for what happened in-

side Standard Gravure this week. All of us came to work Thursday morning expecting a normal day. An hour later someone barely 75 yards away, carrying an AK-47 assault rifle, was gunning down people I had worked with and a man I had played basketball with, a man I had shared beer and laughter with.

It was all so sudden, so random and so senseless.

And then there were ambulances parked in the middle of Broadway, their sirens screaming and their lights pulsing, and wounded men and women were being carried out of our building on stretchers.

And the dead, wrapped in burgundy blankets, were later carried out to hearses waiting silently in the middle of Armory Place.

And we spent a lot of time looking at three jagged bullet holes in a pressroom window near where the wounded and dead had passed.

I didn't really want to write about all that. I didn't want to think about it. But there is nothing else to think about.

Many of us kept saying it didn't seem real, that it was like a movie and all the people in it would get to go home to their families when it was over. We all tried to hide in those places in the mind reserved for tragedy and death.

We were numb—probably more than we realized—and much of the work that was done was completed out of habit. We watched the events over and over again on television, but it still seemed to be happening someplace else; this couldn't possibly be happening here.

What I remember most of that day are the medics,

company employees and policemen who rushed into the building, the concerned, determined looks on their faces, and the chances they took to care for the wounded.

We saw the televised pictures from the hospitals, the army of doctors and nurses who quickly responded to the need, and the family members who gathered there to console one another, and ask: Why?

We saw the hospital administrators, the counselors and the clergy already in place, offering hope, support and understanding.

There were so many individual kindnesses. A downtown motel offered free rooms to anyone with family members who were injured in the shooting. The Bank of Louisville opened its doors to the hundreds of Courier-Journal employees who had evacuated the building, so they could call home and report they were safe, or get a cup of coffee.

Almost 600 people, many of them strangers to the people who were wounded, rushed to Red Cross donor centers to give blood, some waiting as long as four hours before they could give.

Across town hundreds of people offered food, shelter and comfort to the affected families, and prayer services were scheduled in local churches.

These are the kinds of things that happen in any town struck by tragedy; but this was here, it was happening to us, and it was comforting.

The psychiatrists and psychologists say this is part of the healing process. They say that what every member of every family involved in this tragedy feels about their loss will also trickle out into the rest of the community—*the hurt, the anger, the guilt, the rage and the frustration that must be acknowledged and worked out.*

A motel offering its rooms, a bank offering its telephones and its helpful employees, a neighbor offering to bring over some salad and feed the cat, a church opening its doors—that is the way the rest of us will deal with tragedy.

Yet it doesn't seem enough. So many lives have been shattered. There is already so much bitter debate in this country about the need of anyone to ever have access to an assault rifle. This is already such a gun-mad society that it would now seem impossible to ever stop such random carnage. There are too many lethal weapons out there already that we could never get back.

But the help, compassion and prayers we can offer each other in moments of need and tragedy are the things that keep us going. They are what keep us as civilized as we are.

They may not seem like enough, but at times like these they are all that we have, and neither the families nor our community could heal without them.

A stranger in need and a moment of hesitation

Early this week I was heading out to the parking lot after another tough day at the word processor when

I heard a women screaming from the steps of the old post office building across Sixth Street.

I hadn't seen her climb the steps. When I looked up she was twirling around. Her head was tossed back, her arms thrown out like a child pretending to be a whirling top.

Only the woman wasn't playing; her screams were real, insistent and frightening.

The woman was alone. She made three or four tight circles, pirouetting madly in the bright sun, then fell back clumsily onto the top of the steps. As she fell the small purse she had been carrying flew back over her head. It made a low arc—a final, bizarre detail in this bizarre and unexpected urban drama—and landed just a few feet below the bottom step. Then everything was quiet.

I hesitated for a second—a hesitation I've thought about a lot since—and walked across Sixth Street toward the steps. A woman leaving the newspaper building behind me went back inside to call for an ambulance. A slim man in a white shirt—apparently an employee in the old post office building—headed toward the woman ahead of me.

All the pieces were in place. An obviously mentally disturbed woman was in need of help; an ambulance was being called; two of us were approaching her to offer immediate assistance.

As I crossed the street my first thought was: I wonder if she has a gun.

That moment is frozen in my mind because I can't ever remember worrying about the possibility that someone needing help might have a gun. That worry was new to me. A few years ago my response would have been automatic. I would have run across the street toward the woman without reservations. Now I was thinking that I—or the man in the white shirt ahead of me—could get shot for the trouble.

I knew the worry was mostly irrational. It obviously came from being too close to people whose lives were changed forever when a mentally ill man cut loose with an automatic weapon in a printing plant, or having met the family of a young doctor gunned down in his office by a deranged patient. It wasn't until I was crossing Sixth Street that I realized just how much those stories are still living with me.

I don't know what the man in the white shirt was thinking. But as he cautiously approached the fallen woman she jumped to her feet, then drew back into a corner near the locked door.

She was a big woman. She had the eyes of a cornered animal, dark, angry, uncomprehending eyes that flicked wildly back and forth between the man in the white shirt and me. It would have been a real struggle if the two of us had had to hold her there.

I picked up the woman's purse and was going to hand it to her but thought better of it. It seemed to be too light to be concealing a gun, so I laid it on the top step and backed away like a man backing away from a guard dog.

A dollar bill had fallen from the purse. The man in the white shirt picked it up and tried to hand it to her. She would not take it. She and the man circled the landing at the top of the steps, he trying to give her the bill, she refusing.

"I don't want it," she snapped. "You keep it. I don't want it."

By then the woman had her purse back. I kept looking at it, wondering if I had made a mistake in laying it down, mentally planning where and how I would run if she reached inside to grab something.

The woman never did take her dollar bill. The man in the white shirt, looking every bit as uneasy as I felt, went back inside the building. The small crowd that had gathered left. The woman walked down the steps and headed east on Broadway.

"What are you laughing at?" she snarled. "Do you think something is funny?"

Nobody had been laughing.

The woman crossed Sixth Street, briefly stepped in The Courier-Journal lobby, then kept walking east. She was alone again, which made no sense. The drama couldn't—shouldn't—end there.

It didn't. An ambulance weaved through the Broadway traffic and pulled alongside the woman. The two men in the ambulance kept her company, leading her back to wherever she came from or was going.

She probably won't be there long. She didn't belong on the street, but she had broken no laws. She'll be back, no different for the experience.

But I am.

The facts in this column were checked yard by yard

Bob Hill

Good morning, Ms. Hawkins. Please take a memo for Johnson & Johnson. Have it read:

Dear Messrs. Johnson,

Last week in a moment of foul humor I wrote a column saying there could not possibly be 100 yards of dental floss packaged inside one of your baby blue dental-floss containers, a rectangular container measuring roughly 2 3/4 by 1 1/4 inches.

I was wrong. I am Sorry & Sorry. Please call off your lawyers.

This raising of my dental-floss consciousness occurred during a field trip to Cardinal Stadium, our local baseball and football facility, where a container of 100 yards of Johnson & Johnson waxed Denotape selling for $3.86 (a little high, don't you think?) was unrolled amid minimal fanfare; three firemen kicking a football, an entertainment critic from Kansas City and a Louisville Redbirds ticket salesman.

I do not know what the firemen were doing there. The entertainment critic said he had paid as high as $25 to watch rock stars pass out and was thus more than happy to watch a man unroll 100 yards of dental floss for nothing. The ticket salesman, Rob Rabenecker, just happened to be in the wrong place at the wrong time.

"I was just standing around the office," said Rabenecker, "and they told me some

guy wanted to come out here and unroll 100 yards of dental floss. I thought he was promoting dental hygiene or something,"

The plan was devilishly clever: Rabenecker was to stand on one goal line holding one end of the floss. The entertainment critic was to stand at about the 50-yard line to help support the thin, waxy strand. And the columnist would march resolutely toward that far goal line and pay dirt.

"This," said Rabenecker, "is the first time anybody's asked me to do this all year."

It was a wet and blustery day, and there was some fear the dental floss might break before midfield, but history cannot wait for the weather. Rabenecker grabbed his end of the floss, the entertainment critic adjusted his sunglasses, and the march was on. Let me tell you, gentlemen, it is the rare and privileged man who gets to unroll 100 yards of dental floss at once. It literally hummed out of its container, smoothly, evenly and with nary a snag.

John Hughes and Bob Hill doing some serious measuring.

At 50 yards the entertainment critic, a man who looks as if he hasn't eaten a full meal since the '37 Flood, stepped neatly into the picture and grabbed the floss in a reverse, double-knuckle finger hold.

By the time your dental floss had stretched out 80 yards, even the firemen stopped kicking the football to watch, obviously thrilled to have lucked into a small slice of scientific discovery.

As always, it was that last five yards to the goal line that proved the toughest, that moment when the mind is willing but the dental floss may be weak.

But we made it, gentlemen! 100 yards! Then 101, 102, 103 and, finally, 104 wonderful yards!

Rabenecker, even from 312 feet away, looked ecstatic. The entertainment critic was mildly impressed, but said you'd never make it on a Canadian football field. Nevertheless, next week we may take on kite string.

$3.70-per-hour guard watches over high price horseflesh

The man guards at least $2 million worth of Churchill Downs horseflesh for $3.70 an hour, but that's the way *it is in the Sport of Kings, and the guard wasn't complaining. He said he couldn't give his name because his employer, Pinkerton's Inc., said he would be violating company rules, and he seemed to accept that, too.*

At 21, he already has a pretty good idea of what's out there. He stood at the corner of his barn wearing a Pinkerton-blue uniform that was about a size too large, so he looked even smaller than his 145 pounds, and maybe even a little more vulnerable.

He was one of those people who tells you more about his life than you have any right to expect, at least until you realize that he has nothing to hide, no axes to grind; he is just a 21-year-old kid guarding $2 million worth of horses.

His father left home before he was born, reappearing once in a while on Christmas day, leaving only the barest sense of what a father should be.

"He was an orphan," said the guard, trying to explain his dad.

The guard, his sister and their mother lived in the Iroquois housing project until he was 9 years old. When he was 12, his mother remarried.

"She married a black man," the guard said. "My real dad heard about that and he didn't like it. He just showed up one day and took me out to get an ice cream cone. He asked me if I wanted to come live with him, and I told him, no, I'm happy here. That's all there was to it. I haven't seen him since.

"I would like to see him again now, to kinda meet him on more mature terms. I'd like to sit down with him and ask him what went wrong with his marriage. But Mom tells me I might be better off if I didn't."

The guard went through South Louisville grade and junior high schools, and finished two years at Stuart High School.

"I guess they quit on me as much as I quit on them," he said. "I just wasn't going to school. I was getting high a lot, drinking and smoking pot. Sometimes I'd go to school stoned and I wouldn't know what was going on. I had the ability to do the work, but I just wouldn't do it. . . . I'm mostly over that now."

He quit school and lived where he could, bumming off his mother and stepfather, but ignoring their discipline.

"I used to get grounded a lot," he said. "They'd tell me to stay home for a week, but as soon as they went to work I was gone. I wouldn't listen to them."

He left home at 17, moving in with the family of a girlfriend. The girl's father liked him, encouraged him and got him started in heating and air-conditioning repair.

"I moved back home when I was 19," he said, "I was doing more or less odd jobs and working for an outfit in New Albany. I've learned a lot. I could put in central air conditioning myself if I had the boss's tools."

Last April, during a layoff, he went to Pinkerton's Inc. looking for part-time work. He had passed his high school equivalency test ("I never even studied") and did not have a police record, so he was hired.

"I did look like a bum," he said. "I had shoulder-length hair. They told me to cut it, so I got a burr."

There was no training. He was told where to report at Churchill Downs, what barn to watch, and whom to keep away from the horses.

"Mostly I was guarding Royal Roberto," he said. "He came in last. He might still be out there running."

The guard liked the work, the chance to be around famous people, and the horses. And he fit into the picture: the wealthy horsemen and the $100-a-week stable help, the million-dollar horses and the barely minimum-wage security force.

This April he was preparing to call Pinkerton when the company called him, asking him to come back for the Derby. He was issued a uniform, waited about five days, and then the company called him at 10 a.m. asking him to report by noon.

"So I come down," he said.

There have been problems. The guard was late to work several days and did not wear his tie one day, angering his employer. That's also part of the system.

"As far as what the horses are worth and what they're paying me, well, I guess I never thought about it," he said. "If it come right down to it, if somebody wanted to hurt one of my horses, I'd pretty much stand up for the horse. I'd punch somebody's lights out.

"I enjoy seeing my horses run. It makes me feel good just to be here, kinda like I'll always have a memoir. Even if they was paying me $2 an hour I'd protect the horses. I'd have to. It's my job."

STAY TUNED. BOB INTERVIEWS A GAS PUMP

Where do the column ideas come from? With Sharon Baugher, who found an uninvited guest in her house with a gun, a guest for whom she ended up making two bologna and cheese sandwiches.

My alleged conversation with a gas pump named Sheila came because she kept talking to me, and all I wanted was gas.

The column about the guy who returned about $100,000 in somewhat-found cash to a bank that had just been robbed, and then saw the same bank deny him a $500 loan, came from a friend of the rejected honorable man.

Another just-waiting-at-the-bus-stop column was about a woman living on $220-a-month in Social Security payments and clutching 75 cents in her hand to visit her sick husband in a Southern Indiana nursing home. She could only afford to see him twice a week, I was waiting at the same bus stop to take what was then called the Toonerville Trolly to go buy tickets for the Kentucky Derby, admittedly a once-in-a-life extravagance, but somewhat more expensive than 75 cents.

The case of the 'polite' burglar

The man who forced his way into Sharon Baugher's home at 1:10 p.m. this past Wednesday said he had a gun. Baugher believed him. She had no choice but to do what the man said. Her two babies were home with her. She had to protect them.

The Baugher home is in a very nice subdivision of mostly brick homes off Bardstown Road. Baugher's husband, Jim, had left the house only a few minutes before 1 p.m. He had taken their oldest child, Adam, 5, with him. Baugher had Jennifer, age 2 months, in her arms when the man pushed into her home. Their second son, Eric, 22 months, was asleep in his bedroom.

"I heard someone at the front door, and I thought it was Jim coming back home for something," Mrs. Baugher said. "When I went to the door, there was a little man standing there. He wasn't much bigger than I was.

"He had his head down and he mumbled something, but I couldn't understand him. I unlocked the front door, and he pushed me back and came in. That was a mistake. I never should have opened the door."

The man was in his 60s. He wore a brown jacket and baggy gray work pants. He was thin and angular but clean-shaven, and he didn't look like a bum.

"He told me he had a gun," Baugher said. "He told me to go get my purse."

Her purse was in a back bedroom. She was still carrying Jennifer in her arms as she walked back to get it. The man followed her back.

"The man noticed Eric's door was shut when we walked back," Baugher said. "He asked me who was in there, and I told him my son was asleep. He opened the door very carefully, peeked at Eric, then shut his door very quietly."

Baugher grabbed her purse and took it to the living room, where she dumped it on her couch.

"I handed him my money," she said, "and I gave him my change purse, too."

The man took about $30 and some credit cards. By this time, Baugher was a little less frightened. In fact, she thought she could have knocked the man down and escaped.

"I had a can of Mace in my purse," she said. "I always thought I would use it in moments like that, but I didn't. I kept thinking the whole time I could get away from him. But I didn't want to leave Eric."

The intruder took the money and cards, then asked if he could use the Baughers' telephone. Baugher said of course, and showed him the telephone in the kitchen.

"He called somebody and used some kind of nickname," she said. "He mumbled a lot, and all I could hear him say was that he was at a certain address. I was standing by the door. I could have gotten away. But Eric was asleep,"

"He never touched me," she said. "In fact, if you can

call a burglar polite, he was polite. He was like somebody's grandpa,"

Baugher said she was in a state of mild shock, but felt certain the man would not harm her. All she could do was hold her baby and do what the man asked.

But she wasn't ready for his next request.

"Could you please fix me something to eat?" he asked her.

"What?" she said.

"Just some sandwiches to take with me," he answered.

Startled, Baugher went to the refrigerator and took out some bologna and cheese.

"Do you want me to hold the baby while you make the sandwiches?" he asked.

"No!" she said.

She began making the sandwiches, but not to the intruder's satisfaction.

"I would like some mayonnaise," he said.

When she finished two sandwiches, she gave them to the man.

"Don't you have something to put those in?" he asked. Baugher put them in Baggies.

"He asked if I had something to drink," she said. "I told him milk and juice was all I had, but he didn't want that."

The intruder took the two sandwiches and walked slowly to the front door.

"He turned around like he was going to say something," Baugher said. "But he just said, 'Thanks,' and left. I was kinda stunned,"

She said he had apparently parked his car in her

driveway. She waited a few seconds, then ran to the window.

"He was driving slowly down the street, just like anybody else," she said. "I could have gotten his license number, but I never thought about it."

She ran to the phone and called the Jefferson County Police. Then she called her husband, broke down and began crying.

Her 22-month-old son never woke up.

The happy gas you get with 'service' makes it easy not to get too pumped up

I needed some gas early yesterday morning, so I stopped by one of those mega-service stations soon to be fortified with a 10-foot wall of bagged cypress mulch and pulled up to Pump 16.

"How are you?" the pump asked.

"Gas pumps can't talk," I answered.

"My name is Sheila," said the pump. "I can talk."

I looked around. Most modern gas stations have a speaker system where the attendant inside the store can talk to customers at the pumps. The attendant here was busy with a customer, though. He wasn't even looking my way. I was having a conversation with a gas pump.

"So, do you come here often?" Sheila asked.

Actually, I do. The station is handy, open 24 hours a day It sells the working journalist's breakfast: sugar-rich apple turnovers and 96-ounce soft drinks. I can buy a Powerball lottery ticket whenever the jackpot crosses into the $60 million, fool's-gold plateau. But I wasn't going to spill my guts to a gas pump.

"Often enough," I told Sheila.

I was annoyed. I longed for the old-fashioned pump, the simple, honest kind where you pulled up, lifted the nozzle, filled the tank, paid the attendant and left.

Now the self-service customer is forced to make decisions.

The customer must select "inside pay" or "outside pay."

The customer must study octane ratings the way dieting secretaries read "Thirty Days to a Better You."

The customer must choose "unleaded," "better-unleaded" or "super-unleaded."

The customer must request the car wash, the hot wax.

The customer must worry about the environmentally improved nozzles and reformulated gas.

The customer must "Push to Start."

The customer must pay with cash or credit card, punch the right computer buttons, be sure to "Pull receipt firmly."

I don't want to deal with life's complexities at a gas pump. All I want is gas.

"So Sheila," I said, "what's a nice pump like you doing in a place like this?"

Sheila didn't do coy sarcasm. She was pure business, all the way up to her "Stop Engine-No Smoking" sign. But I did wonder if Pump 16 was programmed to be a "Sam" if a woman pulled up. It was just a thought.

"I am the first in a new line of gas pumps," Sheila said. "Our company surveys have shown the average person spends 37 minutes a month just standing beside a gas pump, squeezing the trigger finger. Our company believes we could offer many other personal services during that time."

Actually, if you can ignore the fumes, I mostly enjoy those 37 minutes of down time. Most of the gas-purchasing decisions have been made by then. You get to just stand there, lost in thought, watch digital numbers race past, even play a little game with yourself: Geez, those numbers are cookin'. Can I really stop this sucker right on $10?

All that's left to do after that is to slop some gas on your shoes while replacing the nozzle, then go inside and stand in line another 37 minutes while the guy in front of you buys 9,000 exotic lottery tickets.

But I wanted to play Sheila along, see what else a gas pump might have to offer.

"I understand what you're saying," I told her. "It's the old captive-audience thing, sort of like the advertising on the wall above urinals."

"We prefer to call it marketing the opportunity," Sheila whispered.

"For instance?"

"There's a lot of wasted space on gas pumps. We may sell advertising, add automatic bank tellers, sports scores, motor-voter registration, even give tourist information or stock reports. We could go online, surf the Web, offer airline reservations and 1-900 telephone numbers."

I looked around again. The station was bathed in that peculiar, death-like, all-night-gas-station light. I did not want to be seen arguing with a gasoline pump about 1-900 phone service. I leaned toward the pump:

"Listen, Sheila. We are talking about a major philosophical difference here. All I want to do is buy gas, which already requires an advanced degree in macroeconomics. So stick a nozzle in the rest of that stuff."

Sheila went silent. I went inside to pay my $10 and find a 96-ounce soft drink. When I came back out, Sheila was talking to a good-looking thirty-something guy in a Camaro about Club Med reservations. I couldn't be sure, but I thought I heard her say something about the Caribbean and free suntan oil.

Man returns robbers' loot to bank but can't get loan

What we have here is an O. Henry short story with an ending the Grinch could fully appreciate.

Think of it the next time fate throws $100,000 in cash at your feet.

It began Dec. 20 at the Family Funeral Care funeral home in Louisville's Portland area. Employee Lois Allen had car trouble. Danny Johnson, an old friend, came by the funeral home to fix it. Suddenly, they heard frantic pounding on the funeral home's locked front door followed by breaking glass.

"I freaked out," Allen said. *"I didn't know what was going on."* Four armed men had robbed the National City Bank branch next door. They ran from the bank, needed a place to hide and tried to smash their way into the funeral home. When they saw Allen and Johnson inside, they ran away, two heading across North 26th Street, the other two rushing for a car in an alley.

Johnson started to run after them. Allen screamed at him to come back, that it wasn't safe. Police later found a gun in the alley. Johnson returned to find the robbers had dropped clothing, a knit hat and three bags of money on the porch.

And cash was spilling out of one of them, a plastic grocery bag.

"It was bundles and bundles of cash," Allen said. *"The $10,000 wrappers were filled with $50 and $100 bills. There must have been 10 bundles in that bag."*

Johnson started to return the money to the bank, then thought better of it, fearing that he might be considered a robber. Instead, he put it just inside the funeral home's door. Allen called 911 to advise police of the robbery.

Soon, 2nd District police were swarming into the area. Johnson motioned them down the street toward the area where the men had fled. Police captured two suspects in a car at 34th and Jefferson streets after a chase.

Police now suspect the other two robbers—playing it cool—walked into the nearby Victor Mathis florist shop, where they bought roses and a teddy bear. They paid cash and made two phone calls—one for a cab—before leaving the store on foot. The men are still at large.

With police chasing the robbers, Allen and Johnson stood guard over the astounding amount of cash at their feet. Nearby residents who had seen the four robbers bang on the door came over to look at the money, but Allen and Johnson asked them to leave. Both confessed to a little temptation—police might never know which robbers fled with how much money—but they never seriously considered taking any.

"Oh sure, it was right at Christmas, my car had just blown up, and Danny was having a tough time financially too," Allen said. "But I would never steal any of their money."

Johnson, who works construction during the summer and drives a tow truck at other times—was having a tough enough time that only days earlier he had applied for a $500 loan at the very bank branch that had been robbed.

"I just wanted to get caught up, pay some bills," he said.

Within a half-hour of the robbery, police returned to the funeral home and learned about the money. An officer guarded the money until the FBI came, followed by a bank examiner. That night Johnson got a call at home from a bank officer.

"When the woman identified herself, I first thought it was about my loan. But she didn't know anything about that," he said. "She told me banks don't normally offer rewards, but in this case it was going to give me $100."

Johnson took out the $35 it cost for the parts to repair Allen's car and gave the rest to Allen.

Two days later, the bank told him his $500 loan

had been denied. They said he'd been too slow making payments on previous loans. Johnson admitted being slow to pay but said he had always paid in full by the time the final payment was due. Having chased robbers and stood guard over the bank's money he thought it might cut him some slack, but it didn't.

So George Villiar, Allen's father, lent Johnson the $500. Villiar has co-signed Johnson's notes before, and Johnson has always paid him back.

Human trust over bottom-line business. That's what's known as going the distance.

Inspired thoughts on Derby, fate, fortune

I was waiting for a bus—the Toonerville trolley connector—to take me to Commonwealth Convention Center to pick up tickets for the Kentucky Derby Festival Parade. The old woman said she was waiting for a regular TARC bus to Southern Indiana to visit her husband in a nursing home.

I've never before bought parade tickets, mostly preferring to get out of Louisville before its downtown streets fill with people carrying aluminum lawn chairs and vendors selling aluminum balloons. I love the Great Balloon Race, endure the forced bravado of The Great Steamboat Race, generally like any Great Parade, worry about the Great Sameness of much of the Derby Week stuff.

So this year—our 20th year in Louisville—my wife and I decided on a new tack; attack Derby Week head-on. We invited family and our best friends from high school to the Great Show. We vowed to take in every Derby sight and sound we could manage, leaving no hoof unturned. Instead of fighting Derby Week ennui, we vowed to go with it. On its terms. With feeling. Just this once. Or twice.

The old woman was short—wearing black shoes and a worn blue dress. Her hair was long, uncombed, with wide streaks of gray. She held three quarters in her hands, constantly pressing them together, rubbing them the way a worried man rubs the tips of his fingers. A regular TARC bus had just left the stop, the woman had spoken with its driver, learned she was an hour early for the bus she needed.

I don't wait well, have always marveled at people who could. The woman accepted her situation with the patience—or the resignation—of someone who has waited before. She walked around a little, as if looking for a place to sit, but there were no benches near the bus stop.

She neatly stacked her quarters in one hand, shifted them around, the coins clinking faintly. It would cost her 75 cents to ride the bus to visit her husband between 8:30 a.m. and 3:30 p.m. The return trip—if made between 3:30 and 5:30 p.m.—would be $1.

It was mid-morning, bright and cheerful. Spring—Derby fever—hung in the air like the scent of magnolias. Having gotten into the spirit of the thing, my wife and I had actually begun looking forward to it. She bought new dresses, an official Derby Hat, began pol-

ishing the plastic forks. I vowed to polish my shoes.

We mapped out a Great Plan, eager to show off Louisville, share its two minutes in the world spotlight, become as Derbystruck as first-time tourists. I had just purchased tickets to a Derby Week concert before heading to the bus stop, was mentally lining up other events, other purchases.

With little prodding the woman became talkative. Her husband had been a security guard in another state, had gotten beaten up in a fight, filed a lawsuit seven years ago, it hadn't yet gotten to court. They had moved to Louisville—her hometown—but her husband's health failed. He was placed in an Indiana nursing home because no places were available in Louisville.

She receives $220 a month in Social Security payments, lives in a subsidized apartment. He receives $540 a month, but all but $30 goes to the nursing home; he had $50,000 in medical bills paid by the government. Twice a week she puts aside $1.75 for round-trip bus fare to see her husband, all she can afford.

Perhaps all this is some level of guilt disguised as slice-of-life, but I don't think so. I didn't feel any urge to hand over my concert tickets, give her money, or even a ride to Indiana. I still don't. Our social services net seemed to be doing its job. TARC can handle the rest.

Our lives intersected for about five minutes, but the woman has never quite left my mind. More than anything I guess I wonder how many things must go right—or wrong—to allow some people to be buying Derby Week parade tickets and force others to hoard quarters for bus fare to go see their husbands in nursing homes.

McDONALDS, MY FATHER'S CHAIR, A WEDDING

People often ask me about a favorite column, a task equal to picking a favorite sunrise or sunset. So many, each a little different, some more personal than others. It almost depends on the day, the location, where you or your mind is traveling or resting at the moment.

One was about a woman who handed food across the counter to me at a McDonalds for years. On the fun side I went outside early one Spring morning and sat in a lawn chair waiting, ala Charlie Brown and the Great Pumpkin, for The Great Daffodil.

A tragic column was about a father who accidentally lost his five-month-old daughter. On the reflective side, I sat in my father's chair while he was in the hospital recovering from a heart attack thinking about our relationship. Then came a weekend when we ended up at a family wedding and good friend's father's funeral back-to-back.

Bob Hill

Humanity free with purchase of burger and Coke

If I ever did know her name, I've forgotten it. It doesn't matter much. She was the girl—a young woman, really—who worked behind the counter at McDonald's. I was the guy who always ordered two cheeseburgers and a Coke—more recently amended to two hamburgers and a Diet Coke—to go.

This went on, sometimes three or four times a week, for months. By then, of course, dialogue wasn't necessary. She'd almost have the stuff waiting by the time I walked in the door. I'd have my $1.75 in hand. Rarely has commerce been more swift or satisfactory.

Well, you know how it is with people you meet almost every day in a store or fast-food restaurant. They become familiar. Conversation becomes easy In a way, they become friends, even if you don't know their names. You care about them. You begin to look forward to seeing them. More important, you notice when they are not around.

Alas, a few months ago McDonald's moved her from working behind the walk-in counter to handing hamburgers and french fries out the drive-in window as the public rolled past.

Whatever she had to say after that she would toss over her shoulder while passing white sacks out the window.

Usually the public was backed up bumper to bumper

and nearly out into the street.

You do wonder what America did for lunch before the invention of drive-in windows.

She was amazingly cheerful almost every time I saw her. I know it is not always possible to be that way when a hungry America is continually rolling past your window asking for more ketchup or dropping its change onto the drive.

There must be moments when french fries are best delivered through an open window and into the face of a screaming child at about 40 miles per hour, cold soft drink to follow.

Indeed, the next generation of saints might come from young men and women who spent 5, 10, even 15 uncomplaining years handing round breakfast muffins through rectangular windows.

Imagine, if you can, saying a short prayer to St. Buffy, the patron saint of scrambled eggs.

Yet, and through it all, Our Lady of the Window at least appeared to be happy in her work, even if she wasn't. That's close enough for me. Optimism is often its own reward.

Yesterday, for the first time, we were able to talk a little longer. She had to catch a bus home and had to walk a few blocks to meet it. She was even more cheerful than usual. She said she is getting married in a big ceremony in May. She said she plans on being married for a long, long time.

There was something so appealing and optimistic about that, even from a young woman whose name I did not know, whose fiancé I had never seen, whose family I had never met.

Somehow you never think about all those people behind a counter at McDonald's getting married, raising families and then lining up, bumper to bumper, for dinner at a fast-food restaurant.

I know the statistics about the number of marriages that survive. I know it is not easy. But I would be willing to bet three weeks' worth of lunch that they make it.

April 10, 1984

Where were you, Great Daffodil?

It is 12:06 a.m. Wednesday. I am sitting in the fog and darkness of my backyard. I am facing east toward a distant sun and the dented, galvanized beauty of my half-dozen garbage cans.

I am waiting for spring.

And maybe, so help me Linus, The Great Daffodil.

Good grief!

Spring is due in at 12:22 a.m. I had never waited her in before, just accepting on faith she would show up unescorted some time after "Laverne and Shirley" and before "The Star-Spangled Banner" sign-off.

But this year is different. I have been particularly tired of this winter. A simple yet elegant greeting for spring is in order.

So I am sitting alone on my children's basketball court. My children claim it is their father's basketball court, but that is another story.

I am sitting in a lawn chair, a dubious contraption of tubular aluminum and green and white plastic—all in all the absolute essence of modern spring.

I am wearing my best sport coat, a daring, V-necked T-shirt, jeans that have been washed to the color of wood ashes and red basketball shoes, Chuck Taylor Converse All-Stars.

I am holding a crystalline glass of white wine in one hand. I am taking notes (carefully interviewing myself) with the other. I am feeling a little stupid about the whole thing.

I am wondering if The Great Daffodil will arrive by gardener's wheelbarrow or just will simply push up through the ground and slam-dunk me through my children's basketball goal. I am wondering what I am doing here. I am wondering what the neighbors might be thinking.

My wife accepts my greeting of spring with the normal calm of a journalist's wife. She is in bed asleep. She wouldn't even pour the wine.

It is 12:17 a.m. Wednesday. Night sounds, pressed close to the ground by the heavy fog, carry clearly to my backyard.

A towboat beats heavily up the Ohio River a half-mile away. A farmer's geese stir, cry angrily into the night, tuck their graceful necks under smooth white wings and settle back to sleep.

A jet airplane, a young calf and a distant dog, undoubtedly a denter of garbage cans, perform in turn, a cappella, and the night closes in again.

Our yard light throws long shadows across the back field. Dark shadows from my split-rail fence angle cra-

zily into my tiny patch of woods. The deep shadow of my lawn chair could easily hold The Great Daffodil, lock, stock and stamen.

Advance public-relations types for The Great Daffodil already have been at work. My crocuses, clumped thickly in purple and white patches, arrived last week on slender green feet.

My fairy's circle of tiny daffodils bloomed yellow on dark green for the first time Tuesday. My irises and lilies are stirring light green. My poppies have put on star-shaped leaves and, faithful Republicans that they are, are out looking for more real estate to control.

It is 12:21 a.m. Wednesday. I remain a solitary nut in a lawn chair looking glumly around a fog-filled yard for a great spring flower, my vigil lighted solely by a yard light and Public Service Indiana.

I don't even have a decent speech prepared if The Great Daffodil does show up. I am a man who dislikes speaking before Kiwanis and Lions clubs. What am I supposed to say to a 12-foot green and yellow flower?

Good grief!

So, as the countdown toward spring continues, I am gazing anxiously around my backyard. I am beginning to believe in The Great Daffodil. I am continuing to wonder how a yard that is so friendly by day can be so mysterious at night.

It is 12:22 a.m. Wednesday. Spring has arrived. I lift my crystalline wine glass in the general direction of my dented garbage cans. There is no response. There is no Great Daffodil.

It is 12:28 a.m. Wednesday. I can see my biggest mistake was not bringing the wine bottle out with me.

I shift uneasily in my lawn chair. The fog presses in: I am thinking of my favorite "Peanuts" cartoon strip. I have searched for years for a copy of it. Charlie Brown is pitching in a baseball game. He is, of course, being shelled. The next-to-the-last cartoon box shows a disgusted Charlie saying:

"Good grief, 184 to 0."

In the last box, a forlorn Charlie asks, "How can we lose when we're so sincere?"

It is 12:34 a.m. Wednesday. I am back in the house. But I leave the lawn chair outside on my children's basketball court. You can never tell who might need it.

March 24, 1979

Baby's father deserves compassion, not righteous indignation

When our daughter was about a year old, I made a quick trip to visit her maternal grandfather—one of the few trips we ever made without my wife. Her father was a farmer, a small, wiry, interesting man given to hard work and tall stories—the latter always sprinkled with just enough facts to lend them credibility, but not quite credence.

It was January, the temperature well below zero; cold, but not the type of weather to keep people indoors in Northern Illinois, where frigid weather comes with the corn-stubble. On the way to the farm I spotted my father-in-law's car at the local coffee shop, a favorite haunt for him and his neighbors, especially when the winter winds blew in from Iowa.

By then I had spent days listening to my father-in-law's coffee-shop stories, his eternal claims of poverty, his tales of wandering the country during the Great Depression, working the Kansas wheat fields and the Montana sheep ranches. I could recite many of his stories—as could his audience—but this was a funny, gregarious, story-loving bunch that would invariably indulge him—and thus, themselves. What else was there to do in Northern Illinois in January?

I pulled into the crowded parking lot near the gas station—my daughter in a car seat sound asleep, well-bundled in several layers of snowsuit. I didn't want to wake her, or take her inside.

And I was afraid to leave the car's motor running for fear of engine fumes. I decided I would turn off the engine, run inside to tell her grandfather we had arrived, then come back out.

What I did next has haunted me—if I let myself think about it—for 30 years. I went inside the coffee shop, somehow got to listening to the farm stories, and forgot about my daughter. I don't know how long it was—10 minutes, 15 minutes, 20 minutes—before the name Jennifer suddenly flashed in my mind. I ran outside, opened the car door, and there she was: awake, grinning at me, none the worse for the experience, although her eyes did have a puzzled edge to them. Today, even as I write this sentence, terrible feelings of guilt wash over me.

Those feelings were even more powerful last week-

end as I read the tragic story of Brian Swett, the University of Louisville employee whose 5-month-old daughter died, apparently of heat prostration, after he went inside to work, forgetting she was in the car.

How could that have happened? How could somebody forget a child in a car, forget to take her to a day-care center? Was it some distraction, a preoccupation, a change of domestic routine that had not yet become habit? All I know is that we are human; it can happen; I did it. I love my children more than life itself, but I once left my daughter alone in a car on a frozen January morning.

I was disappointed—but not surprised—at the level of righteous indignation, if not hatred, aimed at Swett by a few callers to local talk shows. We can all be so good at raising other people's children, at pointing fingers, at being judgmental. Swett's friends and co-workers have nothing but praise, sympathy and respect for the man and his family. The murder charge against him—are we worried about another Susan Smith episode here?—is absurd, ludicrous, cruel.

We all—if we are honest—can remember moments when we accidentally placed our children at risk, were not as careful as we should have been, got busy and forgot them.

We can all look back and shudder. How can any parent examine a lifetime of raising children and not feel empathy, compassion and aching sorrow for Brian Swett and his family?

I was lucky; our daughter recently graduated from a fine university; our son breezed home last weekend to leave a gift of what he does best—photo images. Our *family remains intact. Brian Swett will never again know that feeling. Isn't that burden enough?*

July 18, 1995

From my father's chair, a glimpse of genes and generations

I am sitting in my father's chair in my parents' home. The chair is at a corner of the room near the kitchen alcove, a bookcase on its right, a floor lamp by its side. The chair is stiffly upright, more comfortable than it looks, brown in color, with flecks of white.

My father is in the hospital recovering from a heart attack; the prognosis is good, but he is 75 years old. Most of the family has gathered to be with my mother, to visit my father, to wrap our arms around this moment and make it go away.

I've become so accustomed to seeing my father in his chair that I can see his image there even when the chair is empty. He sits in a certain way, his fingers folded prayer-like against the front of his nose, or with his arms at his side, unconsciously rubbing his thumbs against his forefingers, lost in thought.

He will leap into the conversation for a time, then sit back, watch from a distance.

What's odd is that I now find myself doing the same things. Often when I write, pausing between thoughts, I find my fingers rubbing against my face, or *folded on top of each other. Often when I am watching television or lost in thought, I will find myself unconsciously rubbing my thumbs against my forefingers. I will argue for a time—our family gatherings are often closer to group encounter sessions than anything you might see on "The Partridge Family"—then sit back and listen.*

These are obviously hereditary echoes, pulses of my father passed on to me, which I may have passed on to my son or daughter.

They are as easily identifiable as our other similar traits: personality, creativity, work ethic, sense of humor.

It is interesting to think about how far back some of these characteristics might go. Did our great-great-great-grandfather sit around on a bushel of potatoes in Ireland unconsciously rubbing his thumbs against his forefingers?

Did a great-great-great-grandmother in France press her fingers against her face while staring off in thought?

Are men more likely to inherit the unconscious traits and habits of their fathers, daughters the mannerisms of their mothers? It seems to me my wife has more of the gestures, mannerisms and expressions of her mother than her father. Or perhaps I am just more conscious of how I imitate my father's acts, especially now.

Nor do many of these mannerisms seem especially unique to our family. What is it in the human genes that makes us press our fingers against our lips when in thought, or unconsciously rub fingers together?

What is it about humans that collectively make us

throw our arms up in disgust, shake our fists in anger, cover our faces in shame? Why do we purse our lips in thought, scratch our heads when lost for an answer, shrug our shoulders in dismay?

Did we learn those things watching others, or did cave men and women first shake their fists at the inconsiderate heavens and the futile gesture has been passed down to us ever since? Where do the new mannerisms jump on, the old jump off? Maybe there is a common genetic pool only 10 characteristics deep, and all of us are swimming around in it.

What's odd is that I find myself imitating my father's mannerisms more and more as I get older. Or perhaps I am just more conscious of them. One of my favorite essays—it was written by E. B. White—described a father and son walking together, and for just a moment the father could not remember if he were the boy, or the man. He remembered taking walks with his father in the same fashion, and time and genes had begun playing tricks on him. It all seemed so familiar that the generations didn't seem to matter.

I find comfort in this genetic mirroring, the generations forming a tunnel of imagery that reflect forward through time. That feeling is surely heightened because I am sitting in my father's chair and he is in a hospital bed, thoroughly irritated at being there, curious to know the full details of the medical technique aimed at making him well, uncomfortable with his thoughts of mortality.

I like to sit in his chair, although I would prefer that he were in it. It's a good chair from which to think, argue, rub my fingers against my face, rub my thumbs against my forefingers and think about time, family and life.

March 12, 1994

Through tears of joy and sorrow, the common denominator is love

---

Jim and Laurie both liked country music and the boot-scootin' kind of dancing that came with it. He was tall, blond, good-looking and quiet, an ex-professional football player with a wonderful grin. She was tall, very pretty and outgoing.

They were always a handsome couple, two-stepping their way around the outer lanes of country music.

Their wedding was to be a family affair, a big, rolling, much-anticipated event done with style, planning, food and drink, country music and The Lord's Prayer—in somewhat equal measures. That was on Saturday night.

Gary and Sally are old friends. We went to high school in a time and place where our friendship became cemented in common memories. We could be apart for years and be comfortable again in seconds. My wife and I—and our children—were going to stay at their home for the wedding, attend it together. But when we arrived Friday night, we learned Gary's father had died Thursday night. The funeral would be Sunday. A soloist would sing The Lord's Prayer.

The wedding was in a big Presbyterian church with stained-glass windows. Jim stood at the altar in his tuxedo, grinning. Laurie looked beautiful in a white dress that hinted of country music. Her brother played "The Wedding March" on his fiddle. The minister, a man with a gift for being able to say exactly the right thing, stood at the altar, grinning along with Jim. After Scriptures were read and rings exchanged, the soloist sang a joyous Lord's Prayer, her voice filling the church, tears running down the cheeks of the families.

Gary's father, George Scott, had been a farmer, living in the same house for 72 of his 75 years. He had been married to Gary's mother 55 years. His funeral was in the same Methodist church where Gary and Sally had been married, where their daughter had been married, where my wife and I had been married.

The casket was placed in a long hallway near the sanctuary, the funeral flowers crowded close around it: red roses, pink carnations, white lilies. George Scott had died at home, peacefully, surrounded by those he loved, those who loved him. A granddaughter placed a gift in his casket: a jar of dry-roasted peanuts. The family linked arms, smiled at the peanuts—and cried.

The wedding reception was held at a museum-restaurant where tables surrounded a big, oak dance floor. The happy couple were toasted with champagne, then gracefully danced around the floor. The guests watched, smiled, applauded and shared in their happiness.

The minister at the funeral had a gift for being able to bring smiles, even laughter, as the family shared stories of George Scott. He had been a small man;

hard-working, tough, very proud of his strength. One mourner cried and laughed at the same time as he remembered how George would always shake your hand until it hurt. A granddaughter tearfully remembered how her grandfather would pick her up, hold her. A daughter-in-law remembered how, as a joke, she had given him long underwear with an electric cord so he could stay warm at night.

"I don't think he ever used them," she said, and everyone laughed.

Jim and Laurie laughed, danced, linked arms and posed for pictures until well after midnight. They had been certain to thank their parents "who have shown us what true commitment and love are all about," and "God, who brought us together and made this love possible."

The soloist at George Scott's funeral sang "Amazing Grace," and then, near the benediction, sang The Lord's Prayer—tears welling up in the eyes of his family. The service ended with an upbeat, hand-clapping rendition of "Soon and Very Soon."

George Scott's casket was taken to Ohio Grove Cemetery, a country spot near the old home place. One of the mourners held a great-granddaughter in his strong arms, an answered prayer, a continuation, a glory forever, amen.

Aug. 30, 1994

'Everybody thinks their mother is the greatest'

It fell to the Rev. Kevin Cosby, pastor of St. Stephen Baptist Church, to bring together all the tender emotions evoked by the death of Odessa Lee Grady Clay, the woman whose family called her "Mama Bird."

Cosby—a slim, elegant, passionate man—spoke of towering trees, and before him sat Muhammad Ali, whose fame has spread around the world, and his brother, Rahaman Ali, who found his own way in Muhammad's shadow. Speaking of the unseen roots that anchor and nourish great trees, Cosby spread his arms wide over Odessa Clay's gilt-edged casket:

"If the tree stood tall," he said, "it must be because of the roots."

In time Odessa met Cassius Marcellus Clay, a gregarious, fun-loving sign painter with a taste for alcohol. They dated three years before marrying, then lived on Grand Avenue, where their eldest son, Cassius Marcellus Clay Jr. grew up. In time Cassius Clay Jr. took up boxing, won an Olympic gold medal, became heavyweight champion of the world. He declared his Muslim faith and changed his name. Through it all he could always go home, the source of his strength.

Odessa Clay was mother of one of the most remarkable men in sports history, yet she mowed her own grass, cooked her own meals, delighted in her own jam cake and settled for a comfortable, middle-class home *when she could have had a mansion.*

Hundreds of people went to her visitation at A. D. Porter & Sons Funeral Home on Tuesday night, a teeming mix of men in dark suits, women in fine dresses and youths in basketball jerseys. Her death Sunday at 77, almost six months after a stroke had left her unable to speak, was almost a relief.

"We would tell her, 'Grandmother, we love you,'" Alecea Ali said. "She could only nod her head in reply."

Her family, Rahaman and Muhammad among them, had been with her continually at the Hurstbourne Care Centre.

"Everybody thinks their mother is the greatest," Muhammad Ali said to me Tuesday night.

The service was a thoughtful, judicious and ultimately uplifting mix of Baptist and Muslim. The mourners gathered in a long, flowing line down the center of the church; Rahaman and Muhammad slowly bent over the casket to kiss their mother goodbye. David Cosby Jr. sang "Amazing Grace," and Carol Kirby brought joyful tears from the assembly with a soaring, soulful offering of "His Eye Is On the Sparrow."

FULL CIRCLE IN A BOXING RING

Along with his mother's funeral, journalism continually brought Muhammad Ali back into my life long after seeing him in the Courier-Journal lobby in 1975. I was covering a Kentucky Derby, which annually lured some of the most famous and wealthiest people in the country and world—including the usual tweed-and-lace pocket of English royalty.

They all gathered in the modestly declared "Millionaire's Row" on top of the Churchill Downs grandstand. Ali walked into the room, unannounced. All heads turned, conversation stopped, complete reverential silence. The gawking began among the rich and world famous. Ali *was* the rich and world famous.

I sat in the back seat of a car in downtown Louisville with Ali up front, window open, smiling, waving to instant fans, trading excitement and laughter. Then we stopped, and, never missing a beat, Ali pranced up a long set of concrete steps and disappeared into a building.

We later spoke in his mother's house; a Koran and a Bible lay on the table before us. This was a different Ali. It was the teacher Ali, solemn and serious, as he carefully selected different parts of each book, explaining the differences. We spoke for almost an hour about his religion, Ali's speech slow, pausing at times, the part of me listening as a journalist, part of me still a Midwestern kid wondering how this ever happened?

Bob Hill with The Champ.

Ali died June 3, 2016, his mind and body slowly deteriorating due to head injuries and dealing with Parkinson's disease for 32 years. His larger legacy outlasted his slow death. It still does. Muslim mourners from around the world came to Louisville to honor him, with Bryant Gumbel, Billy Crystal and former President Bill Clinton offering eulogies before about 15,000 people in the KFC Yum Center.

Thousands more lined the streets, holding up signs, running alongside the hearse and laying flowers on it as his casket was slowly carried past his boyhood home in West Louisville, then the downtown Muhammad Ali Center created in his honor and supporting his humanitarian work.

The solemn 23-mile procession flowed down Broadway past the very familiar *Courier-Journal* building and continued east into historic Cave Hill Cemetery. His final, unifying parade led Ali to his gravesite atop a flowered, grassy slope.

His grave still receives thousands of visitor a year from around the world, his gravestone carved in a final message: "Service to others is the rent you pay for your room in heaven."

Visitors can sit on two granite benches beneath a magnolia tree. Many of them have left behind flowers, personal mementos and trinkets with meanings of their own for Ali, each picked by daily and preserved by Cave Hill staff.

They include autographed boxing gloves, a bag of marbles reminiscent of Ali's childhood, and ornate butterflies and bees. There are foreign coins, artwork, toy elephants to honor Ali's "Rumble in the Jungle," coffee mugs and, once, a full-sized rocking chair, empty and reverential.

There are now hundreds of personal letters and notes to The Champ preserved in plastic bags, each thanking him for the messages, inspiration and memories he created. Some people also left books.

EPILOGUE

The first thing I feel compelled to say to any readers that made it this far is to assure them this book was not written by an AI machine. My next book, perhaps. Or my obit. But this one was knocked out with my own two fingers.

But that is our unknown future, isn't it? Give an AI machine a bare bones list of facts and characters—confused kid, good jump shot, sofa salesman, skinny journalism professor, two-fingered typer, ice skating, police beat, Supreme Court, Butcher Hollow, Muhammad Ali—and it could come up with a lot better story than this one in 10 minutes. Movie script in five more. And this two-fingered one has required more than 80 years.

Who knows where it's all going, but it won't be much longer until we find out, or maybe we can just ask an AI machine what's up and get the hell out of the way.

Despite all that, but maybe because of it—and my cheerful cynicism required here—I remain optimistic about our future. I believe that we the people—and good journalism—shall survive all this self-serving division, hypocrisy, political lies and demagoguery. Climate change, I'm not so sure. But it will take one cure to solve the other.

Many of the reasons for that belief are the people you just read about—or most of them. Hard workers, believers and problem solvers. The very people and places I preferred to write about. Heros of a sort. Mostly quiet about it. They are still out there. Why get out of the bed in the morning if you can't make it worthwhile?

It is a cinch that journalism delivery itself will not survive in the printed form and substance I have always known, but, as mentioned earlier, neither did the Pony Express. No lamentation there. Move on, help out or get out of the way.

In somewhat the same vein I wrote my final *Courier-Journal* column on Aug. 2, 2008. I was ready to go, to move on to other things. It said, in part:

"Looking back over my 40 years, I share the feelings of so many others who have enjoyed their life's work; I just got away with something. I did what I loved to do—and got paid for it.

In recent years, however, came another thought: What else could I do—and when was I going to start doing it? My past, present and future were continually arguing with one another.

Something had to give.

That something was me.

Change is inevitable. My hope, wish and belief is that the best journalists and citizens will continue to find ways to get the truth out to the masses, or at least those willing to accept the truth, which is the larger problem in a world bombarded daily with "alternative facts."

I also wish those good journalists will have the opportunity, as we did back in the day, to daily gather around a cafeteria or bar table after deadlines, to be in the same room, the same space to laugh and talk together to share thoughts and ideas. In modern journalism, even many of the original newspaper buildings have been sold by marauding capitalists.

Beyond that, the Inner Writer was again banging in my head, insisting I move on, try other things, maybe get a hearing aid, but certainly not a condo on a beach in Florida.

More important, Janet was dealing with breast cancer, of which she has fully recovered. We wanted to travel more, to see family, to better tend to our gardens and friends. I wanted to write more books.

Stay tuned. Next up is "Fifty Years, $500 and a '52 Buick"—a more personal look at our lives, farm, flowers and family over a half-century on our eight acres.

And I really did have very few bad days in the newspaper business.